The Practice of Printing
Reprinted and Enlarged

Ralph W. Polk
1926 Edition

The Practice of Printing, by Polk is considered by many to be the fundamental book on platen press printing. At the time of it's publication offset lithography had not taken hold to become the dominant printing method. Polk's intent with this book was to provide an introduction to young workers who wished to become printers. It is a well respected overview of what we commonly call "Letterpress" printing in the United States. The publisher owns two such of these presses and is delighted to have the opportunity to further the profession and hobby by bringing this book back to print.

Note from the Publisher: The source material is a scanned copy and there are quality issues with the images and text. Short of retyping the text or destroying an existing copy in order to scan it, this is a limitation of the re-print process. Every effort has been made to produce a quality copy of the book.

Should you have suggestions or feedback on ways to improve this book please send email to Books@OcotilloPress.com

---

Edited 2021 Ocotillo Press
ISBN 978-1-954285-58-3

Ocotillo Press
Houston, TX 77017
Books@OcotilloPress.com

William Caxton in Westminster Abbey, showing the first printing done in England to King Edward IV, the Queen, and Members of the Court. Reproduced from a steel engraving by F. Bromley, in the Typographic Library and Museum of the American Type Founders Company, Jersey City, N. J.

The Practice of Printing

By RALPH W. POLK

Principal Robidoux Polytechnic School
St. Joseph, Missouri

Formerly a Typographer
of broad trade experience

The Manual Arts Press
Peoria, Illinois

Composition by the author

Plates by Artcrafts Engraving Company, St. Joseph, Mo.

Presswork and binding by W. B. Conkey Company
Hammond, Ind.

PREFACE

THERE is an urgent need in the printing industry for young craftsmen who are properly trained in the science of printing, and who are acquainted with the details of the basic operations of the trade. It is in answer to that need that this book has been developed. Our purpose has been to select and arrange such material as will be most helpful to the student of printing, whether in the school printshop, or in the apprentice department of the commercial printing plant. The book will be found to contain reliable information and instruction on the various trade processes that are commonly considered as essential to a complete and well-rounded apprentice training in typography.

The material which comprises the text is in no sense in a theoretical or experimental stage. Each chapter has been perfected from practical lesson material which has been successfully used in regular classes, and after taking its present page form, it has been again subjected to the test of regular class procedure. Proofs of each section have also been submitted to outstanding specialists in the trade, and verified as to correctness of technical detail. Some of our best printing instructors, and many printers of national reputation have given much time and attention to the perfection of this material, which co-operation the author very gratefully acknowledges.

Naturally, it is impracticable to attempt to discuss all the details of each process in a book of this nature. At the ends of chapters dealing with special phases of printing will be found lists of reliable trade books which may be used as references, or for a further study of these subjects. These books have been carefully selected, and are recommended for the school, or the printer's library.

Advertising men, salesmen of printing, printing-office executives, and all those who have not been scientifically trained in the mechanics of printing, will find this book full of very helpful information, and it should be available to the workmen throughout the plant.

The pages have been hand-set in foundry type and materials, as a guide and example to the young compositor, and as an inspiration to his typographic efforts.

This work is issued with the sincere desire for helpfulness, to young men who wish to become printers, and to the noble Craft itself, to which I owe a larger debt than I can hope to repay.

RALPH W. POLK.

CONTENTS

Contents

Contents

Contents

Contents · xiii

Contents

CHAPTER I

A Brief History of Printing

"And this our noble art of Printing is the very foster mother
of all learning; for although the few had books before John
Gutenburg gave us our art, not until Printing came could
Learning, yea and Wisdom also, knock at every man's door."
— From the *Latin of Cardelius,* 1546

FROM the very earliest time, men have endeavored to
establish a graphic record of their achievements. It
was not until about the time of Columbus that the
art of printing—as we know it today—was actually
practiced, but many other forms of communication and record existed through a number of centuries previous to the
invention of printing types. A study of these successive
stages in the development of printing is a most interesting
and fascinating one, especially to prospective printers.

It is difficult for us to imagine a time when men had no
knowledge of paper or of any of the writing or printing
materials of more recent years, and when they did not even
have an alphabet, or any equivalent system of symbols by
which knowledge or information might be preserved or
transmitted. Yet this was a condition which existed among
all primitive peoples. All that we now possess of the great
art of printing is a gradual development of crude beginnings, by slow successive stages, through the centuries.

1. **The cairn.** One of the earliest methods of recording
an important event was that of raising a heap of large
stones to commemorate it. A victory over a rival clan, the
death of a chieftain, a treaty, and similar events, were "recorded" in this way by many ancient peoples. This method

was imperfect, to be sure, as the heap was in no sense a graphic reproduction of the event, nor could it be understood by those who knew nothing of the details. These commemorative heaps are known as cairns, from the Gaelic word, *carn,* a heap.

2. **Early records in stone.** Discoveries of crude pictures and symbols sculptured upon rocks, or upon the walls of caves, have been made in various parts of the world, which show us that this was another method of making records in the early days of civilization.

Tablets of stone, carved with symbolic characters, were used for many purposes by the ancient Assyrians, Chaldeans, Egyptians and others. At one time the royal library at Babylon contained numerous "volumes" of stone slabs, on which many important records were preserved. The Ten Commandments, also, are said to have been delivered to Moses on tables of stone.

3. **Tablets of clay.** Later, the Chaldeans made a form of clay tablet to replace the heavy slabs of stone. The characters imprinted on these tablets are known as *cuneiform,* or wedge-shaped, letters, and they owe their shape to the fact that they were originally cut by a chisel into stone.* The charac-

Fig. 1. Clay tablet with cuneiform characters

ters were applied to the soft clay by means of small bronze or copper punches mounted on ivory handles. These were

---

* Letter forms have always been influenced by the manner in which they could be made most easily. It was easier to chisel angular forms into stone, so we find that, in general, these inscriptions are rather plain and consisting of straight lines. Curved characters became more common when records were written on papyrus and vellum with a pen.

impressed singly by hand, after which the tablet was hardened by baking. These cuneiform punches might be called the world's first types. An illustration of a section of a Chaldean tablet is shown on the preceding page.

4. **The first paper.** One of the most important contributions of early times was the manufacture of a crude kind of paper by the Egyptians.* The papyrus plant—a tall reed growing along the Nile—furnished the material for this new substance. The outer rind of the stem of this plant was removed, leaving a number of very thin fibrous layers. These were dried and flattened, then interwoven at right angles into a sort of mat. After this mat of fiber was soaked in water, pressed and dried, it became a sheet of *papyrus,* ready to be written upon.

If a smoother surface was desired, the sheet was rubbed with stone until a satisfactory effect was secured. Papyrus was very widely used by the Egyptians and Greeks, and later by the Romans.

After the making of papyrus, parchment and vellum were also introduced as writing materials. Parchment was made from the skins of sheep and goats, while vellum was from the skins of young calves. The skins were soaked in a solution of lime, then stretched on frames, and scraped thin and smooth. Parchment is still used occasionally in the making of diplomas and certificates.

5. **Early picture-writing.** One of the earliest methods of graphic communication was that of making pictures, or symbols, that would convey ideas to the observer. Most prominent among these systems were the hieroglyphics (literally *sacred-writing*) of the Egyptians, and the picture-writing of the early American Indians. Neither could be said to be an "alphabet," for their separate characters did

*The bamboo tablets of the Chinese, and their paper manufactured from silk, wood fibers, or old linen, were made long before the days of papyrus, authorities assert.

not have definite phonetic value, but were ideograms, representing ideas and not sounds.

Undoubtedly, the early Egyptians developed the most elaborate system of picture-writing known. By means of their hieroglyphics, they were able to express themselves very accurately. They employed these pictorial characters in carving inscriptions on temple walls, about palaces, in tombs, and wherever messages were engraved in stone. They also in-

Fig. 2. Specimen of Egyptian hieroglyphics

scribed them on rolls of papyrus, which served as the books of ancient Egypt. Fig. 2 shows a specimen of hieroglyphics.

The Indian carved his symbols on the trunks of trees, burned or painted them on hides and bark, and wove them into beadwork, or into his blankets.

6. **Development of an alphabet.** A wonderful contribution was made to the graphic arts, as well as to the cause of civilization, when a simple set of phonetic characters was introduced by the Phenicians.* No doubt the development of this alphabet was very gradual, and no exact date for its appearance can be given, although it was long before the birth of Christ. This Phenician alphabet consisted of twenty-two letters, nearly all consonants. Later on, the Greeks took fifteen of these, and originated enough more to make an alphabet of twenty-four characters. Rome adopted eighteen of the Greek letters, and added seven more, some in slight modification of other Greek letters. The Anglo-Saxons took all of the Roman letters, adding

---

*No doubt, the symbols of the Egyptians, Chaldeans, and others, had a direct bearing on the development of the alphabet but it remained for the Phenicians to sim- plify the existing signs and to assign to each character a definite phonetic value. It is for this reason that the Phenicians are credited with the invention of letters.

two new ones but later dropping one, so that we now have an alphabet of twenty-six characters.

7. **Early printing from wood blocks.** Printing from wood blocks seems to have originated in the Orient, and there is evidence of the production of some religious work by that method, in Japan, as early as the eighth century. It is supposed that a knowledge of this process was brought to Europe by traders in the early days of commerce.

Stamping sheets of paper from hand-carved blocks of wood was practiced in Europe as early as 1417. In that year Jan de Printere, of Antwerp, made these wood block prints, and others followed his example. At first, only rude pictures were printed. Later, brief lines of explanation were added, and at last some full pages of reading matter were produced in this way. The work was done entirely by hand, the dampened sheet being laid on the inked block, and rubbed until the image was transferred to the paper.

The manufacture of paper from cloth was first practiced in Europe in the eighth century. It was made by hand. Machine-made paper first appeared in the eighteenth century.

8. **Early books.** The papyrus scroll was the forerunner of the modern book. Long strips of papyrus, or vellum, were written upon by the ancient scribes, and then were rolled up into cylindrical form when not in use. At first the manuscript was written across the breadth of the roll, which was held upright before the reader, and unrolled from the top downwards. Later, the lines

Fig. 3. Early manuscript scroll showing written page

of writing ran parallel with the length of the roll, and were divided into groups, which might be thought of as pages.

The scroll was then unrolled sidewise. In many instances, rollers were fastened to the ends of the sheet, for convenience in handling the scroll. Many had decorated handles.

Gradually the book form was developed, with folded sheets bound together. Books, like the scrolls, were written by scribes, and some of them were illustrated with occasional wood blocks. Most of this work was done under the direction of the medieval Church, within the monasteries and in the ecclesiastical centers of western Europe.

A high degree of skill was attained by these manuscript writers, and many of the early books were very elaborately finished, with large colored initials, and artistically dec-

COPR. ELSON ART CO.
Fig. 4. Reading from scroll

orated headbands and borders. Because of this tedious method of making books, only those of the upper classes could afford to own them. The poor had no books, and could not even read.

THE INVENTION OF PRINTING

9. **The invention of movable types.** In the middle of the fifteenth century the demand for books steadily increased, and men in various countries attempted to work out new processes whereby they could be produced more rapidly than by the laborious manuscript method. The most successful of these was Johann Gutenberg, of Mainz, Germany, who invented the first movable metal types for printing.* His first known work was the "Bible of 42 Lines," which

*Some maintain that a Dutch innkeeper and tallow-chandler, Laurens Coster, of Haarlem, developed a system of printing with movable types before Gutenburg. Although some arguments are made in his favor, his own townsmen made no claim for him until a century after printing was known. The story is generally discredited.

appeared about 1456. It was a book of over thirteen hundred pages, printed laboriously by hand on a crude press, two pages at a time. In style, it was very similar to the manuscript books of the time. This style is shown in Fig. 5.

Dominc qd mfcplicati tribular mes multi inl uerfum me. Multi dicut an nō eft falus ipli in deo eius. Dūe fulcrptor me es: glorie altās raput meū. Toce in minū damaui: z ezaudiuit te lācto fuo. Ego dormiui z lum: z ezfurrexi quia dūs fu

Fig. 5. Specimen from first book printed from movable types, by Gutenberg, 1456

The invention of printing gave a great impetus to the advancement of knowledge and enlightenment, and its influence was immediate and widespread. Books could be had by even the common people, and all the arts of learning were stimulated to new activity. The practice of printing spread rapidly throughout civilized Europe, and although it met with temporary opposition because of the prejudices and superstitions of some of the early peoples, it soon became universally accepted as the "art preservative of arts," and one of the greatest factors in human progress.

The early printers adopted as their manner of lettering the style of handwriting of the scribes of the countries in which they operated. They even assiduously attempted to counterfeit the workmanship of the scribes, as some think, in order that their handiwork might actually appear as manuscript. Not until printing became well established did they begin to make improvements on the old forms of manuscript lettering, and to show individuality in their art.

10. **Origin of Roman types.** Among the first printers to press across the Alps into Italy were Arnold Pannartz and Conrad Sweinheym, who came to the monastery of Subiaco, near Rome, and set up their outfit in 1464. These men first printed from types they had brought with them from northern Europe, but they found difficulty in the fact that the

Italian people were accustomed to a form of lettering far more simple and graceful than the bold, angular Gothic type, and hence their early product was not received with favor. Accordingly, they designed new types after the fashion of the Italian calligraphers, and thus they became the originators of the first Roman types.

11. **Origin of Italic types.** The most famous printer of of Venice, perhaps of all Italy, was Aldus Manutius. Aldus was born in 1450. He devoted his life to the task of improving the quality of printed books, and of producing good literature cheaply, that the masses might obtain knowledge.

In 1501 he printed an edition of Virgil in a new type face which he designed "after the handwriting of Petrarch." This graceful, condensed slanting letter became known as *Italic*, as all slanting letters are now classified.

12. **Italy's master typographer.** Nicholas Jenson, who began printing in Venice in 1470, developed the Roman letter into its finest form and beauty. So perfect was the style of his types that it became the pattern for nearly all the printers of Europe.* Throughout all his work the touch of the master craftsman is apparent. His books, even today, are models of neatness, proportion and balance.

This style of letter is very similar to the type cast by Jenson for use in his books

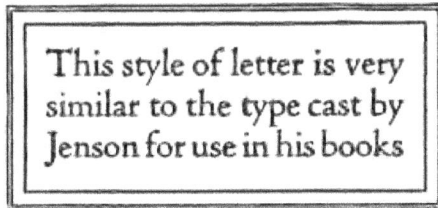

Fig. 6. Cloister Oldstyle type, patterned after the style of Nicholas Jenson

In Fig. 6 a specimen of Cloister Oldstyle type is reproduced. This is very closely patterned after Jenson's letter, and gives a good idea of its excellent style.

13. **Beginnings in France.** One of the prominent early printers of France was Geofroy Tory (1480-1532), who did

* Nicolas Jenson is one of the most celebrated artists on the honor roll of typography. His types are of great beauty, and his impressions great masterpieces. The style of letter he devised is the one we are using today, if we submit to some trivial changes introduced by fashions which do not disturb its general effect.—Bernarde.

much to develop decoration and ornament in typography. His pupil, Claud Garamond, brought out the first French type of distinction, closely modelled after the famous type of Jenson, and with italics very similar to those of Aldus. Garamond came to devote his entire time to producing types for other printers. Up to this time nearly all printers designed and cast their own types, and this marks the beginning of the type foundry as a separate activity.

14. **Beginnings in England.** It was William Caxton who introduced printing into England. Caxton was an English merchant who visited Belgium, and while there became interested in this new art, and in 1472 he produced, in Bruges, the first book ever printed in the English language. Later, Caxton returned to England, taking with him his printing equipment, which he set up in London.

The best known printer of early England was William Caslon, who operated a printing-office and type foundry in the early eighteenth century. His greatest contribution to the craft was the type face which still bears his name. Caslon types today are the most popular of all styles offered by the founders. The Caslon oldstyle faces now used are very similar to the types of this early designer.

> The first modern-face type was designed and used by Bodoni, 1789

Fig. 7. Bodoni type, a modern letter cut after the original of G. Bodoni

15. **Modern-face types.** Giambattista (John the Baptist) Bodoni, who in 1760 became the head of the royal printing office in Parma, was the first to bring forth the style of letter which we class as *modern-face*. His types were cut with light hair-line serifs and bold, uniform body strokes, and while they were more formal and precise than the letters of his predecessors, they had a charm and elegance that has furnished inspiration for many type designers since his time. Modern Bodoni type closely follows his pattern.

16. **Printing in America.** Mexico was the first country in the western world to receive the new art of printing. Its Spanish governor brought over an outfit in 1536, and John Cromberger, America's pioneer printer, issued his first book in 1540.

In the North American colonies, printing made its appearance among the very earliest settlements, and it became a great factor in the development of our nation. The first colonial printer, Stephen Daye, began his work in Cambridge, in 1639. Daye's first production was *The Freeman's Oath*, but his most fa-

Fig. 8. The first printing press in the United States, first used in Cambridge, 1639, by Stephen Daye

mous publication was the Bay Psalm Book, or *The Booke of Psalmes*, issued in 1640. Samuel Green succeeded Daye in 1649, and published a number of notable books.

William Bradford, the first printer of Pennsylvania, set up a shop near Philadelphia in 1687. Six years later, he removed to New York. He was also the only printer in that colony for a period of thirty years.

It is of particular interest to students of printing that Benjamin Franklin, one of the greatest and most typical of Americans, was one of the most notable early printers of America. Nearly everyone is familiar with his life, and his experiences in the printers' trade, through his famous *Autobiography*. There are few romances more thrilling than the story of his life. Modern printing owes much to

THE EVOLUTION OF THE BOOK, *by John W. Alexander*

1. THE CAIRN. Primitive men raising heap of stones as a record

2. ORAL TRADITION. A story-teller relating traditions to his people

3. EGYPTIAN HIEROGLYPHICS. Cutting an inscription on an arch

4. PICTURE-WRITING. An American Indian depicting story on skin

5. THE MANUSCRIPT. Scribe writing book, in cloister of the church

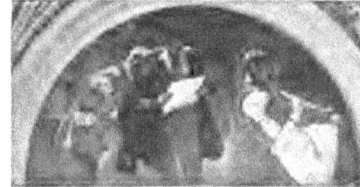

6. THE PRINTING PRESS. The first printing by Gutenberg in 1456

This series of mural decorations illustrating the successive stages in the development of graphic records is of particular significance and interest to students of printing. The originals are in the Library of Congress, Washington, D. C.

From a Copley Print, copyright by Curtis & Cameron, Publishers, Boston

Fig. 9.

this great statesman, as well as to all the good printers of the past, for the contributions each has made toward the development of this great industry.

SUGGESTIONS AND BIBLIOGRAPHY

In this chapter we have been compelled to make only the briefest mention of some of the outstanding facts in the development of printing. Many very interesting and important events are not mentioned. The student, therefore, must not think that he has acquired a full knowledge of this subject when he has studied the foregoing. This brief outline is given him as a guide to further investigation, and as an incentive to learn all he can about this most fascinating subject. An intensive study of the traditions of the trade is necessary if one wishes to become proficient in the art of printing.

Find out all you can about the various processes mentioned in this chapter. Consult all the available references concerning the early typographers mentioned. Also, learn what you can of Plantin, Cot, Ratdolt, Elzevir, Didot, Fournier, John Daye, Morris and others.

The following books contain special material on this subject:

Art and Practice of Typography—Gress. Oswald Pub. Co.
Vols. 49, 50, 51, 52, 53, and 54, U. T. A. Typographic Library
Title Pages—DeVinne. Oswald Pub. Co.
Story of the Alphabet—Clodd. D. Appleton & Co.
The Book; Its History and Development—Davenport. Van Nostrand Co.
Notable Printers of Italy in 15th Century—DeVinne. Oswald Pub. Co.
Pre-Alphabet Days, a booklet by Norman T. A. Munder
Printing Types: Their History, Forms and Uses — Updike. Harvard
      University Press
Franklin's *Autobiography* should be read by all students of printing.

QUESTIONS

1. What were some of the early devices for recording ideas?
2. What was papyrus, and how was it made?
3. Name some advantages of papyrus over stone and clay.
4. Who invented the alphabet?
5. Describe the ancient scroll.
6. When and by whom was printing invented?
7. Name some advantages of printed books over manuscript books.
8. What was the style of lettering of the early books. Why?
9. How did the Roman form of lettering originate?
10. Where did Italic type come from?
11. What was the most important achievement of Nicolas Jenson?
12. Who might be called the "father of type founders?" Why?
13. Who originated the first modern-face types?
14. Tell what you can of William Caslon.
15. Name some of America's first printers.
16. Give a brief sketch of Franklin's life as a printer.

CHAPTER II

The Great Industry of Printing

"The glory and power of printing is not all in the past. Its
influence in the present makes it a powerful conservator
of human progress. It is the handmaiden of all the arts
and industries, and a most effective worker in the world's
workshop, to polish and refine the civilization of the age."
—CARLYLE

IN THE preceding chapter we have followed the development of the printing industry from its beginning to early
colonial times. Printing has rapidly advanced until it has
become one of the leading industries of the United States,
and a foremost factor in the promotion of all phases of commerce and industry, and of all the cultural arts.

17. **Printing ranks sixth among industries.** The census
reports rank printing as the sixth industry of this country
with respect to the value of its product, although in some
other respects it is entitled to be classed as the third great
industry, and in some, even as the second in rank.* There
are about 35,000 printing establishments in the country,
representing a capital investment of over $1,000,000,000.
These plants employ more than 450,000 printers, whose
total annual salaries are approximately $560,000,000.

18. **The allied trades.** Printing, with its allied trades,
includes such lines of work as job and catalog printing,
newspaper, magazine, and book publishing, bookbinding

---

* With respect to the value of their gross
products, the meat industry ranks first;
foundry and machine shops, second; and
printing and publishing, third. When net
products are considered, foundry and
machine shops rank first, and printing and
its allied trades, second. In total capitalization, foundry and machine shops lead;
lumber, steel, and printing tie for second
place. Printing ranks third in the number
of employees, and second in the wages paid
its workmen.

Fig. 10. View of composing room of The International Textbook Co., Scranton, Pa.

and blank book making, photo-engraving (plate-making), lithographing and offset processes, steel and copperplate engraving, type-founding, paper-making, the manufacture of inks, and commercial design and advertising service.

19. **The printing trade.** The printing trade proper, which we shall consider particularly in these lessons, comprises the activities that are carried on in the regular departments of the modern commercial printing plant. The scope of the work done in different plants varies considerably, but all of them include activities which may come under the three main heads, or departments, of (a) composition, (b) press-work, and (c) stockroom and bindery. In the smaller shops these three departments may exist in simple form, but as establishments become larger and more fully equipped, we find increased subdivisions of these activities into a larger number of departments.

In the *composing department*, the jobs of printing are planned, or "laid out," the type is set up, corrected, made up into forms in accordance with the individual specifications, and locked up for the presses. The type may be set entirely by hand, or partly by hand and partly by machine,

Fig. 11. Cylinder pressroom of The Commonwealth Press, Worcester, Mass.

and therefore the work on the linotype, monotype, and all typecasting machines, is considered as in this department.

In the *pressroom* type forms are placed on the presses, made ready, and printed. This work may be done on job presses, or on cylinder presses, and the sheets may be fed into the presses by hand, or by mechanical feeders.

Paper stock is received and stored in the *stockroom*, and is cut to proper size, as needed, for each job. After the printing has been completed, such operations as folding, stitching, tabbing, perforating, trimming, etc., are carried on in this department (or in the *bindery* if it is maintained as a separate division). Packing and shipping ordinarily are functions of this department.

In small plants, a printer may be an all-around workman, setting up jobs, cutting paper stock, feeding presses, and in short, doing any of the necessary work of the shop. In the larger plants, the lines between the departments are more definitely drawn, and men serve in narrower capacities, as specialists. One may be a compositor, another a stoneman, one a lay-out man, a proof-reader, a pressman, a stockman, a linotype operator, or a specialist in any one of the various operations of the printing trade.

20. **Broad training necessary.** In the earlier days of printing, it was common for the apprentice to receive an all-around training, but in this period of specialization and factory production methods, he is fortunate if he obtains a good working knowledge of one process, or at least of one department, in connection with his apprenticeship work.

However, every printer should develop a broad knowledge of the fundamental trade processes, regardless of the department in which he works. The compositor needs to know the problems of the pressman so that he may anticipate them as he pre-

Fig. 12. Stonework in The Scholl Printing Co., Chillicothe, Ohio

pares the forms for the presses; the pressman needs to know the processes of the composing room, so that he can get the best results from the type forms, and can work in close cooperation with the composing department; both must have a knowledge of paper, and of the problems of the stockroom and bindery. Skilled workmen in every deparment must have an understanding of the entire problem of producing printed matter, if they would be efficient printers.

If one does not obtain this knowledge through his regular experiences at his work, then he should make up his deficiencies by extra study and investigation.

21. **Exceptional opportunities in printing.** There is great need in the industry today for well-trained workmen. There is a magnificent array of machinery, type, and of all the

modern appliances of the trade, but a shortage of skilled, competent printers, who can produce work of quality.

The demand for the better grades of printed matter is constantly increasing. The modern business man is asking for quality printing, and he will not accept jobs that are not up to the standard. Employing printers, also, are constantly raising their standards, and improving their plants.

There never was a more opportune time for young men of ability to prepare for the great printing industry, and the prospects for capable, well-trained men are especially good.

SUGGESTIONS

Let the student resolve, at the outset, that regardless of whatever phase of printing has attracted him to a study of this work, he will strive to acquire a broad knowledge of this great industry.

Visit printing plants wherever you can, and observe the work of the various departments. Do not hesitate to ask for this privilege, as any youth really interested in printing is most welcome in any plant.

Read the printing magazines, such as *The Inland Printer, Printed Salesmanship,* and *The American Printer.* Some of our best tradesmen owe a great measure of their success to a careful study of the trade magazines. Study them—ads and all—as you would a textbook. Also, become familiar with the printers' supply catalogs and type specimen books. Such a one as the American Type Specimen Book is a wonderful storehouse of knowledge and information for the young printer.

Read other books on printing. Some of the best ones are listed in this book. Most of them will be found in any library. If possible, start a printing library of your own, adding a book at a time, as you can. It will be a remarkable help and inspiration to you.

QUESTIONS

1. Name some of the allied printing industries.
2. How many printers are there in the United States?
3. What are the three common departments of a printshop?
4. What are some of the activities of the composing-room?
5. Tell what you can about the pressroom?
6. Which department has to do with the handling of paper?
7. Name some process carried on in the bindery department.
8. What are some of the differences between a large and small shop?
9. Why should a printer have a knowledge of the various processes?
10. Does an apprentice ordinarily receive all-around training? Why?

CHAPTER III

Type

LETTER-PRESS printing is accomplished by means of type, of uniform height, assembled into groups, and locked up in a steel frame, or chase, for the printing-press. Ink is applied to the faces of the types, and they in turn are pressed onto sheets of paper, on which they leave their impression. The letters on types are cast in reverse, and the printing surfaces, or faces, of the letters stand out in bold relief above the type body.

Fig. 13. Specimens of foundry type

22. **Kinds of type.** There are different kinds of type, and they are classified in four general groups, as (a) foundry type, (b) linotype slugs, (c) monotype, and (d) wood type.

Foundry type is cast in single characters on individual bodies, and is put up in assortments, or fonts, which are kept in type cases. This is the original form of type, and also the most prevalent one. Foundry type is set by hand, the individual letters being picked out of the type case and assembled into a composing stick.

Mechanical composition, or "setting of type," is done on the linotype and monotype machines. The former casts a slug, or line of type, from soft lead, which may contain a number of letters or words on a single body. The latter actually casts individual types and assembles them into the form desired. Both machines are operated by a keyboard.

Wood type is made in large sizes, and is used for poster printing. Hard, close-grained wood is used, and it is given special treatment to prevent checking or warping. The only advantage in the use of wood type is that it can be manufactured much more cheaply than metal type of the same size, and it is not so heavy. The finest results in printing cannot be obtained from the use of wood type.

The rest of this chapter will deal entirely with foundry type, although some of the information here given is applicable to all classes of type.

23. **Height of type.** All type is of uniform height, which is .918, or approximately eleven-twelfths, of an inch. This is the measurement from the feet, or base, of the type, to the face, or printing surface. It is sometimes called "height to paper," as it represents the distance from the bed of the press to the sheet when in position to be printed. An object of this height is said to be "type-high."

24. **Type metal.** Foundry type is made from an alloy of lead, antimony, and tin. The lead, which would be too soft if used alone, forms the body of the type metal; antimony gives it hardness; tin gives it toughness, and also cements the other metals into a common mass. This mixture of metals fits the mould perfectly, and does not shrink as it cools. It does not rust or corrode. Some founders also add a little copper, or nickel, for greater durability.

25. **Parts of a type.** The principal parts of a type which the student should know are indicated in the diagram in Fig. 14, on the following page.

The *face* of a type is the outlined character, standing out in relief on its upper end, which gives the impression to the paper. It is the printing surface of the type. The face may be subdivided into heavy and light elements, and serifs.

The *heavy elements* are the thick strokes, or heavy lines, of the character, sometimes called letter stems. The *light elements* are the thinner connecting lines between the heavy elements. They may be straight, as in H, M, N, W, etc., or curved, as in such letters as B, P, or R. They are also called the hair-lines of the letters. The proportion between the widths of the light and heavy elements vary in different styles of type.

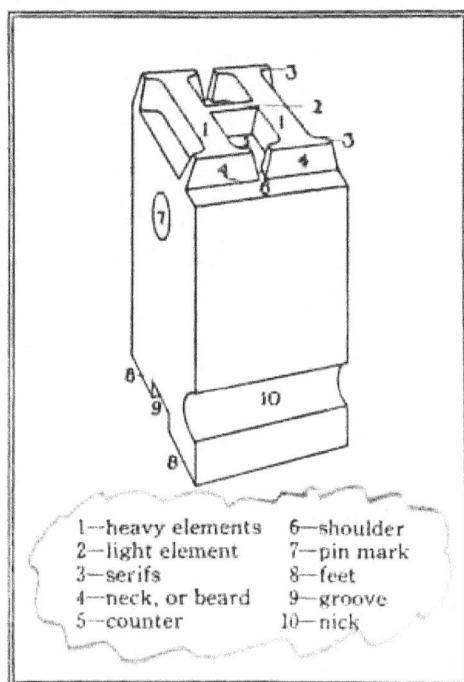

1—heavy elements	6—shoulder
2—light element	7—pin mark
3—serifs	8—feet
4—neck, or beard	9—groove
5—counter	10—nick

Fig. 14

The *serifs* are the short cross-lines placed at the ends of all unconnected body strokes, or elements. Serifs differ widely in different type styles, from a thin hair-line to a bold stroke, sometimes forming a sharp angle at the intersection with the stem, and sometimes being heavily bracketed to it. It is the formation of the serifs that gives the greatest touch of individuality to a type face.

The slope of the metal between the face and the body is called the *neck*, or beard. The *counter* is the depression between the elements of the letter, and the *shoulder* is that portion of the upper surface of the body which extends below the base of the character. There are a few styles of lettering which cover the entire body of the type, leaving no shoulder, but all standard types have

Fig. 15

a shoulder at the foot of the letters, to make allowance for the descending strokes of such characters as g, j, p, q, and y.

In Fig. 15, *a* shows a type without shoulder; *b* a type with a standard shoulder; and *c*, an oldstyle letter with an unusually wide shoulder. In *d*, descending types are shown.

The founder's mark, or *pin mark*, is found on the upper part of the body. It is a circular indention made by the pin which dislodges the type from the mould, in casting. Sometimes it bears the trade mark of the foundry, or a figure indicating the size of the type.

Fig. 16. Types of five different fonts, but of the same size, showing distinguishing nicks

The *feet* of a type are the two projections upon which the body rests. Between the feet is the *groove*, which is formed by the planing tool that removes the jet after the type is cast. Across the front of the body are grooves, or *nicks*, which serve in the double capacity of indicating the correct position of the letter, in composition, and of aiding the printer in identifying the letter with respect to the particular style, or font, to which it belongs.*

All the type of one size and kind are nicked in the same manner, and the nicks are placed toward the open side of the composing stick, as the type is set. A letter bearing a different nick can easily be detected as a "wrong font" letter, even though the face of the letter might seem identical with the font used.†

26. **Type is put up in fonts.** All type is put up in assortments, or fonts. A font contains a complete outfit of letters of one size and style of type, the quantity of each individual character varying in accordance with the frequency of its use in ordinary printing. Usually, a font will include capitals, lower-case letters, figures, and punctuation

---

* In American, English, and German types the nicks are on the front of the body; in the French and Belgian types, the nicks are on the back.

† An extra nick is usually cut on the small capitals—o, s, v, w, x, and z (and also I in oldstyle types)—to distinguish them from lower-case letters of the same font.

marks, or *points*, as the latter are known in printing. Large fonts of Roman, or body, types may also include SMALL CAPITALS, reference marks (* ‡ † § ‖ ¶ ☞"), parentheses and brackets, and sometimes fractions (¼ ½ ¾ ⅛ ⅜ ⅝ ⅞ ⅓ ⅔), dashes (- — —— ———), and sectional braces (— ‿ —). The diphthongs, Æ Œ æ œ, are found in many styles of lettering. In some fonts, also, special characters, such as Qu, ct, st, ", and ", appear. Other characters, including accent marks, commercial and mathematical signs, leaders (_____), etc., are put up in special fonts, and are sold separately from the regular fonts.*

Ordinary Characters in a
Font of Type

A B C D E F G H I J

K L M N O P Q R S

T U V W X Y Z &

Capitals

$ 1 2 3 4 5 6 7 8 9 0

Figures

a b c d e f g h i j k l m

n o p q r s t u v w x y z

Lower-case letters

ff fi fl ffi ffl   . , - ' ; : ! ?

Ligatures   Points

Fig. 17

27. **Weight fonts.** Body type, such as is used for the text-matter of book and catalog pages, is sold in weight fonts of twenty pounds each, or multiples thereof. This is the most economical way to buy type used in quantity.

28. **Job fonts.** Display type, used for open display work, and for general job printing, is put up in smaller assortments, known as job fonts.† As in other fonts, the quantity of each letter is governed by the frequency of its use. Job fonts are made up in accordance with standard schemes for apportioning the amounts of each character, and the quantity of type in a font is indicated by the number of capital A's and lower-case a's it contains. Thus, a font of type may be labelled as 23A, 40a, etc. Such a font would contain

---

*The word "font" is a corruption of "fount," the original term, still used in England.

† The smaller sizes of display type are also made up in weight fonts.

forty of lower-case a; the same quantity of i, n, o, r, s, and t; fifty-three of e (the most used letter); while only seven of q, x, and z. The quantity of each other character in the font would be in proportion to these amounts.

Capitals and lower-case letters are packaged separately by type founders, and may be obtained separately.

Spaces and quads—used for blanking out between words or at the ends of lines—are packaged separate from the letters, and are furnished both in job and weight fonts.

Any individual type character may be obtained separately, on special order. Types so ordered are termed *sorts*.

29. **Kerned letters.** When a portion of the face of a letter projects beyond the body of the type, the letter is said to be *kerned*. Kerned letters are common in Italic, and in other slanting faces. Also, in some fonts of Roman type, the lower-case f and j are kerned at the extremities of these letters. Kerned letters must be handled carefully, as the kerned portions are easily broken off.

30. **Type classified by series and families.** Type is cast in different sizes, in standard graduations, and the various sizes of any one kind, or style, is known as a series of type. Thus, the different sizes of Cheltenham Oldstyle make up the Cheltenham Oldstyle Series, and we have the Venetian Series, New Caslon Series, Kennerley Series, etc.

A number of series of type, having the same general characteristics of design, and bearing the same name, are said to be of that family. For example, the Cheltenham Oldstyle Series, together with Cheltenham Italic, Cheltenham Bold, Cheltenham Bold Italic, and other Cheltenham faces, make up the Cheltenham Family.

31. **Body type and display type.** The two main classifications of type, with respect to both use and style, are: body type and display type. Body type includes all plain, light faced letters of the Roman style, of a comparatively even

tone, that are designed for body composition, in newspapers, books, and wherever large groups of plain reading-matter appear. They are designed for legibility in masses, not for ornament, and their individual letter shapes are not accentuated. When composed in solid groups, or masses, they make an even gray tone on the page, with no outstanding features of design to detract from legibility. The type used in this book—Century Oldstyle—is a body type.

THIS EXAMPLE is set in 8 point Century Oldstyle, one of the most popular series of body types. It is of even tone, or density of color, and is easily read in large masses. Other common body types are: Caslon Oldstyle, Ronaldson, Scotch Roman, Harris Roman, Bodoni Book, and Baskerville Roman.

SPECIMEN OF
DISPLAY TYPE
Being an Example
Set in Different Sizes
of Caslon Type

BOLDER, WITH MORE
EVIDENCE OF DESIGN

Fig. 18. A typical body type   Fig. 19. A style of display type

Display type is bolder in tone than body type, is more decorative, and bears more evidence of design in its construction. In display type, the considerations of legibility and of individual beauty are combined. It is not as legible as body type when composed in solid masses, because its individual shapes do not blend together as naturally, and one is more conscious of the letter forms while reading it. The main purpose of display type is to attract the attention of the reader, and to add beauty and interest to the page. It appears best in open display work.

Fig. 20. Common form of cabinet in which type is kept

SUGGESTIONS

Study well the parts of a type, as you will need to use this knowledge daily in your further work. It is the foundation for typesetting.

Examine the various styles of type in your shop, noting the differences in the faces and nicks. Be sure to replace each character in its proper box.

Study the type specimen books. They contain valuable information for you on type faces, styles, fonts, etc.

BIBLIOGRAPHY

Plain Printing Types—DeVinne. Oswald Publishing Company

Vol. I, Typographic Technical Library. United Typothetae of America

Type Lore—Frazier. The Inland Printer Company

Printing Types: Their History, Forms and Uses—Updike. The Harvard University Press

QUESTIONS

1. Name four general classes of type.
2. What metals are used in making foundry type?
3. Explain what is meant by "type-high."
4. Take a type and point out its various parts.
5. Name the parts which comprise the face of the letter.
6. What are the purposes of the nicks?
7. What is a font of type? A weight font? A job font?
8. What is meant by a series of type? A type family?
9. Distinguish between body type and display type.
10. What is a kerned letter?

CHAPTER IV

Type Cases

THE printers' case is a wooden tray divided into a number of compartments, or *boxes*, of varying sizes, into which the different characters of a font of type are placed. The cases are $1\frac{1}{16}$ inches deep, and a pair of full-size cases will hold about forty pounds of type.

32. **News cases.** The oldest style of cases, and the one from which all others are patterned, is that of the News Cases. They are used in pairs, and one is called the upper case, the other the lower case, because of their relative positions, one above the other, on the case rack. News cases are designed to hold large fonts of body type, and they are not so commonly used in commercial plants today since a large part of body composition is set by machines.

33. **Upper case holds capitals.** The upper case contains the capitals, small capitals, and most of the special characters which accompany a font of body type. The capitals are found in the right side of the case, and the small capitals in the left. The letters are arranged alphabetically, except that the letters J and U appear at the last.* The positions of the fractions, reference marks, commercial signs, and other characters, are shown in Fig. 21. They are very seldom

---

* When type cases were first planned by the early printers, the alphabet of the Latin language—the universal printed language of that time—contained only twenty-four characters, and these were arranged alphabetically in the case. There was no character J, but instead, the letter I was used both as consonant and vowel. Also, the V sound was missing from the language, and the letter U was formed in the angular V shape. For example, the name of the Roman emperor, Julius Caesar, appeared as IVLIVS CAESAR. In the first name, both the consonantal and vowel use of the letter I occurs, and also the sound of the vowel U is signified by the V character. When J and U came into use later as distinct letters, they were assigned the positions in the printers' case which they now occupy, at the last of the group.

used, and their locations need not be learned until the positions of the letters have been thoroughly mastered.

34. **Lower case not alphabetical.** The boxes of the lower case are of varying sizes, in accordance with the propor-

Fig. 21. The upper case

tionate quantity of each letter used in ordinary composition. The letter e, which appears most often in print, is given the largest box, while such letters as j, k, q, x, and z, which are seldom used, occupy some of the smallest boxes. The letters

Fig. 22. The lower case

are not arranged alphabetically, but those which are most frequently used are placed in the handiest positions to reach, while those that are little used are in less accessible places. In a few instances, however, alphabetical sequence is preserved in smaller groups of the letters. For instance, trace b-c-d-e, f-g, l-m-n-o-p, and t-u-v.

Note, also, that the boxes are so arranged that a number of the most common letter combinations are at the fingers' ends, as: and, end, are, the, is, this, that, -ed, -ent, etc.

Fig. 23. The California Job Case

35. **The California Job Case.** In the California Job Case, the capitals are placed in the section to the right, and the lower-case letters, the figures, points, and spacing material occupy the middle and left sections. This is the most popular style of type case, and it is estimated that more than nine-tenths of all cases now in use are California Job Cases. When used for type fonts that contain the small capitals, reference marks, etc., these extra characters are usually put in Small Cap Cases, three of which fill a regular blank case.

This is the style of case that is built into practically all modern composing-room cabinets.

36. **The Triple Case** is used for fonts which contain only capital letters, and it holds three different fonts of such type, complete with figures and points. It is particularly suitable for lining Gothics, Titles, Engravers Romans, and other types that are made without lower-case letters.

Quadruple Cases contain sections for four separate fonts of capitals, but are otherwise similar to Triple Cases.

37. **Sizes of cases.** All standard full-size cases are of the same dimensions ($32\frac{3}{16}$ x $16\frac{5}{8}$ inches), and they may be interchanged in all ordinary case racks. Two other sizes of type cases are made, which are known as two-thirds, and three-quarter, cases. They are made to hold small fonts of type

Fig. 24. The Triple Case

in composing rooms where space is especially limited. The smaller cases are very seldom used, however, in modern printing plants. When one has learned the lay of the News Cases, these smaller styles will offer no new problems, as the same general scheme for the positions of the letters is followed in all standard type cases.

38. **Special cases.** In addition to the ordinary type cases mentioned above, special cases are designed for accented letters, Greek, Hebrew, and other foreign language types, music type, etc. They are made in the same standard size, and wherever possible the standard lay-out scheme is used.

39. **Case racks.** Type cases are contained in stands or cabinets. The older style is the open frame, or case stand, which is designed to hold one or two pairs of News Cases in exposed position on top, and a number of cases below, on horizontal runs. In most modern plants, enclosed cabinets, made of wood or steel, have replaced the open stands. They are more compact, and they protect the cases from dust.

30

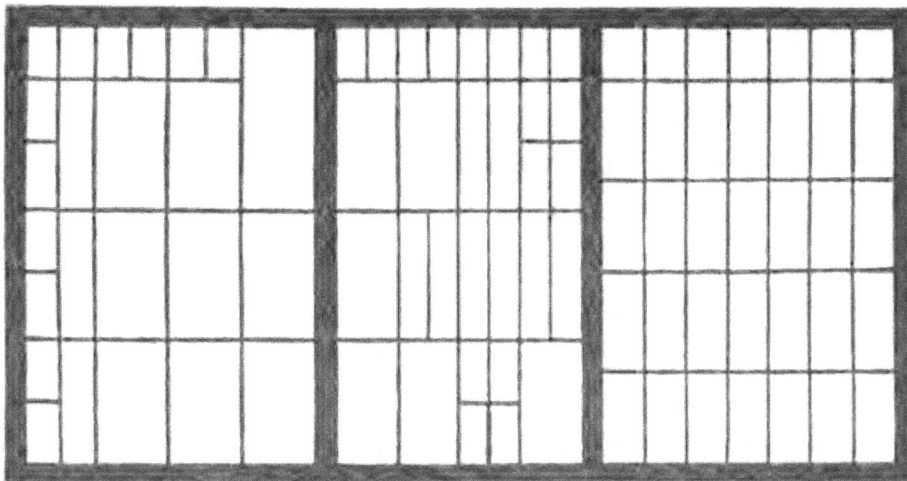

Fig. 25. Outline of California Job Case. A convenient diagram for practice
work, or for testing the student

SUGGESTIONS

It is essential that the student shall have a thorough knowledge of the
lay of the case before attempting to handle type. Various methods are used
by instructors, most of which will bring the desired results in a short time
if followed diligently by the student. A popular method is for the student
to draw a diagram of the case, locating the positions of the letters. The
outline of the case may be printed, if desired. Case diagrams may be built
up with brass rules, or printed from an etching similar to Fig. 25.

If a set of large letters—of 36 or 48 point type—are placed in the case
it will aid in learning the lay-out, and also afford practice in reading type.
Some instructors use a set of letters printed on cardboard, to be placed in
the proper boxes, as a preliminary practice before type is handled.

A careful study of the printed diagrams of the type cases will often be
sufficient, but one should make sure that the boxes are thoroughly learned.

QUESTIONS

1. Describe a pair of News Cases.
2. Why are J and U at the last of the capitals?
3. Is the lower case alphabetically arranged? Why?
4. What letter occupies the largest box in the lower case? Why?
5. Name some letters used most frequently; some least used.
6. Describe the California Job Case.
7. What is the plan of the Triple and Quadruple Cases?
8. What can you say of the sizes of cases?
9. What is the advantage of closed type cabinets?
10. Which style of case is in most common use?

In Races of Type:
1. Roman
2. Block
3. Old English - Tudor - Gothic
4. Script

CHAPTER V

Spacing Material

IN THIS chapter, we have grouped the various items of spacing material used in the composing room under their respective heads. The beginner will not use all these articles in his first few lessons, but we have assembled this material in one chapter for the sake of systematizing it. Accordingly, some of the items may be passed over at first, and taken up later when they are needed in the work.

LEADS AND SLUGS

40. **Leads and slugs** are thin strips of soft type metal, less than type high, used for spacing out between lines of type, or elsewhere in a form, where thin strips of spacing

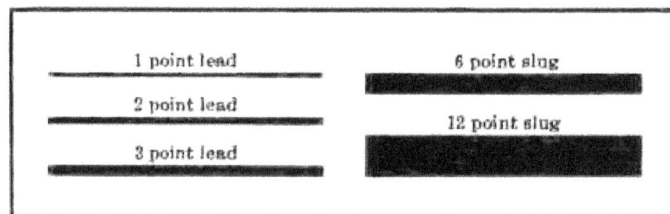

1 point lead	6 point slug
2 point lead	12 point slug
3 point lead	

Fig. 26. Common thicknesses of leads and slugs

are required. They are cast or rolled in several thicknesses ranging from one to twelve points in the printers' measure. If the width is less than six points, the piece is called a *lead;* if its width is six points or more, it is called a *slug.*

By far the most common thicknesses of leads and slugs are two points, and six points, respectively. In fact, the term, "a lead," would be understood to mean a two-point lead, and the term, "a slug," to mean a six-point slug unless otherwise specified. Fig. 26, above, illustrates some of the other common thicknesses of leads and slugs.

Leads and slugs are sold in strips twenty-four inches in length, to be cut to measure as needed, or in labor-saving fonts, ready-cut, in the various standard lengths. Labor-saving material is most commonly used, and it is regularly furnished in graduated lengths, from four to twenty-five picas. Longer lengths are made up as ordered.

Fig. 27. A lead and slug case

41. **Brass leads.** The one-point leads (about 1/72 inch thick) may be obtained in either lead or brass, but brass is ordinarily used, for it is much stronger, and will not become damaged as easily as the soft lead. One-point brass leads are furnished in labor-saving fonts of one to twenty pica lengths, and are kept in small Brass Lead Cases.

Brass leads and slugs are frequently used in place of lead ones, for spacing out newspaper columns, in which spacing material is subjected to particularly hard usage.

42. **Lead cases and racks.** Leads and slugs are kept in cases or racks, which are partitioned for the separation of the different lengths of material. One of the most common styles of lead and slug cases is shown above.

Lead racks, also, are designed in a number of sizes and styles for use with modern composing-room cabinets.

43. **Proper method of piecing leads.** When the leads of any certain length are exhausted, it may be necessary to piece, or splice, leads of shorter lengths to complete a job,

using two shorter leads in place of the longer one. When this is done, the break in the leads should not come at the same place in each line, as this would make the form weak and difficult to handle without becoming pied.* The proper way to piece leads is to use the long and short lengths alternately, as is indicated in the following diagram.

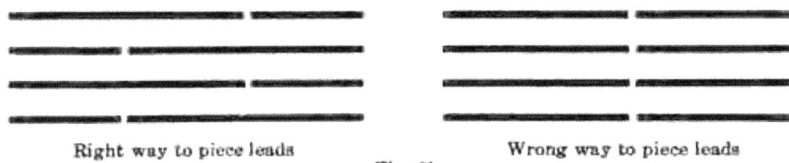

Right way to piece leads   Wrong way to piece leads

Fig. 28

44. **Solid matter.** Type is said to be set solid when no leads are used between the lines. In the figure below, the upper section of a paragraph of six-point type is set solid, i.e., without leads, while the lower section is leaded.

SPACES AND QUADS

45. **Spaces and quads** are type bodies, less than type high, that are used for the purpose of separating the words in a line; for making indentions; and for blanking out the lines of type to any required length. They are of the same body size as that of the type with which they are used, and they are made in six standard widths, for each size of type. Fig. 30, on the following page, illustrates the most common uses of spaces and quads in combination with type characters.

SOLID | Large types and borders that can not be properly placed in ordinary type cases are sometimes stored in blank or tray cases. Some are provided with movable partitions, fitting into slotted sides, and they

LEADED | may be used to advantage for the storage of the larger sizes of type that are infrequently used. Wood type is regularly stored in special blank cases with adjustable partitions. Printing plates, also, are filed in special blank cases or trays.

Fig. 29. An illustration of solid and leaded matter

* Types are said to be pied when they are mixed up or jumbled. To pi a form is to wreck it, or to mix up the letters of which it is composed. Mixed type is printers' pi.

The *em quad* (■) is the unit of spacing material, and it is always a square of the size of the type to which it belongs. An em quad of 12 point type is 12x12 points; an em quad of 8 point type is 8x8 points, etc.

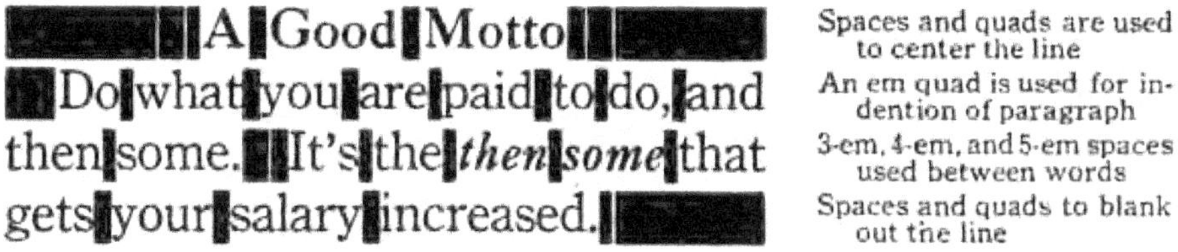

■■■■A Good Motto■■
Do what you are paid to do, and then some. It's the *then some* that gets your salary increased.

Fig. 30

Spaces and quads are used to center the line

An em quad is used for indention of paragraph

3-em, 4-em, and 5-em spaces used between words

Spaces and quads to blank out the line

The *en quad* (▮) is always one-half the width of the em quad. Thus, a 10 point en quad is 10x5 points; a 6 point en quad is 6x3 points, etc. Some printers call this item of spacing the "nut quad," to avoid confusion between the terms "em" and "en," but this is by no means general.

The *3-em space* (▮)* is one-third the width of the square, or em quad. It is the standard space used between words in a line, in ordinary composition, and it occupies a convenient box near the center of the case.

The other spaces are known as *4-em* (▮) and *5-em spaces* (▮) and they are one-fourth, and and one-fifth, of the em quad, respectively. They are located in smaller boxes, in the upper left corner of the lower case.

Standard Scheme of Quads and Spaces

3-em quad	████	3
2-em quad ..	███	2
Em quad	██	1
En quad	█	$\frac{1}{2}$
3-em space	▮	$\frac{1}{3}$
4-em space	▮	$\frac{1}{4}$
5-em space	▮	$\frac{1}{5}$

Fig. 31

Hair spaces, somewhat thinner than the 5-em spaces, are sometimes furnished, especially with types above 12 point.

* The terms 3-em, 4-em, and 5-em are contractions of 3-to-em, 4-to-em, and 5-to-em, indicating three spaces to the em, four to the em, and five to the em, respectively.

46. **Spaces cast to point widths.** As we have previously stated, the em quad and the en quad are always exactly a square, and half-square, of the type body. Spaces, however, are cast according to a standard system whereby the odd

STANDARD WIDTHS OF POINT-SET SPACES				
Body Size	3-em Space	4-em Space	5-em Space	Thin Space
6 pt.	2	$1\frac{1}{2}$	$1\frac{1}{4}$	1
8 pt.	3	2	$1\frac{1}{2}$	$1\frac{1}{4}$
10 pt.	$3\frac{1}{2}$	$2\frac{1}{2}$	2	$1\frac{3}{4}$
12 pt.	4	3	$2\frac{1}{2}$	$1\frac{3}{4}$
14 pt.	5	4	3	2

Fig. 32

fractions of points are dropped, and therefore they are not always exactly proportionate to the em. For example, a 10 point 3-em space, theoretically, would be $3\frac{1}{3}$ points wide, but it is cast $3\frac{1}{2}$ points wide. The 5-em space of 8 point

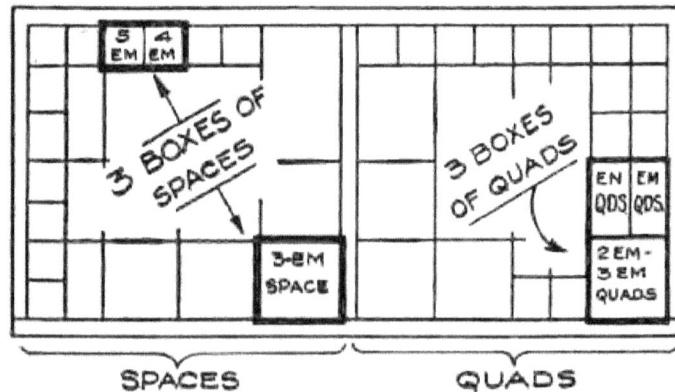

Fig. 33

type is $1\frac{1}{2}$ points wide, instead of $1\frac{5}{8}$ points. This system is particularly helpful in tabular composition, and in making alignments with different sizes of type. The exact widths of the different spaces are given in the accompanying table.

Most spaces are cast without nicks, for this material does not have front or back, head or foot, and a space may be turned in any position in the composing stick.

47. **Location of spacing material.** It will aid the student to note that there are three boxes of quads, in the right section of the lower case, and three boxes of spaces, in the left section. Study the diagram on the preceding page.

BRASS AND COPPER THIN SPACES

48. **Thin spaces,** in graduated sizes from six to seventy-two points, are made up in special fonts, and kept in small cases of the style illustrated here. They are made in one-half point and one-point thicknesses, the former of copper, and the latter of brass. Thin spaces are used for very exact spacing and justification, in tabular and display composition. Brass and copper spaces should not be used by the beginner in ordinary work.

Fig. 34

METAL FURNITURE

49. **Metal furniture** is the name given to metal blocks used for blanking out, wherever an area of white space is desired in a type form. They are made of lead, iron, or steel, and are put up in fonts of assorted sizes, all accurately trimmed to pica widths and lengths. The ordinary font scheme for metal furniture includes the lengths of 4, 5, 6, 8, 10, 15, 20, and 25 picas, in 2, 3, 4, 5, 6, 8, and 10 pica widths. There are also fonts of 6, 12, 18, 24, and 30 pica lengths. Longer pieces are sometimes used, and they are obtainable in special assortments, or fonts.

Fonts of mammoth iron furniture are made for blanking out in large forms. Some are of a pattern similar to this illustration. Sectional iron furniture, consisting of bars of metal, in various lengths, notched at both ends, is also used. Four pieces fitted together form a hollow rectangle.

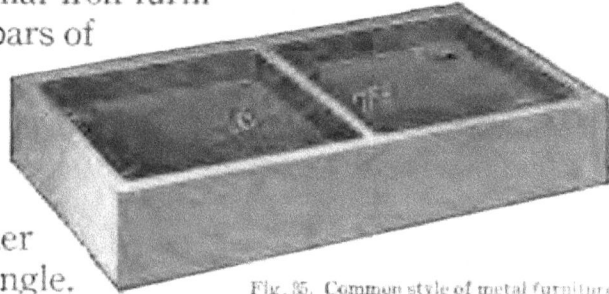

Fig. 35. Common style of metal furniture

WOOD FURNITURE

50. Wood furniture is used principally in locking up forms for the press. It is cut to accurate pica measurements, and is made up in fonts of assorted sizes. There are two font schemes for wood furniture, one in graduations of 5 and 10 picas in length, from 10 to 60 picas, and the other in graduations of 6 picas, from 12 to 60 picas. In both of these schemes the widths are 2, 3, 4, 5, 6, 8, and 10 picas. The length is stamped on the end of each piece. Lengths greater than 60 picas are furnished for locking large forms for cylinder presses.

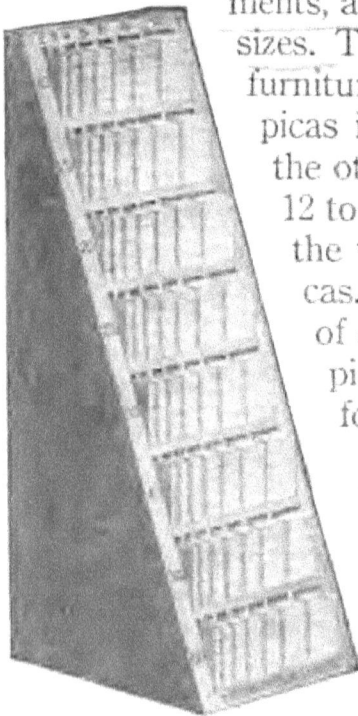

As the 4 pica width is almost as high as it is wide, the top surface is grooved, to insure its correct position in the form. This groove, therefore, should be placed up (or down) to make the spacing right.

Wood furniture is not reliable where absolutely accurate spacing is required, as it is affected by moisture and by changes of atmosphere, and is apt to become swelled or warped.

Fig. 36. A font of wood furniture

A common style of rack for wood furniture is shown in Fig. 36. In most composing rooms, the wood furniture is kept in compartments built into the side of the imposing table, on which the forms are locked up.

51. **Reglet** is wood furniture in narrow strip form. It is made in nonpareil and pica thicknesses, and is used in lock-up work, and occasionally in some other places where accuracy in spacing is not so important.

CORNER QUADS

52. **Corner quads** are L-shaped leads and slugs, sometimes used at the corners of a piece of composition, to hold the form more firmly together. They especially help to hold mitered corners in position, and to align small border units. They are made in 2, 3, and 6 point thicknesses, each piece measuring 4x4 picas outside, and sold in sets of four.

SUGGESTIONS

Get acquainted with the various items of spacing material in your shop. Find out what each is like, and where it is kept. Examine the standing type forms in the chases, or on the stone, and see how these materials have been used in each of them.

Give special attention to the system of quads and spaces. After you have learned the name of each piece, and where it is found, go to the case and learn to distinguish each piece as you handle it.

QUESTIONS

1. What are the principal uses of leads and slugs?
2. In what manner should leads be pieced? Why?
3. What term is applied to matter set without leads?
4. What is the unit of type-spacing material?
5. Name the various quads and spaces in the type case.
6. Tell the relation each bears to the unit of spacing.
7. What significance has the term "3-em space"?
8. Should brass and copper thin spaces be used in ordinary composition?
9. Tell what you can about metal furniture.
10. What can you say of wood furniture?
11. What are corner quads, and what purpose do they serve?

CHAPTER VI

The Process of Setting Type

FOUNDRY TYPE is assembled into forms by hand, the type being picked from the case and placed into a composing stick, in which it is arranged and spaced as desired.

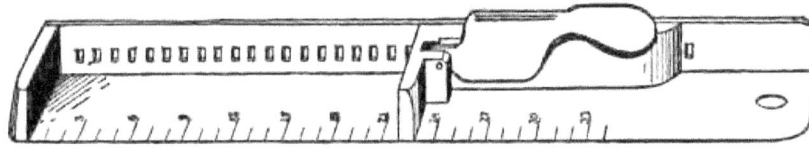

Fig. 37. The Rouse Composing Stick, which sets automatically to standard lengths

53. **Composing sticks.** There are a number of styles of composing sticks. Some of the most common styles are shown herewith. They may be had in different lengths,

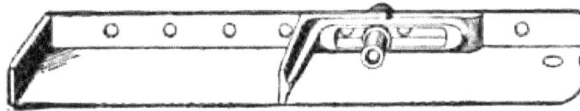

Fig. 38. Common Screw Stick, adjustable to any width

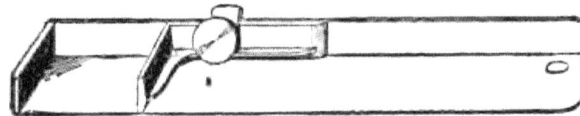

Fig. 39. Yankee Job Stick, a screw-adjusting stick

and in 2, $2\frac{1}{4}$, and $2\frac{1}{2}$-inch widths. The 2-inch width is most common, especially for the use of students. Some sticks set automatically to even pica widths, as the Rouse stick shown above, while others have an adjusting screw by which they may be set to any width. With the latter kind, it is well to allow the instructor to set it to the measure until the student learns to make strictly accurate adjustments.

54. **Method of holding the stick.** See that the composing stick is set to the desired measure. Place a slug of that measure in the stick. Then take the composing stick in the

left hand, holding it with the open side out, i.e., toward the case. Place the thumb of the left hand inside the stick, and close the fingers across the bottom of it, the finger tips clinching the closed side which is held nearest you. Tilt the stick toward you slightly, so that the letters will not fall over when they are placed in position.

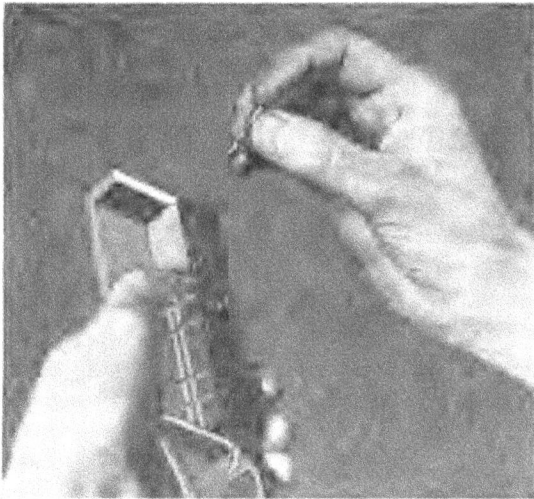

Fig. 40. Proper positions of the hands in typesetting

Always stand erect and do not rest the left elbow or forearm on the case, as you work. The left arm should swing freely above the case, so that the hand grasping the stick may incline to meet the right hand as the types are picked from the various boxes. It is only by this method that one may expect to develop skill and speed in the setting of type.

This method of holding the stick, and especially the tilting of the left elbow, will appear somewhat awkward and difficult at first, but one soon becomes accustomed to it, and then it seems very easy and natural.

Better results will be had if one's coat is removed, and the shirt sleeves are rolled up, as this allows more freedom of the arms, and the cuffs will then not interfere with the movements across the case. This also gives one an attitude of industry that is essential to the mastery of a trade.

55. **Setting type.** In starting to set type, select the letters from the boxes, one at a time, with the right hand, and deposit them in the stick. First, sight into the proper box, and, as you reach toward it, select a type that is lying loose

It is impossible for the beginner to acquire either speed or accuracy in composition until he is able to read type. Type is read from left to right as are the lines on the printed page, but the characters are upside down. With a little practice, the reading of type will become comparatively easy. Do not read type in any other manner than upside down, from left to right.

A paragraph of 12 point type

This is a photograph of the paragraph shown above. Practice in the reading of this type will be helpful to the beginner

Fig. 41

at the top of the pile. Take the type between the thumb and forefinger, and, as you draw it toward the stick, turn it face up and with the nick away from you. Deposit the letter in this position, in the left side of the stick, placing

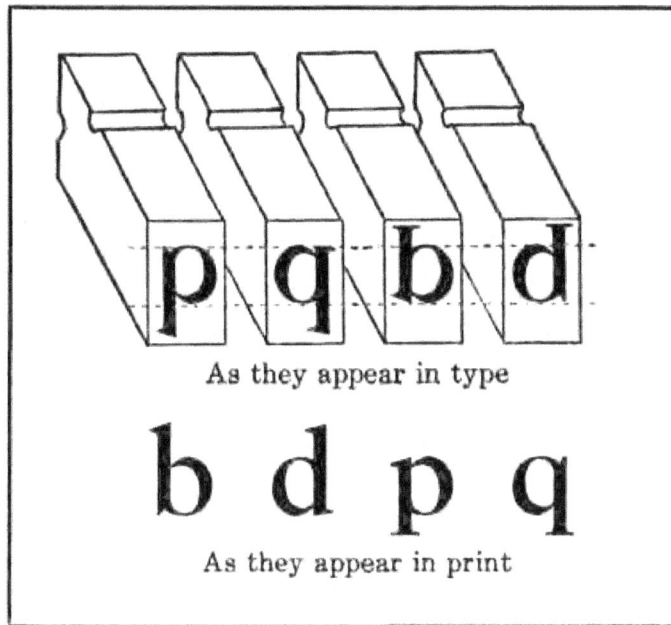

As they appear in type

b d p q

As they appear in print

Fig. 42

the left thumb against it to hold it in position. Place the next letter to the right of this one, moving the thumb into the new position as each letter arrives in the stick, and so on until the line is set. The line of type will then appear in the stick with the letters upside down, but reading from left to right, as is the matter on the printed page.

56. **Always read type upside down.** Fig. 41, on page 41, shows a paragraph of 12 point type in print, and a photograph of this matter as it appears in type. You will notice that both groups read from left to right, but in the type form the letters are upside down. This is the correct way to read type, and with a little practice any student will be

Helpful Exercises in Mastering the "Four Demons"				
bud	drab	equip	pad	pebbled
bind	daub	piquant	quad	quibble
bead	dumb	plaque	drip	pedal
broad	dribble	opaque	bump	piebald

Fig. 43

able to read it easily and rapidly.* Never attempt to read type from the opposite side, as it will interfere with the development of ability to read it easily, and without strain.

57. **The four demons.** There are four letters which are somewhat confusing to the beginner, and which may cause him considerable trouble unless he gives special attention to them. They are the letters b, d, p, and q. Their forms are very similar, but two of them have ascending strokes, while two have descending strokes; in two the bowl of the letter curves forward from the stem, while in the other two it curves backward. If one will keep in mind that the nick of the type is at the foot of the letter, and that, when held upside down, the letter reads from left to right, there will be little difficulty in recognizing any of them. A careful study of the diagram in Fig. 42 will be very helpful.

The letters n and u, also, may be confusing until one has had a little practice in the reading of type.

To the beginner, capital I, lower-case l, and figure 1 may seem similar, but close inspection reveals their differences. The same is true of the capital O, the lower-case o, and the figure 0, but each has its distinguishing size and shape.

*"The young compositor should read over every line as soon as he sets it, and at once correct any detected errors. Before he empties the matter on the galley he should read it again, looking for outs [omissions] and doublets [words repeated]. The time given to correction in the stick is not time lost. It is easier to correct there than on the galley or the stone, and it is worth a deal of trouble to acquire the reputation of a clean compositor."—Theodore DeVinne, in *Modern Methods of Book Composition*.

58. Simple type-assembling exercises. Do not attempt to set any finished work at first. Begin with single words, placing them in the stick in the correct manner, reading them in the stick, and then replacing the type into the correct boxes. By this method, you will become accustomed to the proper procedure of typesetting, and will then be ready for actual work.

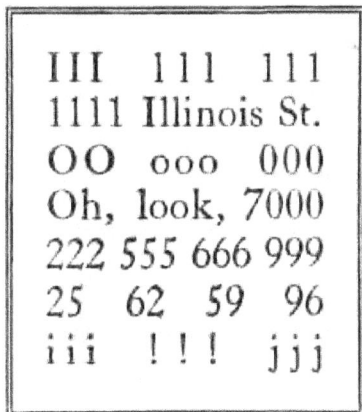

```
III   111   111
1111 Illinois St.
O O   ooo   000
Oh, look, 7000
222 555 666 999
25   62   59   96
iii   ! ! !   jjj
```

Fig. 44

Among other exercises, set up the characters appearing in Fig. 44, one line at a time, and replace them after you have carefully examined and compared the letters.

Follow this by setting up your name, address, and other items that may be of interest, but do not fill in more than a line at a time, and do not attempt to obtain a print from these first few exercises.

JUSTIFICATION AND SPACING

59. Justification of lines. Justification is the practice of spacing out lines of type so that each line will be firm in the stick, and all lines will be set to exactly the same width. Each line must be spaced in such a way that it will be snug and firm, but not too tight. There must be no "play" in the line, yet it should not be difficult to remove any individual letter from the line as it stands in the stick.

If a line is too loose, types may drop out of the form, either when the type is taken from the stick or the galley, or even after the form is locked for the press. Also, the letters may lean slightly toward one end of the line, so that the types will not strike the sheet squarely, causing only one side of the faces to print, after the form has been placed on the press. This is known as the type being "off its feet."

If a line is too tight, it may spring the composing stick, throwing other lines out of true justification. If it reaches the stone without readjustment, it will seriously interfere with the locking up of the form. Also, when types are forced into the stick, they are apt to become bent or broken in the process.

The art of accurate justification is one of the most necessary accomplishments of a compositor. The beginner should especially strive to learn and practice it in the most thorough manner. The proper measure of success in all one's future work in typography depends on the ability to justify lines of type accurately, and no one should slight this important phase of the work.

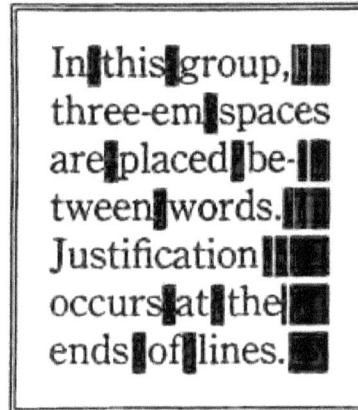

Fig. 45

60. **Justifying work in uneven lines.** Let your first work in composition consist of exercises in using uniform spaces between each of the words in the lines, placing the justification at the ends of the lines. This method is indicated in Fig. 45, above, in which type-high spacing has been used.

Use 3-em spaces between words, and an em quad between sentences. Space out all the lines with quads and spaces, always putting all the largest pieces to the outside, and the thinner spaces next to the type, as has been done in this illustration. Be sure that each of the lines is justified *perfectly* before you leave it, regardless of the amount of effort, or time, that seems necessary to accomplish it.

As a project in this simpler style of composition, set up the exercise given in Fig. 46. Set it line for line as it now appears, placing all the extra spacing at the ends of the lines. If you use 8 point type, set your stick 18 picas wide; if 10 point, set it to 20 picas; if 12 point, set it to 23 picas.

THE AMERICAN'S CREED

I believe in the United States of America as a government of the people, by the people, for the people, whose just powers are derived from the consent of the governed; a democracy in a republic; a sovereign nation of many states; a perfect union, one and inseparable; established upon those principles of freedom — equality, justice and humanity, for which American patriots have sacrificed their lives and fortunes.

[*Your name here*]

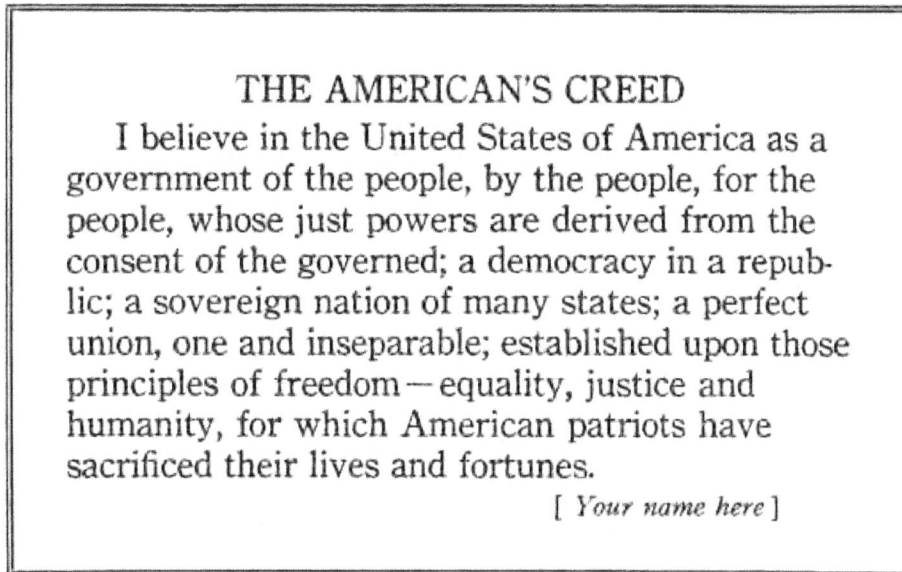

Fig. 46. An exercise in 10 point type, justified at the ends of the lines

61. Justifying straight composition. Nearly all printed matter is set in paragraphs, the full lines of which are set flush, or the full measure of the stick, as is the paragraph you are now reading. Indentions are made at the beginnings of paragraphs, of one em quad or more, according to the width of the lines, and the compositor starts out with 3-em spaces between words. When he arrives at the end of the line, he places no spacing material after the last word (or syllable of a divided word) as has been done in Figs. 45 and 46, but he justifies the line in such a manner that the last word extends flush to the end of the line. If the 3-em spaces between the words are not sufficient to accomplish this, other spaces, or combinations of spaces, are substituted for the 3-em spaces, until the line is sufficiently firm.

Sometimes the last word on a line must be divided, in order to avoid awkward and unsightly spacing. In every case, the word must be divided correctly between syllables and a hyphen placed after the first section of the word. A syllable of one letter is never separated from the rest of the

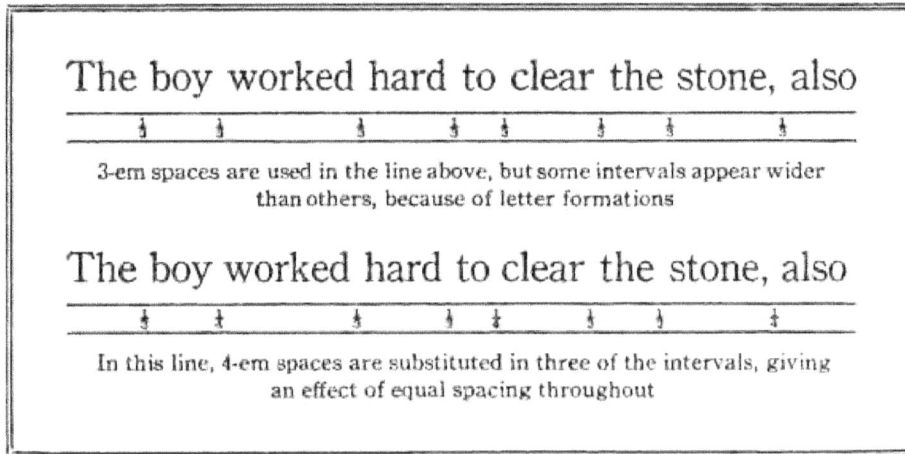

The boy worked hard to clear the stone, also

3-em spaces are used in the line above, but some intervals appear wider than others, because of letter formations

The boy worked hard to clear the stone, also

In this line, 4-em spaces are substituted in three of the intervals, giving an effect of equal spacing throughout

Fig. 47

word, and syllables of two or three letters are not commonly separated in wide measure composition. Also, hyphens are not placed at the ends of a number of consecutive lines, if it can be avoided without awkward spacing.

62. **Equal spacing between words.** In justifying a line, it is necessary that an equal amount of space shall appear in each interval between words. An unevenly spaced line is unsightly, is more difficult to read, and brands the work as inferior and uncraftsmanlike. While it is impossible to reach the point where the spacing will be absolutely exact and uniform, good composition demands that this goal be constantly in mind, and that the spacing shall at least appear uniform to the eye, when the matter shall be printed.

63. **Letter forms affect spacing.** In spacing lines, it is necessary to consider that although one might have a line spaced mechanically perfect, it might not appear so to the eye because of the differences in individual letter formations. One will find more white space between a word ending with a rounded character (as c, e, or o), or a slanting character (as v, w, or y) and the next word beginning with either style of letter, than will be found where the endings are full-faced, or flush with the type body. Study Fig. 47.

For example, when a word ends with the letter d, and the next word begins with b (as in wood block), the space between these words must necessarily be wider than that between a word ending with e and the next one beginning with c (as in the case). In capitals, this difference is much more clearly noticeable.

Less space may also be had in intervals that include such punctuation marks as a period, comma, or apostrophe, because the face covers so little of the body.

COMPARATIVE WIDTHS OF SPACING BETWEEN WORDS		
Combinations of Spaces Between Words	Fraction of Em	Per cent of Em
3-em _ _ _ _ _ _ _	$\frac{1}{3}$	_ _ .33+
5-em+5-em _ _	$\frac{1}{5}+\frac{1}{5}$	_ _ .40
4-em+5-em _ _	$\frac{1}{4}+\frac{1}{5}$	_ _ .45
En quad _ _ _ _	$\frac{1}{2}$	_ _ .50
3-em+5-em _ _	$\frac{1}{3}+\frac{1}{5}$	_ _ .53+
3-em+4-em _ _	$\frac{1}{3}+\frac{1}{4}$	_ _ .58+
3-em+3-em _ _	$\frac{1}{3}+\frac{1}{3}$	_ _ .67-

Fig. 48

If only a very small amount of space must be added to a line, it may be placed between the shorter words, without a displeasing effect. Spacing on both sides of short words such as in, of, and at, should always be exactly the same, as any variation will be noticeable.

64. **Correct method of spacing out.** If it is found that the 3-em spaces placed between words do not completely fill out the line, they should be supplanted by combinations of a 4-em and 5-em space in each interval; if wider spacing is necessary, en quads may be used instead of the 3-em spaces. For still wider spacing, the combination of a 3-em and a 4-em space, or of two 3-em spaces, may be used.

65. **The wrong method.** When the beginner finds that 3-em spaces between words are not enough to fill out the line, he may be tempted merely to add thinner spaces to the 3-em spaces, until the line becomes firmly justified. This is a slovenly and inexcusable practice which causes part of the line to be more widely spaced than the rest, producing

a broken-up, uneven effect which even to the casual reader is quite displeasing. Unless spaces can be added to all the 3-em spaces in the line, then *none should be added,* but substitutions should be made for some or all of the 3-em spaces.

When less space is required between words, 4-em spaces may be substituted, and in special emergencies, 5-em spaces may be placed between certain words. However, unless very small shrinkage is necessary, it will be better to increase the space than to decrease it.

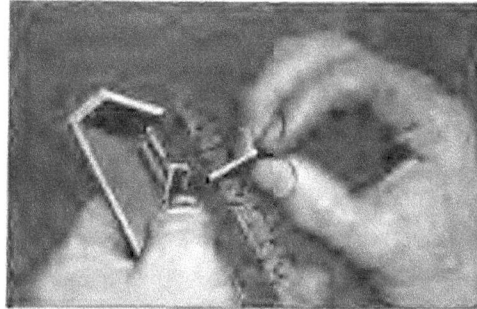

Fig. 49. Proper method of substituting one space for another, in a line of type

In Fig. 48 the various combinations of spaces are listed in the order of their width, and their ratios to the em quad are given in fractions and decimals. A study of this table will aid the student in selecting the proper spaces.

When substituting spaces in the line, hold the stick as shown in Fig. 49. Tilt the stick toward you, and hold the line in position with the left thumb while dislodging the 3-em spaces with the spaces to be inserted in their places. In this way the original spaces are pried out, and the new ones inserted without disturbing any of the letters.

SUGGESTIONS

Practice the reading of type forms about the shop. Remember *never* to allow yourself to read type otherwise than upside down, left to right.

Never be satisfied with "good enough" in justification. Make every line perfect. This cannot be too strongly emphasized, as your success as a printer depends on your ability to do the most accurate work.

As an aid to learning the positions of the letters in the case, the list of exercises on the following page will be helpful, as each of the sentences in this list will be found to contain all the letters in the alphabet.

Fig. 50. View in composing room of the Stone Printing & Manufacturing Co., Roanoke, Va.

1. The quick brown fox jumps over the lazy dog.
2. I endeavored to puzzle the ex-spy by quickly jumping forward!
3. A quick movement of the enemy would jeopardize six gunboats.
4. The public was amazed to view the quickness and dexterity of the juggler.
5. Dexterity in the vocation of printing may be acquired by judicious work and zealous effort.

QUESTIONS

1. Demonstrate and explain the method of holding the stick
2. What should be the position of the compositor at the case?
3. How are types placed in the stick?
4. In what position is type always read?
5. How can you distinguish between the letters b, d, p, and q?
6. What is meant by justification?
7. Why is accurate justification necessary?
8. How do letter forms affect spacing?
9. Name the space combinations in the order of their width.
10. Explain the procedure of justifying a line.

CHAPTER VII

The Handling of Type Forms

AFTER the type-matter has been set up in the composing stick, it is removed from the stick and placed on a flat, rectangular tray with three sides, called a *galley*. It is then tied up, and a proof of it is taken. If any corrections are necessary, they are made, and the form is then placed on the stone to be locked up for the press, or is stored away for future use.

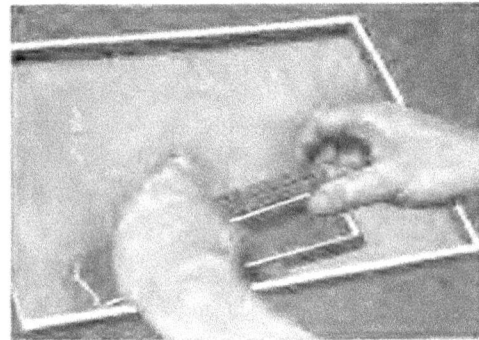

Fig. 51. Removing type from stick to galley

66. Removing type from the stick. The composing stick is placed flat on the galley or stone, with the open side away from the compositor, and the type is removed from the stick in the following manner:

a. Grip the type with the thumbs at the head, and first fingers at the foot of the matter, and with the tips of the second, or middle, fingers pressing against the open edge of the composing stick.

b. Pry the type to the outer edge of the stick by pressing out with the thumbs and holding the stick in position with the middle fingers. Be sure that the thumbs are low enough to press against the body of the type.

c. Continue to press the type matter out of the stick, retaining a firm grip of the thumbs and first fingers at the head and foot, and, as the matter leaves the stick, let it slide between the sides of the middle fingers, as shown above.

Fig. 52. View in Composing Room of the Dietz Printing Co., Richmond, Va.

d. Retaining the positions of the thumbs and fingers, press the type firmly on all sides, and you may pick it up without any difficulty, or risk of pi-ing the type, unless the lines have been very poorly justified.

It is well for the student to begin with only one or two lines at first, until he becomes accustomed to this procedure. It is possible to remove only a portion of the matter in the stick at a time, if there is more of it than can be safely handled in one lift. Never unlock the composing stick before removing the type.

Be sure that there is a slug at both the head and foot of any type form before attempting to handle it.

Some compositors lift the type upward and outward from the composing stick with a sort of rolling motion, instead of sliding it out along the floor of the stick, but it is safer for the beginner to follow the practice here described.

67. **Placing type in galley.** The galley should always be placed in a tilted, or slanting, position, on the type case or workbank, with the head, or closed end of the galley, to the right, and the left side of the galley at the bottom.

To place type on the galley, grip it on all sides in the manner described above, and lower it in such position that the left side of the form rests against the left, or lower, side of the galley. Then slide it into the corner, with the head of the form against the head of the galley. Make sure that the matter is snug in its position, and that the type is firm, and square on its feet.

The proper position for type in the galley is shown in Fig. 53. It should never be placed otherwise than with the head of the type against the head of the galley, and with the type matter resting on its left side, as indicated.

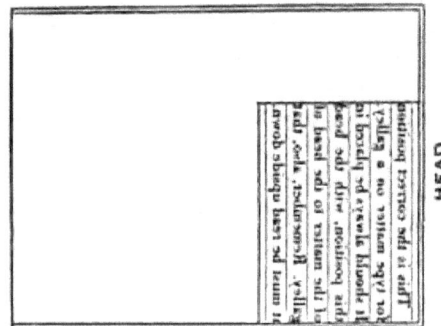

Fig. 53. Proper position of type on galley

68. **Tying up the form.** To prevent the type from being pied in further handling, a strong, light cord is wrapped tightly around it a number of times and then the loose end is wedged underneath the strands of the cord, to hold it securely in place. No knot is tied. The first end is caught at the corner and held by the second and subsequent laps of the cord, and the other is drawn or pushed through the thicknesses of the cord, in the form of a small loop, or noose, which is pulled out when the form is to be untied.

The cord is usually wound clockwise around the form, beginning at the upper left-hand corner. After the second or third lap, the left hand will be free to steady the form, and to assist in securing an even tension of the cord. If it is drawn tightly just before each corner is turned, the form will be firmly and securely bound together.

As the details for the tying of forms differ slightly in different shops, it will be well for the beginner to take his pattern from his instructor. With a little practice in tying up forms, he should soon be able to do it quite well.

Type matter should never be tied up in the composing stick, but always when on the galley, in proper position.

Forms that are tied up should be handled carefully, as they may become pied quite easily, even though wrapped in this way. When picked up in the hands, they should be grasped firmly, in the same manner as though not tied.

69. **Emptying the galley.** To remove the form from the galley after it is tied up, it is only necessary to place the open end of the galley flatly on the surface of the stone, or the letterboard, and slide the form out of it. With large forms, it is easier to place the galley on the stone, move the type to the edge of the galley, and then to draw the galley out from under the form.

SUGGESTIONS

Somewhat of practice is required in removing type from the stick, before it can be done gracefully, and with safety. It is well to practice a number of times with only one or two lines of type, and then gradually increase the amount handled as one's ability develops. Some instructors recommend that linotype slugs be substituted for type, for the first few times. When lines are pied, usually it is because the beginner exerts too little pressure against the ends of the lines with the middle fingers.

In learning to tie up type, preliminary practice with a type-high cut, or with linotype slugs, instead of a type form, will prevent the possibility of pi-ing a form. In some shops, the tie-up cords are saved and used more than once. When removed, they are tied in the "printers' knot," which your instructor will teach you to tie.

Caution, care, and judgment go a long way in the development of the ability to handle type forms successfully.

QUESTIONS

1. What operations follow the setting of type in the stick?
2. Explain and demonstrate how type is removed from the stick?
3. How does accurate justification assist in this operation?
4. Explain how type is placed in a galley.
5. What is the proper position of a galley for holding type?
6. What is meant by tying up a form?
7. Explain the method of tying up a form?
8. Should type be tied up in the composing stick?
9. How would you pick up a small form that is tied up? A large one?
10. How are forms removed from the galley to the stone?

CHAPTER VIII

Proofing and Correcting Forms

AFTER a job is tied up, a proof is taken, and corrections, if necessary, are made. In modern plants practically all proofs are taken on proof presses, but occasionally it is necessary to take a proof by hand, at the stone, and the young printer should know how to "pull a proof" by either method.

Fig. 54. A brayer

70. **Taking stone proofs.** In taking proofs at the stone, the type is inked with a small hand roller, known as a *brayer* (Fig. 54), and then a sheet of paper is laid over the face of the type, and an impression is made by the use of a proof planer* and a mallet (Fig. 55). The planer is lowered gently on the form, and is held firmly in position while it is tapped with the mallet. If the form is large, the planer will be moved into new positions across the form, but it must not be allowed to strike the form, or to rebound with the stroke of the mallet. The force of the mallet

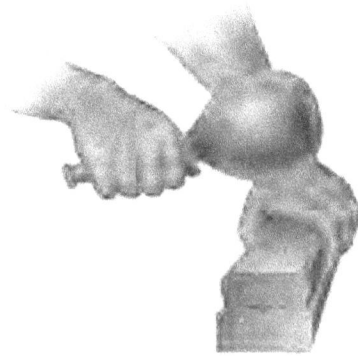

Fig. 55. Method of taking a stone proof

should be delivered perpendicularly to the center of the planer, and should not be stronger than is necessary to get

---

*The proof planer must not be confused with the regular type planer. The face of the former is covered with a thick padding of felt, for receiving an impression of the type. The latter is made of hard wood, and is used for the planing down, or levelling, of type in the chase. Proofing of type must never be attempted with a type planer.

a fairly clear impression on the paper. Printers frequently strike the planer with the end of the handle—the mallet being held in a perpendicular position, with the head up—rather than with the head of the mallet, as a steadier blow may be given in this manner, with less danger of slurring.

Special care must be taken when proofing forms that have small groups of type, surrounded by blank space, or those containing kerned or delicate letters, as much damage may be done them by careless handling of the planer, or by striking too hard a blow with the mallet. End letters, also, are very easily damaged.

The ordinary paper used for stone proofs is a thin stock, glazed on one side and rough on the other, commonly known as dry proofing paper. The smooth side is laid on the face of the type. When other kinds of paper are used, soft paper should be chosen, and it should be dampened on one side, and then the dry side applied to the type. A sponge is used for this purpose.

Fig. 56. Taking a proof on the Potter Proof Press

Sufficient margins should be allowed on all proofs for the marking of any corrections that may be necessary.

The art of pulling a stone proof is acquired by diligent practice, and at best, the proofs are only passing fair, and are never obtained without more or less injury to the type.

71. **Using the proof press.** In taking a proof on a proof press, the galley containing the form is placed on the bed of the press, the type is inked with a brayer, a sheet of proof paper is laid on the inked form, and an impression is taken by turning the cylinder over, thus bringing it into contact with the type form on the bed of the press.

Some proof presses provide grippers for carrying the sheet around the cylinder instead of laying it loose on the type form, and some, like the Vandercook Composing Room Cylinder Proof Press as shown in Fig. 57, also ink the type forms automatically.

The amount of impression is regulated by the thickness of the packing on the cylinder, or a sheet may be placed under the galley, if additional pressure is needed. This should never be done in any case without the consent of the instructor, for if the impression is too great, type will be ruined.

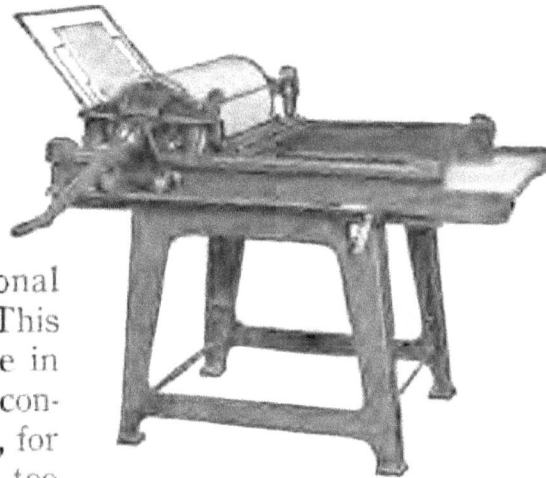

Fig. 57. The Vandercook Composing Room Cylinder, a self-inking proof press

For proofing long columns of body composition, such as large masses of straight matter in news and book galleys, a galley press as shown in Fig. 58 is sometimes used. The galley of type matter is placed in the bed of the press, the type is inked and a strip of paper laid over it, and then the heavy iron roller, covered with a thick padding of felt, is rolled over the type. This is the style of proof press commonly used in the smaller newspaper offices. Small type forms, or open display matter, should not be proofed on the galley press.

Fig. 58. A galley press

72. **Type must be thoroughly cleaned.** As soon as proofs have been taken, the type should be cleaned in a thorough manner. A cloth dampened with benzine should be used to

wipe the ink from the faces of the letters, and if this is not sufficient, the brush may be used to clean the shoulders of the type. The brush should never be used first, as it will only drive the ink from the faces of the letters down into the body of the form. Finally, the type should be wiped with a clean, soft cloth, removing all particles of dirt.

Fig. 59. Replacing a line in the stick, for correction

If ink is allowed to dry on the type, it will become very difficult to remove, and good printing is impossible if types are caked with ink.

73. **Making corrections.** After a proof of the job has been taken, it is read for errors, and is then placed in the compositor's hands, that he may make the desired corrections. The type form is replaced upon the galley, in the correct position, untied, and the corrections are made.

A few corrections can be made without taking the type back into the stick. If a letter is upside down, it may be turned about without changing the justification of the line; a damaged letter may be replaced by a sound one; a period may be substituted for a comma, as they are of equal width; one figure may be exchanged for another; or any character may be inserted that is *exactly* the width of the one taken out. For all other corrections, each line to be corrected must be taken back into the stick, and rejustified.

To replace a line in the stick, open the piece of composition to that line, in the manner illustrated in Fig. 59. Tilt the line forward and, gripping it on all sides, lift it back into the stick. When the line is corrected, replace it in the form.

Haphazard "justifying" of the lines in the open galley is inaccurate, slovenly, and a source of difficulty in all subsequent handling of the form. It will save time and trouble to make corrections in the stick, as is here recommended.

74. **Revised proofs.** When the corrections have been made, they should be checked with the proof to make sure that none have been overlooked, and then a second, or revised, proof should be taken. The original proofs should always accompany revised proofs, when they are submitted for approval.

75. **Use of tweezers.** Tweezers are sometimes used to pick wrong or damaged letters from the type form, or to penetrate into intricate parts, where the fingers cannot very conveniently reach, to make alignment or adjustment of the matter. While they are convenient tools in the hands of careful, trained workmen, they may cause considerable damage, if

Fig. 60. In the composing room of The Lakeside Press, Chicago. Notice the position of workman at the galley

Fig. 61. Printers' tweezers

used awkwardly or carelessly. If the type does not respond to the pull of the tweezers, the points are sure to slip over the shoulders of the letters, ruining the faces of the type. Fig. 62, on the following page, shows what happens when the tweezers slip.

Tweezers should never be used on type in the composing stick; in any form that is tied up tightly; or in any place where the letters are not comparatively loose. Do not use tweezers for anything fingers can do, and

then if they *must* be used, untie the form, and make sure that the types are quite loose and yielding before gripping them with the tweezers.

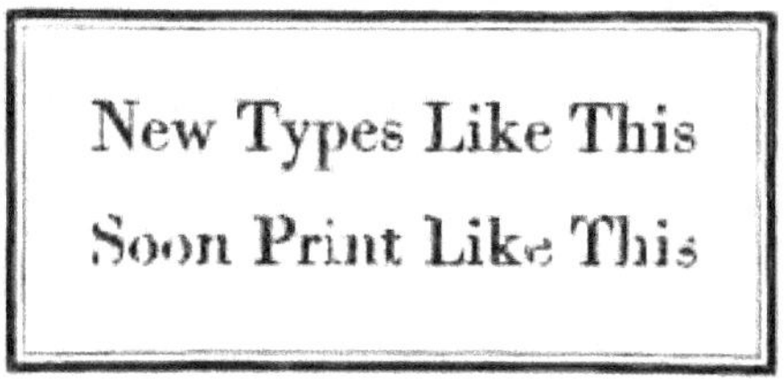

New Types Like This

Soon Print Like This

Fig. 62. What careless use of tweezers will do

In many composing rooms the use of tweezers is absolutely prohibited. While this may seem somewhat drastic, it at least indicates that tweezers may do considerable damage, and that they should be used sparingly, and always be handled with the greatest of care.

SUGGESTIONS

Practice pulling stone proofs on a page of old linotype matter, or an old type form, for the first few times, until you form the proper habit of handling the planer and striking it. There will be little to trouble the beginner in the use of the proof press, provided he makes sure that he understands how to operate it, before making the attempt.

In making corrections, see that the form is in the proper position in the galley, and stand facing the head of the galley as you work. (Study Fig. 60). Do not read the form in any other position. If you pi any type in making corrections, distribute it carefully in the case, and reset such lines as are pied. Then mark them "pied" in your revised proof, so that they will be scanned again by the proofreader.

It is a good plan to retain all one's early proofs in a notebook, in order that reference may be made to them when desired, and one's progress in composition may be readily noted.

QUESTIONS

1. What is a brayer, and how is it used?
2. What is the difference between a proof planer and a type planer?
3. How is a stone proof taken?
4. What caution need be exercised in taking a stone proof?
5. What kind of paper should be used for proofing?
6. Why are margins necessary on all proofs?
7. What is the general principle of the proof press?
8. How and when does one clean a type form?
9. What kind of corrections can be made in the galley or on the stone?
10. Why should corrections be made in the stick?
11. What is a revised proof?
12. Tell what you can about the use of tweezers.

CHAPTER IX

The Distribution of Type

WHEN a piece of composition has been printed, or has served its purpose, the type is put back into the case, and the leads and slugs used with it are sorted and returned to their places.* The process of returning the type to its proper boxes in the case is called *distribution* of type.

76. **Distribution from galley.** The form to be distributed should be placed on a galley in correct position, the string removed, and the form pressed snugly against the head of the galley. Lifts of type will then be taken from the foot of the matter, and the head will not be disturbed until the last. This procedure minimizes the possibility of pi-ing the lines when sections of the matter are lifted out.

If it should be necessary for the type to be distributed from the stone, it should be surrounded with furniture on three sides, so that the matter will remain intact.

77. **Identify the type.** Before proceeding with distribution, be doubly sure that you know the size and style of the type in the form, and just where it belongs. Study the face and nick of the letter, compare it with the type in the case, and then if you are not absolutely sure of its identity, consult your instructor. The old adage, "Be sure you're right, then go ahead," is especially applicable to distribution.

If the form contains more than one size or style of type, each kind should be separated, and placed together on the galley, to avoid any mistakes in the distribution.

---

*When a type form has been printed, or for any reason is not to be used further, it is known as a "dead" form. All type that is ready for distribution is called dead matter. To "kill" a type form is to designate it for distribution.

78. **Holding the type.** Grip the lines of type between the thumbs and first fingers, and press in on the ends of the lines with the middle fingers, just as you have done when placing the type on the galley. Lift the type to a horizontal position between the hands. With the type in this position, retain a firm grip of the right hand, and shift the left hand

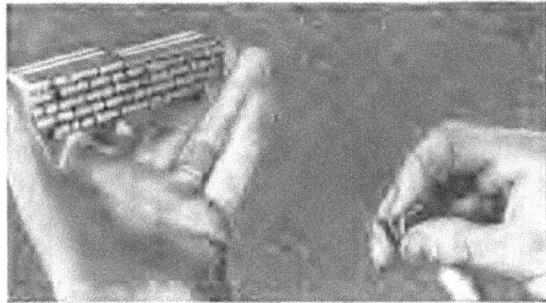

Fig. 63. The proper method of distributing type

into a new position, palm up, the left thumb against the left ends of the lines, the middle finger pressing against the right ends, and the head slug of the type matter supported by the index finger. In Fig. 63 this position is shown. This places the type in the same position as in the stick, the letters upside down, and the lines reading from left to right as on the printed page. Never hold type in any other position, for distribution.

79. **Distributing the letters.** With the type in the left hand, as above described, pick off the letters with the right hand and place them in the proper boxes. Always begin at the *right* side of each line, and take off a word or so at a time, holding the letters, with nicks up and faces toward you, between the thumb and first finger. Let the middle finger assist in tilting the letters apart, so that one will drop at a time. A study of Fig. 63 will help to make this clear.

If words in Italics, or of other fonts, appear in the composition, watch for them as you distribute, and place them in a stick or galley until you are free to put them away. Do not put thin spaces, or other special material, in the case.

Begin by taking one line at a time, and steadily increase the amount as you become accustomed to this procedure, until several lines are taken. *Proceed slowly and carefully.*

Speed must be acquired gradually, and it must not be had at the risk of "dirty" distribution. Accuracy is all-important. One careless distributor can handicap the work of a number of compositors, and throw a whole shop in confusion. All good printers will unite in the declaration that the art of good distribution is a most necessary accomplishment.

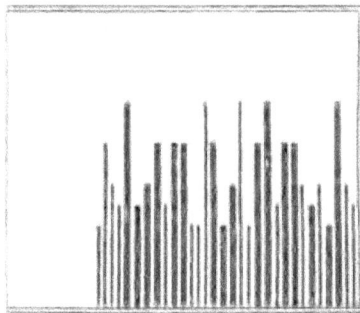

Fig. 64. Proper method of placing leads and slugs in the galley

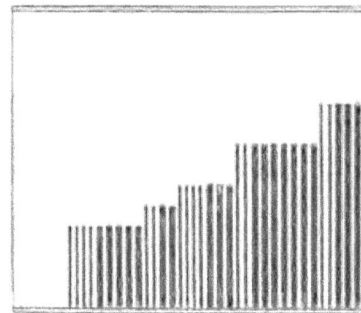

Fig. 65. Leads and slugs sorted and ready for the case

80. **Distributing leads and slugs.** In clearing away leads and slugs, the proper way is to jog them into an upright position in a galley, as is indicated in Fig. 64. First, pick out the longest ones and place them at the head of the galley, then pick out the next in length and line them up against the longest pieces, and so on until each size has been collected and placed in its particular position on the galley. Pick out the slugs and the leads separately, as you proceed, and when you have finished, the entire group of material will be ready to be put away in the case or rack without any further sorting, as it will be graded as shown in Fig. 65. This is not only a more orderly method, but it is also a decided time-saver, as compared with the chance matching of unsorted leads at the case or rack.

Miscellaneous lengths of brass rule should be sorted in this same manner, in the galley. Their surfaces should first be wiped with a clean, soft cloth saturated with gasoline, to remove any dirt from the shoulders or sides of the rules.

SUGGESTIONS

The importance of the most careful distribution of type cannot be over-estimated. It is one of the most vital operations in printing, and the ability to do clean, accurate, dependable work in distribution is an asset that is recognized in the trade. On the other hand, a careless distributor will find no worth-while opportunities awaiting him.

Watch particularly the letters b, d, p, and q, as well as other troublesome characters, and master them. If a word containing any of these letters is picked from the line as a unit, as it should be, the identification will not be difficult. Give particular attention to the various spaces, also, and learn to recognize each with the touch of the fingers.

If some types fall away from the form, and are distributed into the case separately, hold them in the same position as type picked from the line, with nick up and face toward you, as you distribute them.

Do not be discouraged if, at the first, some lines become pied. Most beginners pi some type in their earlier attempts at distribution, although some never do. A thorough understanding of the method, and careful, patient performance, will soon bring the desired results.

DeVinne, in *Modern Methods of Book Composition*, gives the following good advice to beginners: "The novice should distribute carefully and make sure that every type is put in the right box. Speed can be acquired only by practice. As every type wrongly placed makes serious delay in its correction, it is of no advantage to hurry distribution. It will take more time to change one wrong type in the proof than it does to set a dozen letters in the stick. If this wrong letter compels a respacing of the line in the stick, the time so spent will be as great as that taken in the setting of twenty letters. When distributable type contains unusual words, the spelling of these words should be understood before their types are parted. It is better to read the line, and to take up the full word when it can be done."

QUESTIONS

1. What is meant by dead matter?
2. Why is it better to place type on a galley for distribution?
3. How would you proceed to distribute type from the stone?
4. How may one be certain of the indentification of type?
5. If more than one font is represented in a dead form, what should be done?
6. How is a lift of type held for distribution?
7. With which hand are letters placed in the case? How?
8. What should be done with special materials in the form?
9. How does careless distribution interfere with composition?
10. How should leads and slugs be handled?

CHAPTER X

The Printers' System of Measurement

THE unit of measurement for type and all other items of composing material is the *point*, which is approximately 1/72 of an inch. All standard types are cast on the Point System, and all leads and slugs, brass rules, furniture, and other items, are measured in multiples of points.*

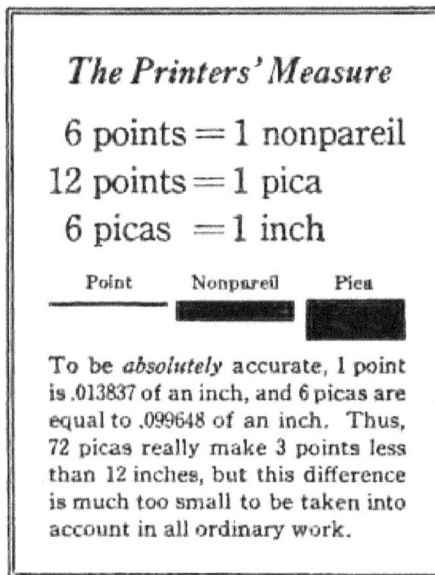

The Printers' Measure

6 points = 1 nonpareil

12 points = 1 pica

6 picas = 1 inch

Point	Nonpareil	Pica

To be *absolutely* accurate, 1 point is .013837 of an inch, and 6 picas are equal to .099648 of an inch. Thus, 72 picas really make 3 points less than 12 inches, but this difference is much too small to be taken into account in all ordinary work.

Fig. 66

A thickness of 6 points is a nonpareil (*non-per-el'*). A 6 point type is known as nonpareil type, a 6 point slug is a nonpareil slug, etc.

The next higher denomination in the printers' system of measurement is the pica (*pi-ca*), which is the width of 12 points. Practically all of the items of composing material (except type, which is always designated by points) is measured in picas. A piece of metal furniture may be made exactly 6x10 picas; a lead, slug, or piece of brass rule may 18 picas long; a type form may be 20x32 picas, a margin 3 picas wide, etc. Sizes of paper, and page sizes, however, are designated in inches.

81. **The line measure.** The standard measuring tool of the printer is known as a line gauge, or line measure. In

* The Point System for sizes of type bodies was adopted in America in 1878, although French type founders, Fournier and Didot, developed similar systems much earlier.

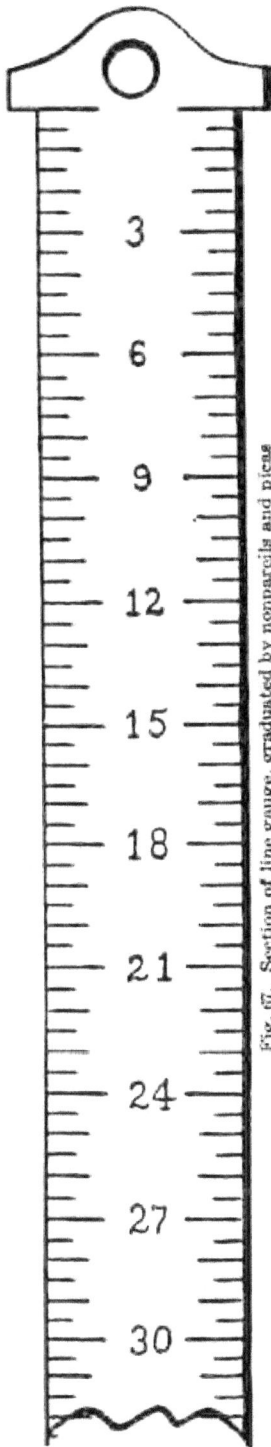

Fig. 67. Section of line gauge, graduated by nonpareils and picas

some shops, the term "pica stick" is used. These gauges, made of wood or metal, ordinarily measure up to 72 picas, or approximately 12 inches, and are graduated by nonpareils and picas. On some styles the inch measurements are stamped on one side, and picas on the other.

82. **Type sizes.** Type sizes are always designated in points. The smallest common type is 6 point, and the sizes in a series of type usually will range from 6 to 72 point. Some series include sizes as large as 96, 120, or 144 point. This book is printed in 10 point type, with the footnotes in 6 point, and chapter initials in 24 point. The ordinary sizes of type are: 6, 8, 10, 12, 14, 18, 24, 30, 36, 48, 60, and 72 point. A few special sizes, such as $4\frac{1}{2}$, 5, $5\frac{1}{2}$, 7, 9, and 11 point, are made for special purposes, but are not common.

Before the Point System was established, sizes of types were designated by names, and some of these names are still used occasionally. A table of the most common type sizes, listed by both points and names, appears on the opposite page.

83. **Measuring of type matter.** The amount of type on a page, or in a group, is calculated in terms of the em, or square, of the size of the type used. One thousand ems of 8 point type, therefore, is equal to the space that would be covered by one thousand 8 point em quads. In estimating printed matter, the body type is regularly calculated by the thousand ems.

Type Body	Size of Face	Size in Points	Name*
	Hm	6	Nonpareil
	Hm	8	Brevier
	Hm	10	Long Primer
	Hm	12	Pica
	Hm	14	English
	Hm	18	Great Primer
	Hm	24	Double Pica
	Hm	30	Five-Line Nonp.
	Hm	36	Three-Line Pica
	En	48	Four-Line Pica

Fig. 68. Table of common type sizes

* The names for some of the other sizes of type are as follows: 4½ point is Diamond; 5 point, Pearl; 5½ point, Agate; 7 point, Minion; 9 point, Bourgeois; and 11 point, Small Pica. Agate type is largely used for the composition of classified advertising in newspapers and magazines of larger circulation. It is fourteen lines to the inch.

THIS PAGE is made up to give the student an idea of the areas covered by one thousand ems of different sizes of type. The first group is in 6 point Century Oldstyle type, leaded with 2 point leads; the second is in 8 point, leaded; and the third is in 10 point, leaded. In each area, a dotted line is inserted to indicate the extent of the matter if the type were set solid, i. e., without leads between the lines.

In the first group, there are thirty-nine lines of 6 point type, set 13 picas wide. There are 13 ems pica per line, or 156 points. Dividing by 6, we find 26 ems of 6 point per line. In the thirty-nine lines we have 39x26, or 1014 ems of type.

In the second group, the 8 point type is set 18 picas wide. Accordingly, there are 27 ems of 8 point per line. In the thirty-seven lines of type are 27x37, or 994 ems.

The third group is set 23 picas wide, in 10 point type. Since there are 276 points in the line, there will be 27.6 ems of 10 point per line, and in the entire page of 35 lines, will be 966 ems.

There would be 690 ems of 12 point, leaded, in this size of page, or 805 ems of 12 point, solid.

Widths always designated in picas. The width of a piece of composition is always designated in picas (or ems pica), regardless of the size of type used. Ordinarily, the measure will be stated in picas, as "18 picas wide", but sometimes it is desig-
—If 6 point is set solid, it would extend to here—
nated as "18 ems." In either case, ems pica is meant. An exception is found in the designation of indentions. If instructions are given to indent two picas, it is of course, understood that there will be a 24 point indention. If a two-em indention is called for, it refers to an indention equivalent to a two-em quad of the size of type used. If it is 8 point type, the indention would be 16 points; if 10 point, it would be 20 points, etc.

l body of that all the ends of nonpareil, and s the distance nd the foot of early touches aces of white ary, thickness the ascending corresponding ith very thin, obably leaded portant ways, llowing tables straight com- atures of this lier described. sizes of types ondensed face old text-letter s usually give multiplication another word, limited to the re descriptive rounded off in rp impression with the ends sually include described this ••••••••••• ortant bodies,

inted matter quickly, and wears better wo thousand llowing table to find these comments on ely extended the common, ight of leads ied one-third n the leading this addition leads needed os already to ion increases composition. he weight of thickness of addition of a considerable full capacity rgely extend py one-sixth intermediate when in the an nonpareil, he following composition sizes of type •••••••••• which case it

this m *1000 ems 6 point, leaded* ost satisfactory to use. an nonpareil,

An em of any type is the square of the body of that type. As it is impracticable to count all the separate bits of metal in a page, the em is made the unit of measure. The space that can be covered by one thousand em quads is reckoned as one thousand ems of type.

is the am *1000 ems 8 point, leaded* vered by the body matter.
Care should be taken not to confuse the terms "picas" and "ems," when they have reference to details of composition.
as the fo *966 ems 10 point, leaded, in the page of 23x35 picas* er group

Fig. 69

A page of matter 24 picas wide is the width of 24 ems of 12 point. If the page is set in 8 point type, the number of ems of type per line will then be increased to 36 (because $24 \times 12 \div 8 = 36$). By multiplying the number of 8 point ems per line (36) by the number of lines of type on the page, the total number of ems for the page will be found. If the type used should be 6 point, there would be 48 ems in the 24 pica line; and if 10 point type were used, there would be 28.8 ems per line. A simple formula for calculating the number of ems per page is as follows:

Length of line $\times$ 12 $\div$ Size of type = Ems per line

Ems per line $\times$ Number of lines = Ems per page

On the opposite page, examples are set which show the areas covered by one thousand ems of 6 point, solid; 6 point, leaded; 8 point, solid; 8 point, leaded; 10 point, solid; and 10 point, leaded. Dotted lines indicate the limits for each group, when the matter is set solid.

SUGGESTIONS

This is one of the most simple, yet most important, chapters in the book. The beginner should learn the details of the printers' system of measurement as thoroughly as he knows his alphabet, and he should be prepared to use them just as readily. He will have constant and increasing need of this knowledge in his work, and cannot succeed without it.

For practical drill work in the use of the printers' measure, problems to be found in Ginsbach's *Print Shop Arithmetic* will be especially helpful.

PROBLEMS

1. With a line measure draw the outline of a page 15x24 picas; of one 6x9 inches; of one 24x36 picas; of one 3½x5½ inches.
2. How many leads equal a slug? How many leads to the pica? How many slugs to the pica?
3. How many 8-point lines to an inch, set solid? How many leaded?
4. How many ems in a line of 10 point type, 20 picas wide? Of 6 point, 14 picas wide? Of 8 point, 22 picas wide?
5. How many ems of 8 point solid in a page 21 picas wide and 33 picas long?
6. Take a page of another book, and report the size of a given page; the size of type used; and the number of ems on the page.

CHAPTER XI
Common Usage in Composition

THIS chapter deals with some of the typographic phases of division, punctuation, abbreviations, etc., which are apt to be confusing to the beginner. It does not attempt to cover the rules of grammar that govern this field. It is presupposed that the student of printing has at least a fair working knowledge of English grammar; that he is a good speller; that he is able to divide ordinary words, and to punctuate sentences; that he knows the common abbreviations; and that he can use these tools of the language in an acceptable manner. Without such a knowledge, one may not hope to be a successful printer. Any deficiencies in grammar, therefore, should be made up by the youth who aspires to enter the printing trade.

84. **Office style.** Some of the details in the style of composition differ slightly in different printing establishments throughout the country. As an example, one shop will advocate printing the abbreviation A. D., following a date, in capitals, while another will favor the use of small capitals (as 1456 A. D.). The procedure of a shop with reference to matters of style in composition is called the *office style* of that shop. It will be well for the young printer to acquaint himself with the office style of the shop in which he works, and to follow it carefully in his typesetting.

The rules laid down in this chapter are quite generally followed in the shops throughout the country, and they are therefore recommended for use in the classroom.

THE DIVISION OF WORDS

85. **Words divided into syllables.** One of the strictest rules of grammar is that no word shall be divided at any

other place than between syllables, and that words of one syllable must not be divided. In general, the syllables are determined in accordance with the pronunciation of the word, although some are influenced by derivation. Office style in a shop will usually follow one dictionary as its guide in the matter of divisions, and the student should accept this as his authority in his work. He should consult the dictionary often, and especially study troublesome words.

The following words are separated into syllables. They may not be divided at any other places than between these syllables, where the hyphens are now placed.

con-di-tion-al	typ-o-graph-ic	should
bor-rowed	ty-pog-raph-er	through
con-tin-ued	oc-ca-sioned	thronged
syl-la-ble	dis-re-gard-ed	schemes

86. **Typographic considerations.** In addition to the rule as stated above, good typography recognizes some further considerations with regard to word divisions, which follow.

a. The division of words should be avoided whenever possible, without detriment to the even spacing of the page. Divided words break the continous flow of the thought, and make the matter more difficult to read. They also mar the appearance of the page. It is a general rule that hyphens should not be placed at the ends of more than two consecutive lines, unless the measure is extremely narrow.

b. A word of only one syllable, though long, may not be divided. Also, a plural or past tense ending which contains a silent vowel is not a separate syllable, and therefore it may not be separated from the rest of the word. Examples:

be-longed	cat-a-logued	par-a-sites

c. When the first or last syllable of a word consists of but one letter, that letter must *never* be divided from the rest of the word. Never divide eas-y, might-y, or E-gypt.

A Good Motto for Young Compositors:

Carve carefully; words have joints!

EDWARD N. TEALL

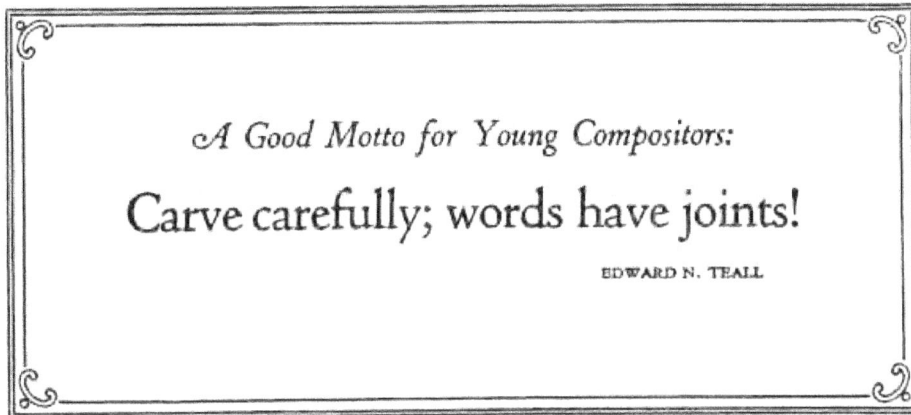

d. Unless absolutely necessary, do not divide such short words as ev-er, on-ly, ve-to, up-on, and in-to.

e. Do not carry over the last syllable of a word, if it contains only two letters. Either space it all into the first line, or carry the next preceding syllable over with it.

DO THIS	DO NOT DO THIS
provision-ally	provisional-ly
respect-fully	respectful-ly

f. Words which end in -able and -ible should be divided before the a and the i, respectively, always grouping these last four letters together on the second line.

account-able	*not* accounta-ble
access-ible	*not* accessi-ble

g. In all words not ending in -able or -ible, in which an inner syllable consists of a single letter, always retain that letter on the first line, breaking the word after rather than before that letter. Examples:

comi-cal	*never* com-ical
monopo-lize	*never* monop-olize
explana-tory	*never* explan-atory

h. Proper names should not be divided at the ends of lines, if it can be avoided without awkward spacing.

i. If the division can be made at the accent of the word, it is advisable, as it increases the legibility of the matter. The following words are divided at their accent:

contribu-tion	apos-trophe
locomo-tive	appro-priate

j. Compound words should be divided at their point of union, in order that they will not be confusing to the reader.

DO THIS	DO NOT DO THIS
paper—making	paper-mak—ing
semi—annual	semi-an—nual
under—writer	un—derwriter

In setting narrow measures, some of these rules must be violated occasionally, but every effort should be made to follow them as far as possible.

ABBREVIATIONS

87. Avoid abbreviations. Only a few abbreviations are regularly used in printing of a formal nature. All words should be spelled out unless there is a particular reason for not doing so. The abbreviations Mr., Mrs., Hon., Jr., and Sr. are permissible in all classes of work.

Rev., Capt., Maj., Prof., and similar titles usually will be abbreviated when they precede the full name of the person, but will appear in full when used with the last name only:

Rev. J. Warren Leonard	Professor Elwell
Maj. Orville B. Kilmer	Sergeant Lynch

Co. may be used when it occurs in the official title of a firm, but otherwise it will be spelled, except in tables, etc.

Honorary titles, as A.B., M.A., LL.D., and D.D., usually take only a thin space between the letters, as here printed. Some printers put no spacing between them, as: A.B., Ph.D.

88. Abbreviations not capitalized. A.M. and P.M., when used in a line of capitals, will be set in capitals for the sake of uniformity, but when used with lower-case, they usually are set in small capitals or lower-case (A.M. or a.m.). The letters are regularly separated by a thin space, but they may be set without any space, if that is office style. The following abbreviations are always set in lower-case:

i. e. (that is)	viz. (namely)	etc. (and so forth—
e. g. (for example)	vs. (versus)	never &c.)
per cent (per centum; no period follows this abbreviation)		

Such abbreviations as D.D., i.e., p.m., and e.g. must not be divided at the end of the line.

USE OF PUNCTUATION MARKS

89. Use of the period. The period denotes a full stop in reading matter. In regular body composition, a period is placed at the end of each sentence, unless the exclamation point or the question mark is used.* Periods also follow all abbreviations, wherever they appear. Numbered and titled paragraph headings regularly take periods, to sepa-rate the heading from the text, as in this paragraph. With figures, periods are used as decimal points. A few proper uses of periods are as follows:

1. Minerals	Sept.	M. B. Wallace	$14.35
a. Copper	Mass.	i. e., etc.	3.1416

In tabulated matter, wherein full sentences are not used, the periods are usually omitted from the ends of the lines.

In display composition, such as a title-page, or an item of stationery, periods are never used, as the breaks in the wording are clearly indicated by the grouping of the matter.

90. The comma. Commas are used to indicate slight pauses in the thought, for the sake of clearness. Words in

---

*The interrogation point, or question mark, finds its origin in the Latin word *quaestio*. meaning *to seek*. The word was abbreviated into $\frac{2}{o}$ and eventually to ?. The Latin word *io*, signifying *joy*, is the forerunner of the of the exclamation point. It was written *I*.

apposition, non-restrictive, absolute, and participial phrases, words in direct address, dependent clauses preceding their principal clauses, interjections, etc., are set off by commas. Generally speaking, the comma is permissible wherever its use will serve to make the meaning clearer to the reader.

When a series of words is separated by commas, with a conjunction between the last two, the conjunction does not displace the comma in the last interval. Both comma and conjunction should appear. Example:

Liberty, justice, and equality are the heritage of all citizens.

A comma must always be placed between the name of city and state, in setting an address. Also, a comma must be used between day and year, but not between month and day, in setting a date of month, day and year. Examples:

Peoria, Illinois   Washington, D. C.   May 18, 1910

91. **Semi-colons** and **colons** are used to indicate greater pauses, or breaks, in the thought. Colons are also used to separate chapter and verse, in references, and to separate hours and minutes, in recording time (except in standard time tables, in which periods are generally used).

Genesis 2:17-18   xxiv : 12   2:15 p. m.

92. **The apostrophe** is used to mark the possessive case; to form the plural of letters and figures (as E's and 5's); or to indicate the contraction of a word.

Don't and can't should be treated as single words, with no spacing around the apostrophe. Such forms as I've and you'll take a thin space preceding the apostrophe. Isn't, wasn't, etc., take a thin space between the two words only, with no space around the apostrophe.

In job printing, the apostrophe is sometimes used to denote a contracted or abbreviated word. This practice is frowned upon by many of our best printers, however, who recommend the use of the period instead of the apostrophe for all abbreviations.   Both period and apostrophe should never appear in an abbreviation.   Note these examples:

WORD	CONTRACTION	BETTER FORM	NEVER DO THIS
Secretary	Sec'y	Secy.	Sec'y.
Association	Ass'n	Assn.	Ass'n.
Department	Dep't	Dept.	Dep't.
Manufacturing	M'f'g	Mfg.	M'f'g.

93. **Quotation marks,** as commonly used, consist of two inverted commas |"| at the beginning of the citation, and two apostrophes |"| at the end.   Within the last few years, typefounders have begun to cast special quotation marks (" ' ' ") for some fonts of type, and it is to be hoped that they will eventually come into general use.   The quotation marks are commonly known as *quotes,* among printers.

When one quotation occurs within another, the double quotation marks appear at the beginning and end of the whole group, and single quotes set off the inner quotation. A thin space separates the single and double quotes, when they come together in the sentence.   Examples:

> "'Ever onward' will be my motto," he said.
> "The A. B. means 'Always Busy'," declares Mr. Doerty.

Periods or commas should always be placed inside the last quotation marks.   Semi-colons, colons, question marks, and exclamation points will go inside if the mark belongs to the quotation itself, but on the outside if they serve as punctuation for the entire sentence, of which the quoted matter is only a part.

> "This is correct."   "This is incorrect".

94. **Parentheses** and **brackets** appear in most body fonts of type.   In some, they are cast in pairs, as (), [], but more often only one character is made, as),], and a pair of them may be assembled by inverting one of the characters.

95. **Hyphens** and **dashes.** The hyphen (-) is used in the formation of compound words, and to indicate the division of a word at the right end of a line.

There are four dashes in a weight font of body type, the en dash (–), em dash (—), 2-em dash (——), and 3-em dash (———). They are used principally in job and tabular work, but occasionally one serves in the capacity of punctuation.

The en dash is sometimes used to indicate a period of time when placed between two dates, as in 1776–1926, or as a hyphen in lines of capitals. In both of these places, however, it is fast being replaced by the hyphen.

Em dashes are used by some almost in the capacity of parentheses—a practice not so common today as in earlier times—to set off parenthetical or irrelevant matter. They are also used to unite different items in lists and tables, as author and book in bibliographies, or date and event, etc.

Two-em and 3-em dashes may be inserted in printed matter to indicate missing words, or parts of sentences.

USES OF OTHER CHARACTERS

96. **The use of ampersand.** The ampersand, or "short and," is a development of the Latin word *et*, meaning and. This can be clearly seen in its present form, especially in the Italic faces. Some of the common forms follow:

Some Roman characters: & & & & & & & &

Some Italic characters: & & & & & & & &

The ampersand is used in the setting of firm names, as Swift & Company, or Barnhart Bros. & Spindler, in which the short form is regularly used by the corporation. It is not permissible as a short cut for "and" in body matter.

In display work, it is sometimes permissible to use this as an abbreviation. When it is used, the Italic form should be chosen, since it is more graceful than the Roman style.

97. **Expressing numbers.** In body composition, numbers will be spelled out in the majority of cases, but the following exceptions are found in common practice:

Complete dates, as in August 21, 1893
Street numbers, as in 2828 Duncan Street
Dollar and odd cents, as in $58.75

Ordinarily, numbers that can be expressed in one or two words will be spelled out, while those requiring more than two words will be set in figures. The following are correct:

I.......1	XI.....11	XXX...30
II.......2	XII.....12	XL.....40
III......3	XIII....13	L........50
IV......4	XIV....14	LX.....60
V.......5	XV.....15	LXX...70
VI......6	XVI....16	LXXX.80
VII.....7	XVII...17	XC.....90
VIII....8	XVIII..18	C........100
IX......9	XIX....19	D........500
X.......10	XX.....20	M....1000

Fig. 70. Table of Roman numerals

Eighty-four dollars	3740
$101	One million
Sixteen thousand	$840,000

However, no hard-and-fast rules can be made which will cover all cases. When numbers appear frequently in a piece of composition, they may be put in figures if the thought can be made clearer in that way. In matter containing statistics, or in work of a technical nature, figures may be used more freely than in other kinds of composition. It is necessary to exercise one's judgment in the matter, and use the method that is most consistent.

A number expressed in five or more figures should include the comma, as in 22,500, or 500,000. Amounts in four figures should not include the comma, except when placed in tables or columns with larger figures, when the comma should be used in all, for the sake of uniformity.

98. **Roman numerals** are used principally for chapter headings, and for the numbering of the pages preceding or following the main body of a book or magazine. Capitals are used in chapter headings, but lower-case (as xxviii) is used for the paging of prefaces, and introductions. Acts of plays, and sections of outlines or tabulated matter, may be

designated by Roman numerals. These are not followed by periods unless their positions in the matter require it.

INDENTIONS

99. **Purpose of indentions.** The purpose of indention at the beginning of a paragraph is to call the reader's attention to a change in the thought, or in the subject matter. Early printers used the paragraph signs (¶, ⫫) for this purpose, placing them in the text at the points where changes of thought occurred, but in the modern printing, indentions serve for this purpose. Paragraph signs are still used in some kinds of display work, but they may now be classed as typographic ornaments.

Fig. 71. Portion of page [reduced] by Bazalerio. of Bologna, 1498, showing paragraph signs

100. **Widths of paragraph indentions.** In narrow measures of composition, it is customary to indent the first line of each paragraph one em of the type body used. When the matter is set wider than 18 picas, the indention is widened to one and one-half ems; or if wider than 24 picas, to two ems. Large sizes of type will take proportionately less indention, while 6 point should be indented more widely than we have indicated.

This is a general rule that will not fit all classes of work, but it is a safe guide for ordinary composition.

101. **Hanging indentions.** The hanging indention is just the opposite of the regular paragraph indention, in that the first line of the paragraph is set full width of the stick, and all of the following lines are indented uniformly. The foregoing rule for indentions also applies to this style.

Hanging indentions are used in the setting of such work as directories, dictionaries, price lists, and catalogs.

Cut-in notes may also be considered under the head of indentions. They represent a style of composition, which, **102. The** like the paragraph sign, was in more common **cut-in note** use in early typography, but which is now used principally for decorative effect. The note is ordinarily preceded by two or three full lines of text, and the margin of space around the group is made uniform.

103. **Indention of poetry.** Indentions in the composition of poetry do not follow any fixed rule, but are established by the author, or by the style and rhythm of the lines. In some, alternate lines will be indented; in others, only occasional lines will be indented, in accordance with the plan of the verse and the positions of the lines that rhyme; and in some poetry, including blank verse, a uniform indention is made of all the lines throughout the poem.

The body of the poem should appear centered on the page, and this makes necessary the centering of a line of average length, in order to determine the standard indention for the job. The other indentions may then be made.

A study of the specimens on the opposite page, or of a book of miscellaneous poems, will help to guide the student in the general principles governing this kind of work.

104. **Indention of quoted paragraphs.** When quotation marks appear at the beginning of a paragraph, the first letter of the paragraph should be indented equally with those of the accompanying paragraphs. This alignment, or uniformity of indention, may be had by placing the quotation marks within the blank space of the indention. This is done by building Fig. 72 out the inverted commas, or quotes, with spacing material until the combination equals the regular indention for all the paragraphs. In Fig. 72 this method is illustrated.

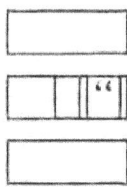

My country 'tis of thee,
Sweet land of liberty,
   Of thee I sing.
Land where my fathers died,
Land of the pilgrims' pride,
From every mountain's side
   Let Freedom ring!

Build thee more stately mansions, O my soul,
   As the swift seasons roll.
Leave thy low-vaulted past!
Let each new temple, nobler than the last,
Shut thee from heaven with a dome more vast,
   Till thou at length art free,
Leaving thine outgrown shell by life's unresting
   sea!

Under the greenwood tree,
Who loves to lie with me,
And tune his merry note
Unto the sweet bird's throat,
Come hither, come hither, come hither,
   Here shall he see no enemy
But winter and rough weather.

"Speak! speak! thou fearful guest!
Who, with thy hollow breast
Still in rude armor dressed,
   Comest to daunt me!
Wrapped not in Eastern balms,
But with thy fleshless palms
Stretched, as if asking alms,
   Why dost thou haunt me?

Whither, midst falling dew,
While glow the heavens with the last steps of day
Far through their rosy depths, dost thou pursue
   Thy solitary way?

Fig. 73

This style of indention is more pleasing than that of using uniform spacing before both quoted and unquoted matter, especially when paragraphs are short, or when large type is used. An example of this style follows:

Theodore L. DeVinne, in his *Correct Composition*, makes the following suggestion for handling quoted paragraphs:

"Put the quotation marks in the space made by the indention, so that the first letter of each line shall line vertically."

This gives a much more pleasing effect to the page, and it tends to unify the whole composition.

Fig. 74

SUGGESTIONS

A printer is expected to know the rules of grammar, and the common usages in composition. The printing student, therefore, must develop this part of his training, as it is fully as important as the mechanical side.

Form the habit of consulting the dictionary frequently. It is one of the printer's best friends. Also observe the details of style in the printed matter you handle. You will learn a great deal by forming such a habit.

An especially good series of lessons on this subject has been prepared by the Education Department of the United Typothetae of America, in Group XII—*English for Printers*, of their Standard Apprentice Lessons.

QUESTIONS

1. What is meant by "office style"?
2. What is the grammatical rule for division of words?
3. Name some typographic usages in division.
4. What are some abbreviations not capitalized?
5. In what kind of printing may periods be dropped?
6. Punctuate: "On May 1 1927 we arrived at Lima Ohio."
7. Give proper abbreviations for Secretary, Department, Manufacturing.
8. How are quotation marks made? How used?
9. When should punctuation be placed within quotes? When outside?
10. Where may the "short and" be used?
11. What is common practice in expressing numbers?
12. What letters comprise Roman numerals? What is the value of each?
13. Name some uses of Roman numerals.
14. What can you say about paragraph signs?
15. What is the general rule for the indention of paragraphs?
16. What are hanging indentions used for?
17. Tell what you can about indention of poetry.
18. What is the preferred method of indenting quoted paragraphs?

CHAPTER XII

Reading Printers' Proofs

IN ORDER that the compositor may know what errors he has made, and what changes are desired, such corrections are indicated on the proof of the job, by certain standard marks which are understood by all printers.

In the larger printing establishments, reading of proofs is done by special proofreaders in the editorial or business department, but where proofreaders are not employed, the proofs may be read by one in the business office, by the superintendent, by the foreman of the composing room, or even by an experienced compositor. Every printer should be capable of reading proofs whenever necessary.

105. **Proofreaders' marks.** On the following page, a list of the standard proofreaders' marks is given, with their uses and meanings. These marks should be thoroughly learned, and then used in all composing-room practice.

It should be particularly noted that each of the various punctuation marks is indicated by a special sign, to avoid misunderstanding. The period and the colon are always enclosed in circles, to distinguish them from the comma and the semi-colon. The comma is followed or (according to some printers' usage) preceded by a diagonal stroke, while the apostrophe is placed above an inverted caret, so that each may be recognized at once. Some place a caret over the comma to distinguish it from the apostrophe.

When the compositor has omitted a number of words, it is better not to crowd them into the margin of the proof, but to mark the omission "Out; see copy," and thus refer him to the matter as it appears in the original copy.

84

Standard Proofreaders' Marks

MARGINAL SIGN	MARK IN THE TEXT	MEANING
x	The practice of that	Take out defective letter
⊥	early colonial period	Push down space
⊙	beginning with the	Invert a letter
δ	establishment oof a	[dele]; take out; delete
wf.	shop in Cambridge,	Wrong font letter
tr.	in year the of 1637,	Transpose
stet.	was not so different	Let it stand
///	from the present-day	Straighten lines
[	methods as might	Move to left
	be supposed by the ⊐	Move to right
¶	casual reader. In a	Make a new paragraph
No ¶	to the present. When this invention became	No paragraph; run in
Caps.	In the united states,	Use capital letters
s.c.	The Inland Printer,	Use small capitals
Ital.	Frazier's Type Lore	Use Italic letters
Sp.out	Ross Publishing Co.	Spell out
Out; see copy	this time, settlement	Omission of part of copy
?	of Pilgrims in Maine	Query; is this right?
#	was one of the first	Equalize the spacing
#	to be made. In the	Less space here
#	mean time, Virginia	Close up entirely
□	was settled. In most	One em of space

TO INDICATE PUNCTUATION MARKS

⊙	Period	✓	Apostrophe
✓	Comma	-/	Hyphen
;/	Semi-colon	✓✓	Quotation marks
:/	Colon	/—/	Em dash

Fig. 75

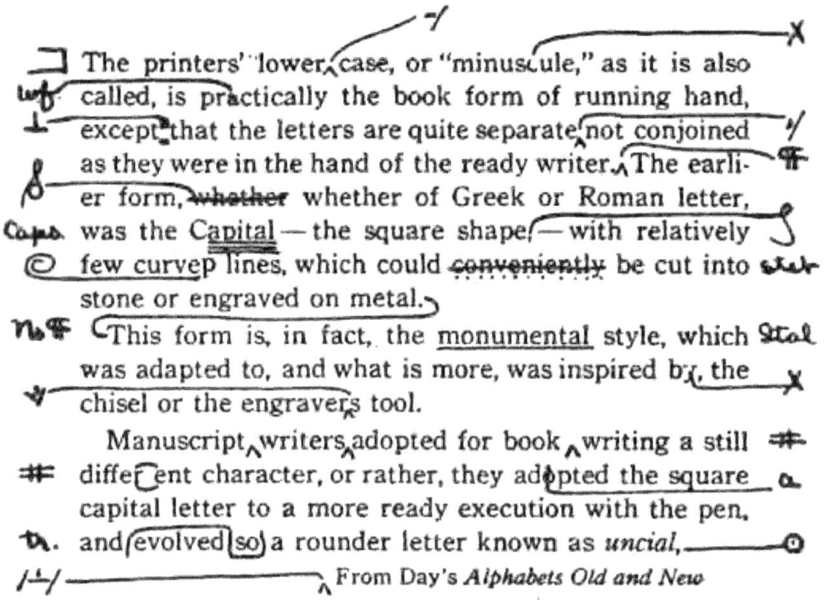

The printers' lower case, or "minuscule," as it is also
called, is practically the book form of running hand,
except that the letters are quite separate not conjoined
as they were in the hand of the ready writer. The earlier form, whether whether of Greek or Roman letter,
was the Capital — the square shape — with relatively
few curved lines, which could conveniently be cut into
stone or engraved on metal.
This form is, in fact, the monumental style, which
was adapted to, and what is more, was inspired by, the
chisel or the engravers tool.

Manuscript writers adopted for book writing a still
different character, or rather, they adopted the square
capital letter to a more ready execution with the pen,
and evolved so a rounder letter known as *uncial.*

From Day's *Alphabets Old and New*

Fig. 76. The customary method of marking errors on a proof

The printers' lower-case, or "minuscule," as it is also
called, is practically the book form of running hand,
except that the letters are quite separate, not conjoined
as they were in the hand of the ready writer.

The earlier form, whether of Greek or Roman letter,
was the CAPITAL—the square shape—with relatively
few curved lines, which could conveniently be cut into
stone or engraved on metal. This form is, in fact, the
monumental style, which was adapted to, and what is
more, was inspired by, the chisel or the engraver's tool.

Manuscript writers adopted for book writing a still
different character, or rather, they adapted the square
capital letter to a more ready execution with the pen,
and so evolved a rounder letter known as *uncial.*

—From Day's *Alphabets Old and New*

Fig. 77. Form corrected in accordance with marks made above

When a word or letter is to be changed, the old one is crossed in the text, and the new one written in the margin.

If it seems evident that a mistake occurs in the copy, it is customary to set the matter according to copy, and then to mark the place with a question mark, for the attention of the author. In making such a query to the author, make sure that the point you raise will be clearly understood. If necessary, add a brief note in the margin.

106. **Marking errors.** For every error, a mark should be placed in the margin; otherwise, it may be overlooked. If possible, the marginal mark should be directly in line with the error. Never write any notations or instructions within the body of the text, but always put them in the margins.

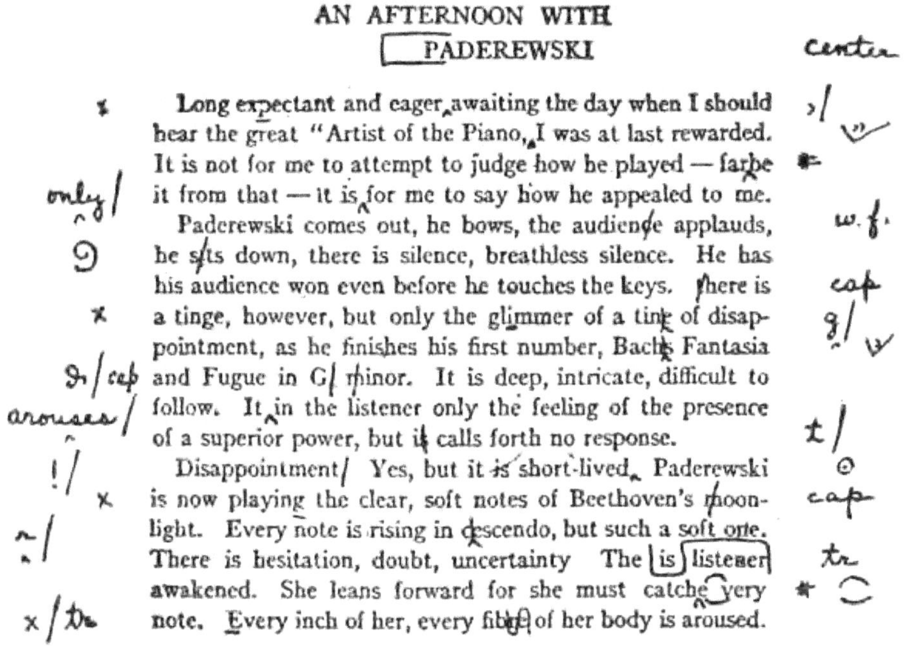

AN AFTERNOON WITH
PADEREWSKI

Long expectant and eager, awaiting the day when I should hear the great "Artist of the Piano, I was at last rewarded. It is not for me to attempt to judge how he played — far be it from that — it is for me to say how he appealed to me.

Paderewski comes out, he bows, the audience applauds, he sits down, there is silence, breathless silence. He has his audience won even before he touches the keys. There is a tinge, however, but only the glimmer of a tint of disappointment, as he finishes his first number, Bach's Fantasia and Fugue in G minor. It is deep, intricate, difficult to follow. It in the listener only the feeling of the presence of a superior power, but it calls forth no response.

Disappointment/ Yes, but it is short-lived, Paderewski is now playing the clear, soft notes of Beethoven's moonlight. Every note is rising in descendo, but such a soft one. There is hesitation, doubt, uncertainty The is listener awakened. She leans forward for she must catch very note. Every inch of her, every fibre of her body is aroused.

Fig. 78. Method of marking proof without use of guide-lines

The guide-line from the error to the marginal sign should not be drawn through the lines of matter where it can be avoided. It should lead to the nearest margin unless the space on that side should be crowded with other notations.

107. **Marking without guide-lines.** In some shops, the lines are not drawn from the error in the text to the marginal sign, but errors are simply underlined, or indicated by a caret or diagonal stoke, and then the standard mark is placed at the end of the line. When there is more than one error in a line, the marks in the margin are entered in the order in which the errors occur, and they are separated by a diagonal stroke between each mark. Fig. 78 shows this.

108. **O. K. ing a proof.** If a proof contains no errors, it should be marked "O.K.," with the signature or initials of the reader, in the lower right-hand corner of the sheet. If only minor changes are required, and another proof is not necessary, it may be marked "O.K., with corrections."

109. **Proofs to authors.** Revised proofs of book or catalog pages, or of intricate or technical matter, are sent to the author for corrections, or final O.K., after the office corrections are made. If the proof of a job is to be sent out, instructions to that effect will usually appear on the job ticket.

SUGGESTIONS

The student should learn the standard proofreaders' marks, and use them for indicating all changes. He should also cultivate the habit of scanning printed sheets for errors. Experienced printers are able to detect typographical errors in printed matter at a glance.

In marking proofs, keep the sheet as neat and orderly as possible. Draw light lines from errors to margin signs, in such a way as to clearly lead the eye to the error. Do not cross through lines of printed matter.

QUESTIONS

1. Where should errors be marked on a proof?
2. What are the various marks for punctuation?
3. Show the mark for wrong font letter; for damaged letter; an inverted letter.
4. How do you mark a space to be pushed down?
5. How would you mark a transposition?
6. How are caps indicated? Small caps?
7. How should you mark an abbreviation to be spelled out?
8. Show how to indicate a new paragraph.
9. How is attention to spacing indicated?
10. If considerable copy is left out, how should the omission be marked?

CHAPTER XIII

Locking Up Forms for the Press

WHEN the type form has been proofed, corrected, and O.K.ed, it is ready to be printed. If it is to be locked for the press, it is then placed upon the stone.

110. **The imposing stone,** or imposing table, is a heavy table or cabinet consisting of a smooth slab of stone set in a wooden frame. It usually contains drawers for holding quoins, planers, etc., and compartments for wood and metal furniture. Larger stones also have racks for holding chases and galleys, and letterboards for storing live forms. Flat surfaces of iron and steel are fast replacing the stone slabs, but in either case, the cabinet is usually called a stone. A printer who prepares the forms for the printing presses is called a stoneman, or lock-up man.

111. **Stone must be clean.** Make sure that the stone is perfectly clean before depositing the type form on it. Even though it seems clean, experienced printers will invariably wipe the surface with a rag or brush, or blow upon it, before sliding the type from the galley. A very small particle of grit on the base of a letter will cause it to be damaged when the form is planed down, or it will make that letter punch into the paper when the impression is taken.

112. **Position of the form in the chase.** The chase is the steel frame in which the form is enclosed and locked up for the press. In preparing to lock up a form, lay the chase over it, with one of the longer sides nearest you, and the ends to the right and left. The side nearest you will always be the bottom of the chase, while the side away from you will be the top, when it is placed in the press.

Locate the form in the center of the chase, or slightly above the center. If it is wider than it is long, place the head of the form toward you. This will head it toward the bottom of the chase.* If the form is longer than it is wide, place the head toward the left end of the chase. This will place the form in the proper position in the press.†

Fig. 79. A steel imposing surface

113. Placing furniture around the form. Wood furniture is placed on all sides of the form in the chase. If the width of the form happens to coincide with a standard length of furniture, then only two lengths of it will be required for the lock-up. Pieces as long as the width of the form will be placed at the top and bottom of the form, and other pieces of suitable length will be inserted on the two sides. Fig. 80, on the following page, illustrates this style of lock-up.

When neither of the dimensions of the form coincides with any standard length of furniture, then either of the methods shown in Figs. 81 and 82 will be followed. The first is merely that of building out one of the dimensions of the form to a length of furniture, usually with metal furniture, and then proceeding as in Fig. 80. In centering the

*This rule would not hold in cases in which a wide form is printed on a long sheet, or vice versa. Paper is fed into the press much more easily when the long edges are horizontal, and forms should be so locked as to permit this whenever possible. Such jobs as letterheads, in which wide forms are printed on one end of the sheet, are often printed with the sheet in vertical position, and the form locked below the center.

†When the forms are locked with the head toward the bottom or left side of the chase, the pressman is able to read the matter on the tympan sheet of the press, and on the sheets of stock as he prints them, enabling him to make sure that the impression is satisfactory, and that no accident has occurred to the form, such as letters pulling out, etc. It also aids him in keeping the right amount of ink on the press.

Fig. 80. Proper method when form is exact width of furniture

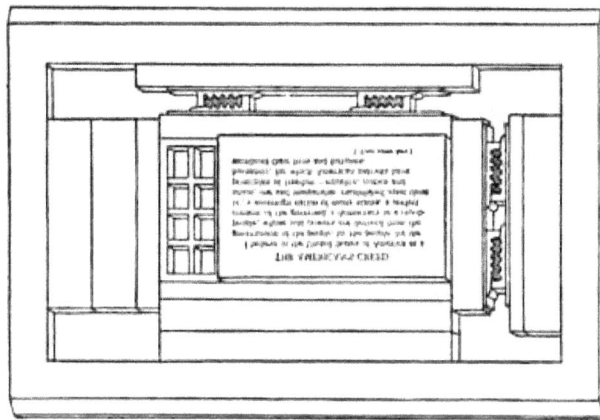

Fig. 81. Form built out to a standard length of furniture

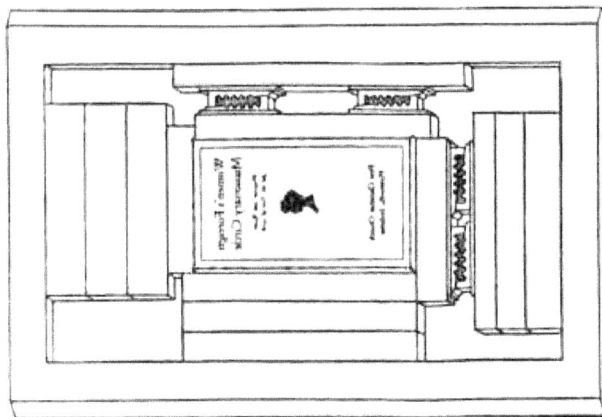

Fig. 82. The "chaser" method of locking up a form

form, allowance will be made for the metal furniture that has been placed at one side, to fill out the measure.

The method shown in Fig. 82 is that of the overlapping of pieces of furniture, longer than the form, in such a way that they do not bind at any of the corners. You will notice that the piece above the form extends to the right, while the one below extends to the left of the form. The pieces at the ends are placed in a similar manner. This is known by some printers as the "chaser" method of lock-up. It is by far the simplest, and most used, method of locking small forms for the job press.

Fig. 83. Common style of quoins, with key

Regardless of the method followed, the furniture must not bind when the pressure of the quoins is applied. The pressure must be on the form itself, from both directions, and not on the ends of the furniture beside the form. If it does bind, spacing material should be added to the form so that it will receive the full pressure of the quoins.

114. **Positions of the quoins.** Quoins (pronounced *coins*) are used to lock the form in the chase. They are made in different shapes and styles, but the most common is the wedge-shaped style as illustrated in Fig. 83, above.

Quoins should be placed near the form, at the top and right sides of the chase. If placed too far from the type, much of the firmness and rigidity of the lock-up will be lost. In practically all cases, two pairs of quoins are placed at the side, and two at the top, to give adequate and even pressure. For large forms, additional quoins will be used.

Always place the quoins so that they will press the form toward the solid part of the chase. In all ordinary lock-ups this means that the top quoins will be turned with the inner pieces pointing to the left, and with the inner pieces at the right side pointing toward you. It is an absolute rule that *the inside quoins must always point toward the solid side of the chase.* If the student has any difficulty in remembering

Fig. 84. Diagram showing proper positions of the inner quoins in the chase

this, he should memorize the details of this diagram, in Fig. 84. When the quoins are turned the wrong way, they tend to defeat their own purpose, as they wedge the type away from the solid part of the chase. It is practically impossible to lock a form securely with the quoins turned wrong.

Always insert strips of reglet between the quoins and the furniture, to protect the surfaces of the furniture.

115. **Locking up the form.** After the furniture has been placed in position around the form, the string may be removed, and the quoins pressed firmly together with the fingers, bringing all the matter snugly into proper position. If any matter is out of alignment, or if rules are not joined properly, adjustments should be made at this time. Then the quoins should be locked tightly, and when it is certain that the form will lift, it should be turned up on edge, and the feet of the type wiped with hand or a brush. The form should then be replaced on the stone, and the quoins gently loosened. It is now ready to be planed.

Never plane a locked form. Push the quoins together firmly with the fingers, or give them a *slight* turn with the key, but never lock up the form and then attempt to beat the letters into position. It should require only a few light taps of the mallet on the planer, to level the type form, if the quoins are just firmly set, as they should be.

After the form is planed, it may be locked up tightly for the press. This requires a little patience, if it is to be done correctly. A strong turn of one of the quoins when others are loose will throw the material out of line, and interfere with the proper pressure of the other quoins. One should be given a very slight turn, then another, and so on, until all are turned, and this rotation should be repeated until all the quoins are equally and tightly locked. Careful, even locking up of the form is very important.

Fig. 85. The Notting Quoin

Before the job is placed on the press, it should be tested, to see that all the material is perfectly tight in the chase. This is done by raising one edge of the chase slightly and resting it on the quoin key, then pressing on the faces of the letters with the fingers, to see if any can be pushed down. If any part of the form is loose, it should be made secure before it is put on a press, as much damage may result from type pulling out while the press is running.

116. **Locking forms for cylinder presses.** When forms are locked for cylinder presses, they are not centered in the chase, as is the case with platen press jobs. A chase of a suitable size is placed over the form, and the head of the matter is turned toward the workman, or to the left side, according to the dimensions of the paper on which it is to be printed. The form is placed close to the near side of the chase, and this becomes the guide edge, or gripper edge, of the form. Quoins are placed at the right, and the far side.

Ordinarily, the form will be placed in such position that the distance from the outer edge of the chase on the gripper side to the edge of the form will be about three inches. If the chase fills the bed of the press, the form must then be set in far enough to miss the gripper fingers that hold the sheet in position as it passes around the cylinder. The necessary margin for the safety of the form varies in width with different presses. This information may be had from the stoneman or the pressman, or the form may be tested by a gripper gauge of the press to be used.

Some Hints on Imposition of Forms

117. **Imposition of forms.** When two or more pages are locked up together, as pages of a book, catalog, or program, the matter of spacing and margins must be considered. The laying out of pages in the proper order for printing, spacing them correctly, and locking them in the chase, is known as the *imposition of forms.* This is a special phase of stone work — practically a specialty in itself — which requires a great deal of skill and experience, so only a few of its problems will be considered here. When the student is ready for a study of imposition, he will do well to make use of the references at the end of this chapter.

118. **Locking up two pages.** When two type pages are locked up together, spacing must be placed between them sufficient to allow for the inner margins on the pages when the job is printed and folded. If the type is to be centered on the page, then the space between the type pages will be twice the width of one page margin; or it will equal the total width of the two margins on one page. Therefore, if the page is six inches wide, and the type page four inches wide, there will be two inches of space between the type pages, in the chase. Proper allowance for margins may be made by measuring the width of the paper page and type page, and then inserting spacing equal to the difference between them. Another method is to fold the paper to page width, and to use the top edge as a gauge for the distance from the outer edge of one type page to the inner edge of the other. If the inner page margins are to be smaller than the outer margins, simply double the width of one inner margin, and put that amount of space between the pages.

The most common method of locking up two pages in the chase is shown in Fig. 86. Note that the wood furniture is placed in such a manner that it cannot bind, in locking, even though a page might be slightly lacking in length.

A two-page form may be used for the printing of a single sheet, on both sides, in which case a double-sized sheet is printed on one side, then turned and printed with the same form on the other side, and cut in two, each full sheet making two complete copies; or it may be used to print one side of a four-page folder, the other side being printed with another form of two pages. Pages 1 and 4 would comprise one form, and pages 2 and 3 the other one.

Fig. 86. A popular method of locking up two pages together

When a sheet is printed on both sides with the same form, then cut in two, it is called a *work-and-turn* job. When it is printed on one side with one form, and is then printed on the other side with a different form, the job is said to be printed *sheetwise*. Thus, a two-page form used to print a single sheet on both sides would be a work-and-turn form, while a four-page folder that is printed two pages at a time would be printed sheetwise.

119. **Locking up four-page forms.** When four pages are printed at a time, work-and-turn, two different lay-outs are possible, and these are shown in the diagrams that appear in Fig. 87, on the following page. Of these two schemes, the first, marked *a*, is in the most common use.

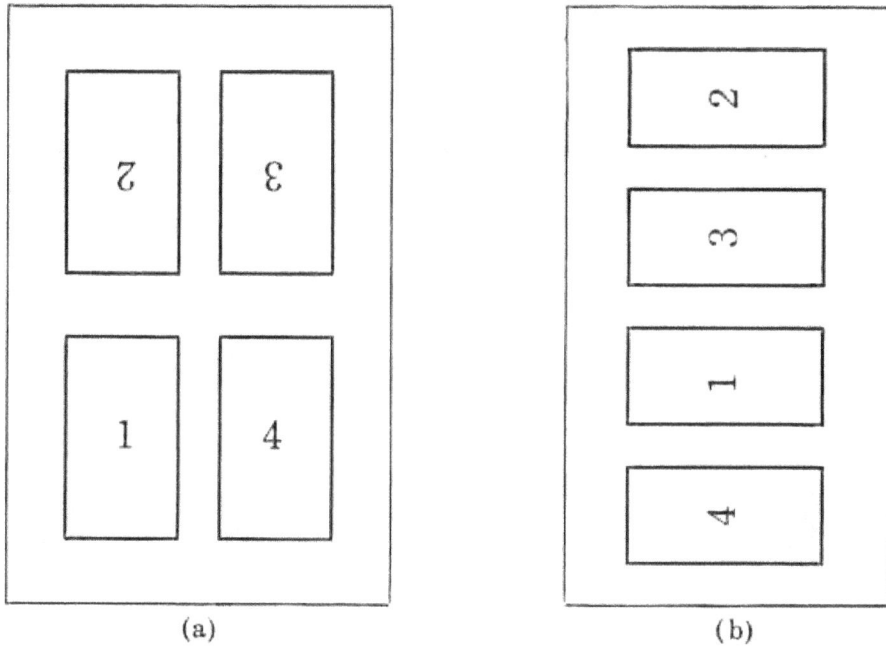

(a)　　　　　　　　　　　　　(b)

Fig. 87.　Two lay-outs for printing a four-page folder, work-and-turn

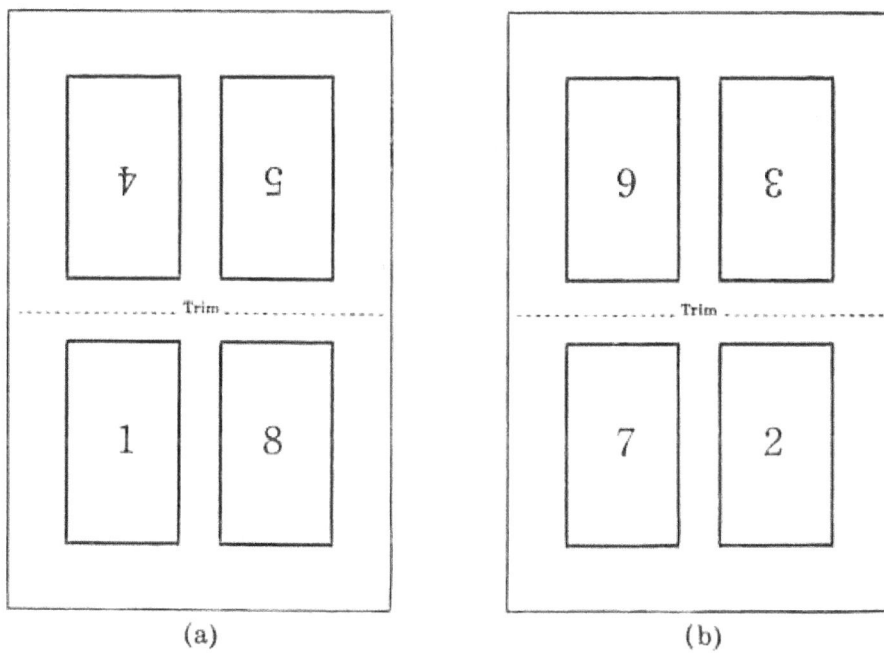

(a)　　　　　　　　　　　　　(b)

Fig. 88.　Lay-out of forms for an eight-page folder printed sheetwise

The ordinary lay-out for an eight-page folder, printed in two forms (i.e., sheetwise) is shown in Fig. 88. In addition to the space for margins, an extra allowance must be made for trimming the pages, after the sheet is folded. Usually, a quarter of an inch is allowed for trim. When this is the case, twice that amount, or three picas, will be added between the heads of the type pages, for this purpose. Dotted lines indicate margins in which trim must be allowed.

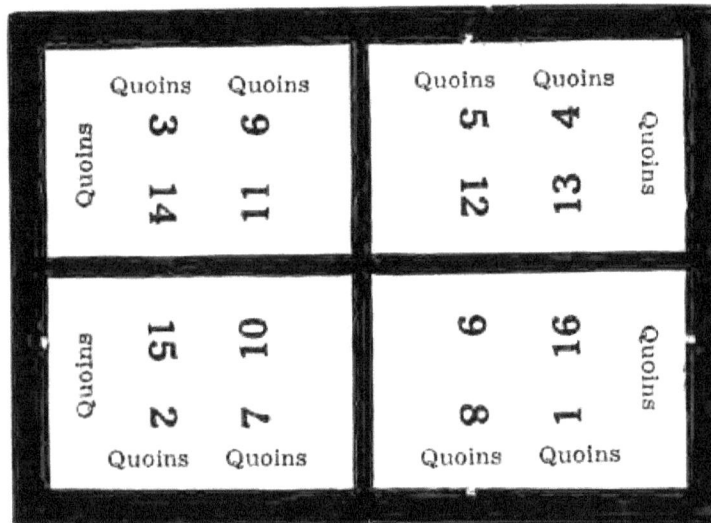

Fig. 89

If the lay-outs *a* and *b* are united by placing their inner edges together, they then form a standard lay-out for an eight-page folder, work-and-turn. An extra allowance for trim must then be made, along the line of their union.

Large forms containing a number of pages are locked up in chases with crossbars, which give strength to the form, and furnish a straight-edge to which the pages may be aligned. A book chase with removable crossbars is illustrated in Fig. 89. Also, a lay-out for a sixteen-page form, work-and-turn, is indicated in this figure. The pages are pressed toward the crossbars, and the quoins are placed at the outside edges, around the form, as indicated.

120. **Determining the lay-out.** The proper order for the arrangement of pages in a form will depend upon how the sheet is to be folded after printing. There are different schemes for folding, depending upon whether the work is to be done by hand or machine, and the style of machine to be used. A safe guide for the lay-out of a form is to take a sheet of the stock to be printed, fold it in the proper manner, and then mark in the page numbers. Open the sheet and lay it face down over the type pages on the stone. If the positions of the type pages coincide with the page numbers on the sheet, the lay-out is correct.

SUGGESTIONS

Examine the various items of lock-up material in and around the stone, and make sure that you are thoroughly acquainted with chases, quoins and keys, reglets, mallet, planer, etc., and that you know how each article is used. Study the locked forms that are to be found in the chase racks, or about the stone, and see just how they are built up.

Take standing forms of different dimensions and build wood furniture about them in a chase, just as you would lock them up, and then have the arrangements approved by the instructor. Use as few sizes and pieces of furniture as possible, and arrange them in a neat manner in the chase.

Practice placing quoins in the chase, the inner ones always pointing toward the solid sides, until you are thoroughly familiar with their use.

REFERENCES ON IMPOSITION

Group VI, Standard Apprenticeship Lessons, United Typothetae of America
Imposition—Tresize. The Inland Printer Company
Vest Pocket Manual of Printing. The Inland Printer Company

QUESTIONS

1. What is a stone? What are the duties of a stoneman?
2. Why must the stone be clean under the type form?
3. Describe the position of a form in the chase.
4. What can you tell of the arrangement of furniture around the form?
5. Describe the styles of quoins to be found in your shop.
6. What is the proper position of quoins in the chase?
7. What caution is given for the planing of the form?
8. Explain the process of locking up the form.
9. How is a locked form tested for loose letters?
10. What is meant by the imposition of forms?
11. Describe the method of printing a job work-and-turn.
12. What is the method of printing sheetwise?

CHAPTER XIV

Printing Presses

PRINTING presses may be divided into three main types: (a) platens, (b) cylinders, and (c) rotary presses. The principle upon which each operates is indicated below.

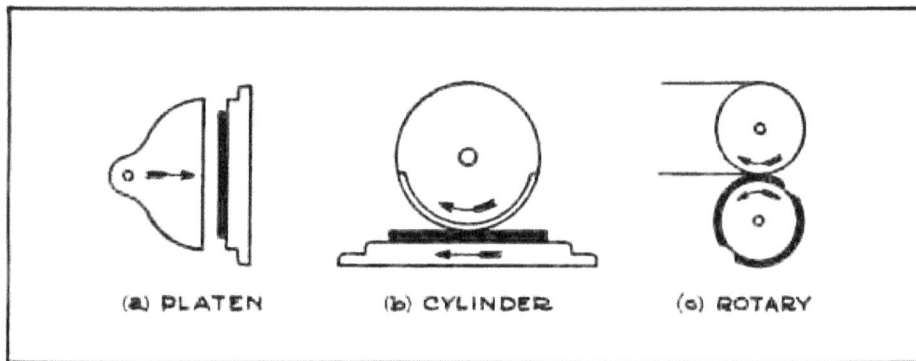

(a) PLATEN   (b) CYLINDER   (c) ROTARY

Fig. 90

121. **The platen press** holds the form on a flat bed, and obtains its impression by the impact of a flat platen, the entire surface of which meets the form squarely in a single thrust. Practically all the small presses for general job work are of the platen type. They are also called job presses.

Three of the popular makes of platen presses particularly represent this style of press, namely, the Golding Jobber, the Colt's Armory, and the Chandler and Price Gordon Presses.

The Golding Press is used in many shops for small miscellaneous job printing. It has what is known as the "clam shell" movement of the platen, and its

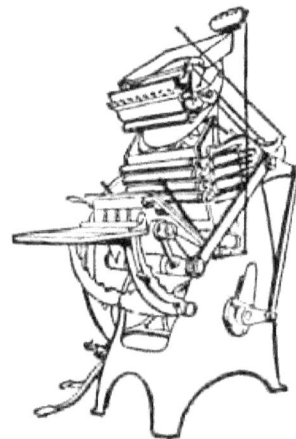

Fig. 91. The Golding Job Press

bed is rigid. Its system of ink distribution is very good, and it is capable of doing a high grade of work.

The Colt's Armory Press represents the heavier type of job press, in which the platen slides into printing position in a manner directly parallel with the form. It is a power-ful press, particularly suitable for the printing of large forms re-quiring heavy impression. Other presses of this heavy type are the the Laureate, the Gally Universal, and the Hartford Presses.

The Chandler and Price Gordon is the best known and most com-monly used press. It is a strongly built machine, easy to operate, and capable of a wide range of work. This press is considered more in detail later in the chapter, as it is apt to be found in most of the school printshops. See Fig. 98.

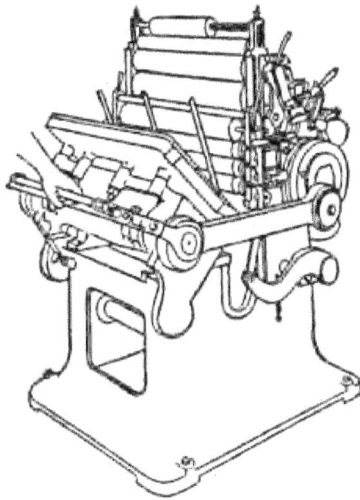

Fig. 92. The Hartford Press

122. **Cylinder presses** hold the type form on a large flat bed, which moves backward and forward upon a track beneath an impression cylinder. Sheets of paper, fed in at the top, are carried around the cylinder, and receive their impression by a rolling contact with the type. Only a small segment of the cylinder touches the form at one time.

This type of press is made in two styles: (a) the single revolution, or "drum" cylinder press, the impression cylinder of which makes one revolution for each impression, and (b) the two-revolution press, the cylinder of which makes two revolutions for each impression.

123. **The drum cylinder.** The "drum" press has a large cylinder which revolves once for each sheet printed. The paper is placed on the feed board at the top of the press, and one sheet at a time is moved down to the adjustable

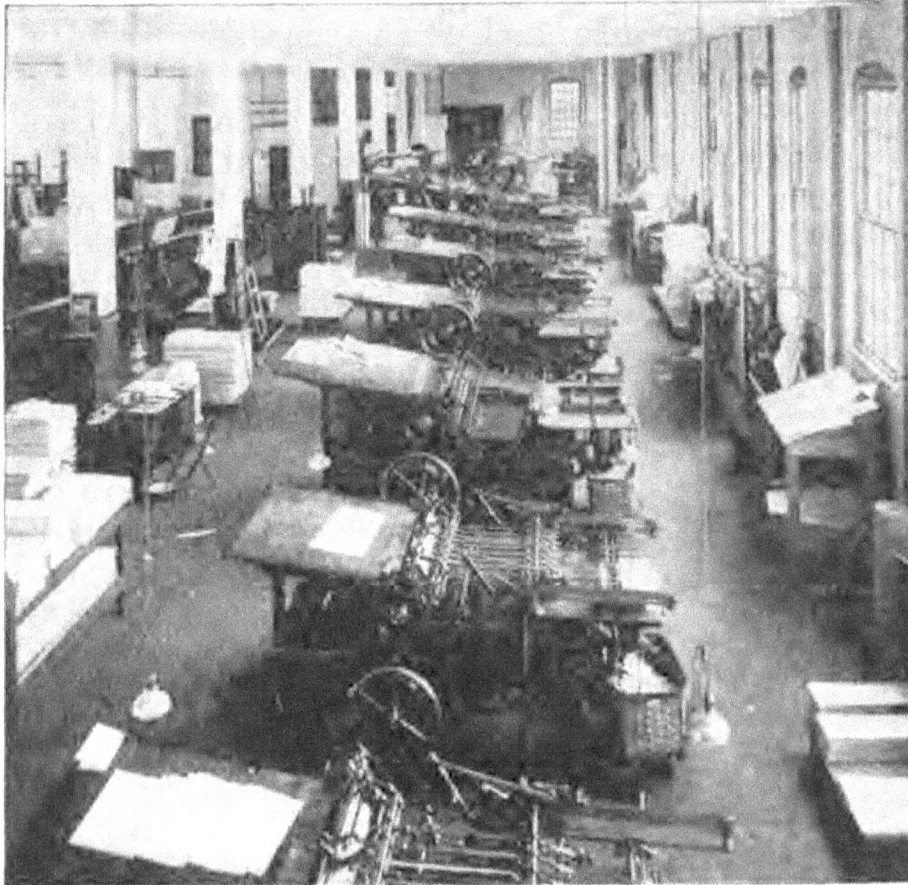

Fig. 93. Miehle cylinder presses in pressroom of the Stone Printing & Manufacturing Co., Roanoke, Va.

feed guides which rest on metal strips at the lower edge of the board, directly over the cylinder. As the press operates, gripper fingers on the cylinder engage the sheet, and at the same time the feed guides rise to allow the paper to pass under them, and then the guides drop back into position to allow the pressfeeder to bring down his next sheet.

The bed of the press containing the form moves back and forth on its track beneath the cylinder, passing under the ink rollers at each forward thrust. On its return trip, its register gears engage the corresponding ones on the impression half of the cylinder, and as they travel together the sheet receives its impression from the moving type form.

The grippers continue to hold the sheet until it comes up under the feed board, and then they release it to another set of grippers which carry it back over a delivery reel and down onto the long fingers of the fly. At the proper time, the fly turns rapidly downward, depositing the sheet, face down, on the delivery table at the rear of the press.

Showing Gear Side

Fig. 94. The Lee Cylinder Press, a two-revolution machine

In the meantime, the grippers have engaged the next sheet, and are carrying it through in the same manner.

124. **The two-revolution press** has a much smaller cylinder than the drum press, and is capable of much greater speed. In this style of press, the cylinder prints while it is making one revolution, and it rises during the second to allow the form to make its return trip. The printed sheets are delivered to the front instead of the rear of the press, and are stacked with printed side either up or down. Most of the modern cylinder presses are two-revolution machines.

Make-ready and feeding of cylinder presses requires a great deal of study and practice, under the guidance of a skilled pressman. Some very helpful books on this subject, by experienced workmen, are listed in the bibliography.

125. **The Kelly Press.** A small job cylinder press, found in a number of school shops, and in many commercial shops where space is limited, is the Kelly Press. It takes a form up to 15x20 inches, and is capable of making considerable speed on all ordinary work. It may be fed by hand or by mechanical feeder. Fig. 95 illustrates the Kelly Press.

Fig. 95. The Kelly Press, a small job cylinder press

126. **Rotary presses** are built for high-speed work, and are used mainly for the printing of large editions of newspapers and magazines. The impression is taken between two cylinders which roll together. One holds curved printing plates of the matter to be printed, and the other carries the packing, or make-ready, against which the impression is made. The paper passes around this latter cylinder and comes into contact with the automatically inked plates.

Type forms cannot be used in the ordinary rotary press. For newspaper work, stereotype plates are made from the type pages, but for magazine and book work, electrotypes are used. The plates are curved to fit the plate cylinder, and are locked upon it with adjustable clamps.

There are rotary presses (called sheet-fed rotaries) which print sheets of paper previously cut to size, but most of them print from large rolls of paper, which feed a continuous *web* through the machine at a high rate of speed. These are known as web presses. If they print the paper on both sides as the web travels through the machine, they are called web perfecting presses. In web presses, the paper is cut into sheets automatically after passing the impression cylinders, and in many cases it is folded, and even collected, pasted, and trimmed, and then stacked in the delivery tray.

Another style of rotary press with a flat bed that admits regular type forms, without stereotyping, is built especially for use in medium-sized newspaper plants.

Fig. 96. The Klymax Automatic Feeder on a platen press

127. **Automatic mechanical feeders** are frequently used on both platen and cylinder presses. They feed sheets of all kinds of stock, with remarkable accuracy, and often at much greater speed than can be had by hand feeding. In Fig. 96, an automatic feeder is shown on a job press.

PARTS OF THE GORDON PRESS

In Fig. 97, a diagram of the Chandler and Price Gordon Press is shown, in which the principal parts are labelled.

128. **The chase** is a detachable rim of steel in which the type form is locked. It fits snugly against the solid bed of the press, resting on projecting lugs just below the bed, and

held securely in place with a strong spring clamp at the top. It is removed by releasing the clamp and tilting the chase slightly forward, then lifting it clear of the grippers.

129. **The platen** is the flat metal surface which approaches the form to make the impression. As the press revolves, the platen swings to a vertical position as it approaches the press bed, meets it squarely, and then returns to the open

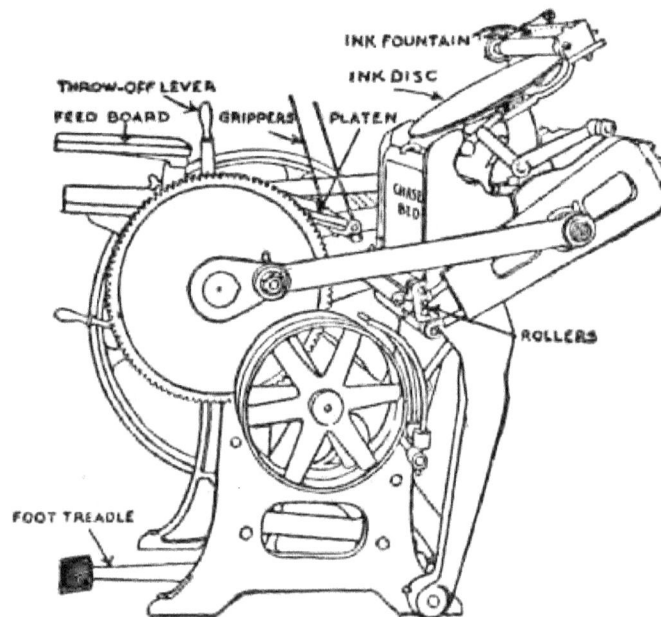

Fig. 97

position for receiving the next sheet, as illustrated in the above diagram. Upon the platen is clamped a packing of paper and pressboard, covered with a sheet of heavy oiled manila paper. This packing is known as the *tympan*, and the top sheet is called the tympan-sheet, or draw-sheet.

The paper to be printed is laid on this draw-sheet, into which gauge pins have been inserted to hold it in proper position, and it receives its impression as the platen presses it against the type form. The amount and nature of the impression given is regulated by the nature and thickness of the packing that is placed under the draw-sheet.

130. **The feed board** at the right side of the press holds a pile of the stock to be printed. The board can be turned to any angle, and locked with a set-screw at its base. The paper is taken from the feed board, one sheet at a time, and fed into position on the tympan. As the sheets are printed, they are drawn out of the press and placed on the delivery board directly in front of the feeder.

131. **The grippers,** or gripper fingers, automatically close against the platen when the press closes for an impression, and they serve to hold the paper flat against the tympan throughout the operation. They may be moved in or out along the bar to which they are secured, so that they may be made to strike the sheet at any desired place. They must be set to strike on margins of the sheet, clearing the type form and also the guage pins, as either of them would be smashed if the grippers were driven into them.

132. **The throw-off lever** is at the left side of the press. It is pushed toward the rear of the press whenever it is desired to miss an impression while the press is running. When it rests in the normal (forward) position, the platen strikes the form at each revolution of the press, but when it is pushed to the rear, the form misses the platen on its forward trip, and no impression is made on the sheet.

133. **The fly-wheel** balances the press, and gives it steady, even motion when in operation. It may be used to turn the press over by hand to take a trial impression, or to see that the grippers will clear the form. It should always be given a turn by hand when starting the press, to take the load off the motor. The fly-wheel on the Chandler and Price Gordon turns over and toward the rear, i.e., away from the feeder.[*]

134. **The ink rollers** pass over the type form twice—down and up—between each impression, bringing an even distribution of ink from the revolving ink disc above. While

[*]On some platen presses, including those of the heavy Universal type, and earlier makes of Gordons, the fly-wheel turns to the front instead of to the rear of the press.

printing a job, ink may be added, in very small quantities, on the left side of the disc, or the ink fountain may be set so that it will feed the proper amount of ink to the rollers regularly as they come in contact with the fountain roller.

135. **Composition of ink rollers.** Printers' rollers consist of a soft, elastic composition cast around steel cores. The material of a used roller closely resembles rubber. However, rubber is not used in making rollers. Glue is the principal ingredient, and it forms the body of the composition. Syrup in some form is added to give the rollers "tackiness," or power to take up and spread ink. Glycerin is added to give them greater durability and a longer period of freshness and elasticity, as it absorbs moisture and keeps the composition from becoming hard and dry. Varnish, paraffin, wax, borax, and castor oil are also used in rollers.

Fig. 98. The Chandler and Price Gordon Press

"Summer rollers" and "winter rollers" are cast for the different seasons, and each kind is made to give the best results in the temperatures and weather conditions that prevail in its season. Summer rollers are more solid, and contain less glycerin, to withstand the heat and humidity of summer days. Winter rollers, on the other hand, are of softer composition, so that they will remain sufficiently soft and tacky during the cold winter season.

136. **The care of rollers.** Rollers are easily injured, and should receive the best of care. They should always be thoroughly cleaned with oil or gasoline after a run, or at the close of the day, and it is a good practice to cover them with a thin film of oil for the night, to keep them from drying out. Water should not be used to clean rollers.

The rollers must never be left up on the disc, even for only a few minutes, as this will flatten them. Also, they should never be left against any part of the type form in the chase. The proper position for the rollers at all times when the press is not in motion is at the extreme bottom of the track, below the form, as is illustrated in Fig. 97.

When rollers are removed from the press, if there is no roller rack they should be placed in a perpendicular position, and no pressure should be put on the composition.

CARE OF THE PLATEN PRESS

All machinery must have care, if it is to give the kind of service it is built to render, and the printing press is not an exception. It will not do the work it is intended to do unless it is kept in first-class condition at all times.

137. **Oiling the press.** There are a number of oil holes about the press into which a little oil should be dropped daily. The student should learn to locate all of them, and then see that none are neglected. In addition to these, the cams and rollers which cause the platen to move should be kept well oiled, as these are parts of the press in which the first signs of wear are most apt to appear.

Do not oil too heavily. If oil runs from the hole, wipe off the surplus with a soft cloth. A few drops in the right place will do more good than a bath of oil, carelessly applied. After oiling a few holes, it is well to turn the press over by hand to allow the oil to soak into the proper places, but *never attempt to oil a press while it is in motion.* It is a dangerous practice, both for press and workman.

Occasionally, the entire body of the machine should be wiped with rags and waste, and all grease, dirt, and dust removed. If the press is kept well lubricated, cleaned, and polished, it will add a number of years to its life of service. More school presses are worn out from the lack of oiling and cleaning than from any other cause.

138. **Washing the press.** The ink must be removed from the press every day, as it would dry on the rollers and the disc and become quite difficult to remove. Some quick drying inks must be washed off as soon as the run is finished. The form should be taken out before washing the press.

There are various methods for washing a press. Some prefer one method, and others another. If the student finds that his pressman or instructor has a certain way of doing this work, he should carefully follow his example. Otherwise, he may use the following method.

Drop a little kerosene, or light machine oil, on the disc, and let it be worked well into the ink with the press moving slowly. Then shut off the power, and wipe the disc clean with a soiled rag. Move the rollers slowly over the disc, wiping them as they roll upward. Change the grip to a clean part of the cloth, and continue the operation as the rollers descend from the disc, finishing each as it turns free of the disc. Then again wipe off the disc with a fresh spot on the rag. The ink should now be practically removed.

Repeat this operation with a clean rag and a little gasoline, and the press will be thoroughly clean. If it is to be idle for some time, or left for the night, most printers will cover the rollers with a thin film of oil, for preservation. It must be carefully removed before the press is again inked.

In some shops, the oil is worked well into the ink at the close of the day, and then the press is left in this condition over night, and is cleaned off in the morning before fresh ink is applied. This preserves the rollers, and necessitates only one washing of the press. Many shops use gasoline exclusively for cleaning presses, and no kerosene or oil.

Do not let the inky mixture run down on the press bed or platen. If any should reach the bed, be sure to clean it off at once. The bed must be kept clean at all times, as a true impression depends upon the condition of this surface.

SUGGESTIONS

Visit some of the printing plants in your city, and study the action of the presses seen. Classify each press, and the type of work done on each.

Particularly study the C. & P. Gordon Press—or the job press in your shop, if it is another make. Turn it over slowly, without a form in it, and get well acquainted with the action of each of its parts.

Watch your instructor or guide oil the press, carefully noting all the places, and then see if you locate all of them. Oil the press yourself, later, under supervision, and thus learn just how it should be done.

Learn the correct name for each part of the press, and always use the correct term when referring to that part.

BIBLIOGRAPHY

The Practice of Presswork—Craig R. Spicher. Published by the author
Vols. 6 and 7, U. T. A. Typographic Technical Library
Group VII, Standard Apprentice Lessons. United Typothetae of America
Modern Presswork—Gage. The Inland Printer Company
American Manual of Presswork. Oswald Publishing Company
Presswork—Robb. Dunwoody Institute

QUESTIONS

1. What are the three general types of presses?
2. Name some makes of platen presses.
3. Tell the difference between a drum and a two-revolution press.
4. How does a drum cylinder press operate?
5. What kinds of work are printed on rotary presses?
6. What is a web perfecting press?
7. Name some of the principal parts of a job press.
8. Tell how the job press operates.
9. What are the chief ingredients of ink rollers?
10. How and where should presses be oiled?
11. Should one oil a press while it is running?
12. Describe a method of washing the press.

CHAPTER XV

Make-Ready and Feeding Platen Presses

AFTER the student has become well acquainted with the press, he is ready to proceed with the printing of small jobs, under the supervision of the instructor.

139. **Inking the press.** After making sure that the press is clean, and that no oil is left on the surface of the rollers or disc, put a small quantity of ink on the disc, and let the press run at a moderate speed until the ink has become evenly distributed over the face of the plate. A very small lump of ink has great power of distribution, and the beginner is apt to apply too much. For a small form on a small job press, a lump the size of a pea is about right. Always remember that it is easier to add more ink if too little has been applied at first, than to remove it if the press is inked too heavily. After the first few experiences in inking the press, the beginner will know what quantity to use.

Always ink up before the form is placed in the press; otherwise, large splotches of undistributed ink would be deposited upon the faces of the type, and forced down into the counters and shoulders of the letters.

To add ink during the run, put a very small quantity at a time on the lower left side of the disc, just out of line with the form, so that the rollers cannot carry any of it into the type. As the disc revolves, the new ink will travel up and around to the right, becoming broken up and distributed before it finally comes into line with the type. For long runs, it is customary to set the ink fountain so it will feed the proper amount of ink to the form rollers at each impression. This insures a more even distribution of ink.

Fig. 99. C. & P. Gordon Presses in plant of Hillison and Etten, Chicago

The pressfeeder should keep an even "color" on his job, not letting some sheets be printed in full color while others are gray from lack of ink.* For this purpose, he watches the impressions as he proceeds, and adds ink when necessary.

140. **Putting in the form.** The type form is locked in a chase with the head of the matter toward the bottom or the left side, and the quoins at the top and the right side. It should be placed in the press, therefore, with the quoins up, and the solid furniture down. One should always be sure that the form has been correctly locked up, and that the feet of the type are free from any dirt or grit, before putting the chase into its position in the press.

To insert the form, run the rollers down to their lowest position, and rest the bottom of the chase in the grooves of its supporting lugs. Push it back solidly against the bed, and clamp it at the top. The type form must not scrape the grippers as it is being lifted across them. Do not leave the chase until you are sure it is solid and secure in its place.

It is well to form the habit of pushing the chase over against the left side of the press bed, so that if it should be removed before the job is done, it may be replaced in its exact position. This is especially important in color work.

*In presswork, the term "color" refers to the quantity of the ink printed on a sheet, and not to its hue. If the print is gray, one "adds color," i. e., he puts on a little ink.

Fig. 100. Laureate Presses in operation in the Tabard Press, New York City

Before proceeding further, sight across the grippers and see if they will safely clear the form. If they will not, move them well out of the way. They may then be set in proper position after the guides are placed in the tympan. *Always move back the grippers or they will smash the type form.*

141. **Regulating the impression.** After the form is placed on the press, the job must be *made ready.* This process consists of regulating the impression so that all parts of the form will print with a firm, even pressure. If sheets are added to the packing under the draw-sheet, the impression will be increased, but if some are removed, it will become lighter. The amount of packing for any job will depend largely upon the size of the form. The larger the form, the more pressure will be necessary to print it satisfactorily. A line or two of type will require much less than half the packing needed for a large form. Then, in addition to placing the proper amount of full sheets in the packing, with many forms it is necessary to cut out smaller sections of the impression which are printing too heavily, or to overlay, or build up, other sections that lack pressure. Some forms require very little make-ready, while others take considerable work before the impression is satisfactory.

The tympan usually consists of one or two sheets of pressboard, possibly a sheet of tag, and three or four sheets of book paper, under a heavy manila draw-sheet. A hard tympan, i. e., one consisting of hard materials, is ordinarily better than a tympan of soft packing, as the former gives a sharp, strong impression, without punching the type into the paper. It also causes much less wear on the type.

Before taking an impression, remove the draw-sheet, and put a new one in its place. Examine the sheets, and remove

Fig. 101. Spring Tongue Gauge Pin

Fig. 102. Flexible Side Gauge Pin, for narrow side margins, under grippers

any that are worn or of uneven surface. Build up a tympan for a *light* impression. If in doubt about any part of the packing, leave it out, for it is always better to take a light impression, then build it up, than to damage the type and ruin the packing by making the impression too heavy at the start. Always be sure that the draw-sheet is uniformly tight, and that the tympan is flat and firm. If it is warped, or wrinkled, or spongy, a slurred print will result. After the tympan is prepared, a trial impression should then be taken, on paper of the thickness and texture of the sheets to be printed. This will indicate the necessary make-ready.

The make-ready of various kinds of forms is an intricate process which can best be learned in practical experience at the press, under the guidance of a competent pressman.

142. **Setting the guides.** Guides are placed on the tympan to hold the sheet in the proper position to receive the impression. These usually are gauge pins of the pattern shown in Fig. 101. An impression is taken on the tympan, margins are outlined with a pencil, and then three gauge pins are inserted, two at the bottom, and one at the left side. After a trial impression or two, the pins may be adjusted to their exact positions. Then they are tapped with the press wrench, to fasten them securely into the tympan.

The lower right pin should be located near the right corner of the sheet, but the lower left one should be placed a little away from the corner, for convenience in feeding the paper to the guides. The guide at the left side should be placed a little below the center, for the same reason.

Quads, glued to the tympan, were the original guides, and they are still used in many shops. Glue is applied to one side of the quad, and then it is pressed firmly to the draw-sheet. Adjustments are made before the glue sets.

Other guides to be found in many shops are the Lees Adjustable Guides illustrated in Fig. 103. These guides are fastened with adjustable screws

Fig. 103. The Lees Adjustable Guides in position on platen

to the lower edge of the platen, and they are independent of the tympan, although held firmly in position against it.

143. **Feeding the press.** A pile of the paper to be printed is placed on the feed board, and "fanned out" so that the near edges of the sheets will project slightly over one another, and the pile will incline toward the feeder. This separates the sheets, and makes it easy to pick them up.

The sheets are taken up, one at a time, with the right hand, and fed down to the guides with a swinging motion. They should be fed to the lower guides first and then slid into exact position against the side guide. When the sheets are printed, they are removed from the tympan with the left hand, and placed on the delivery board.

With a little practice, one may learn to time his movements with those of the press, and thus work easily and accurately. It is best to start with the press going at a very low rate of speed, giving special attention to development

Fig. 104. View in cylinder pressroom of The International Textbook Co., Scranton, Pa.

of accuracy and rhythm. Greater speed may be acquired as the proper habits in the mechanics of feeding are formed.

The best manner of gripping the different kinds and sizes of stock, and of swinging the sheets into position on the platen, must be learned in actual practice at the press.

In removing sheets from the platen, care must be taken not to touch the freshly printed parts, as this would smear the printing. Sheets may be gripped in a convenient margin, or a covering of sandpaper may be placed on the first or second finger to draw out the sheets without damage.

144. **Offsetting.** Sheets are said to be *offset* when ink from one is transferred to another. If freshly printed sheets are stacked too high, they will offset on one another.* Soft or rough finish papers can be stacked in rather large piles without danger of offsetting, but hard finished and smooth coated papers offset very easily, and must be spread out in very thin piles, until the ink becomes thoroughly dry.

*Beginners often notice the offset on the back of the sheet, and say that the form has "printed through" but it is always ink transferred from the copy below it in the pile, or from an impression on the tympan. Type never "prints through" the paper.

When a lift of printed sheets is removed from the press, it should be carried loosely on the hands, to avoid offsetting.

145. **Slip-sheeting.** Some jobs, on smooth, hard paper cannot be stacked at all as the sheets come from the press, without having sheets of coarse paper laid between them as they are put on the board. This process of interleaving a job with other paper is known as *slip-sheeting*.

SUGGESTIONS

Probably the best method of learning to feed the press is to run it at a very low speed, without a form, and to feed blank stock into it. If a sheet misses the guides, or if it does not touch the side guide, *do not reach after it*, but wait until the platen opens again, and then make the needed adjustment. If a sheet falls through the press, let it go until the machine has been stopped. The platen press is not a dangerous machine, if this advice is followed, but one must not reach into the press after the platen begins to close for the impression.

After some practice with blank stock, the student should start with small live jobs that are easy to feed. Cards, tickets, and similar work are good projects for the beginner. Large sheets of thin paper should not be handled until after one has had a little experience in feeding.

Do not make the mistake of trying to develop speed too hurriedly. Speed will come as a natural thing, if correct habits of feeding are acquired.

BIBLIOGRAPHY

The Practice of Presswork—Craig R. Spicher. Published by the author
Modern Presswork—Gage. The Inland Printer Company
The School Print Shop—Stillwell. Rand McNally & Company
Presswork—Robb. Dunwoody Institute
Practical Printing—Sherman. Oswald Publishing Company

QUESTIONS

1. How does one ink up the press for a job?
2. How and where is ink applied during a run?
3. Explain how the form is placed in the press.
4. What is the caution about the grippers?
5. What is meant by making ready on the press?
6. Tell some of the principles of make-ready.
7. How are the guides located on the tympan?
8. Explain the process of feeding the press.
9. Tell what is meant by offsetting.
10. What is slip-sheeting? What paper requires it?

CHAPTER XVI

Printing Inks

PRINTING INKS are supplied to the printer in barrels, pails, cans, and tubes. Most of the inks that are used in job printing are put up in small cans and collapsible tubes.

146. Composition of printing inks. Printing inks are mainly composed of color pigments and varnish ground together in proper relation to one another to suit the various grades of work for which they are intended. The pigments furnish the color, and the varnish the binder which holds the color to the paper. Pigments for the various colors are obtained from various objects in the mineral, vegetable, and animal kingdoms. Pigment in black ink is lampblack, produced by the burning of fats or oils in such a manner as to secure a heavy deposit of soot, or carbon.

The varnishes used are principally linseed oil, or rosin oil. The former is used in the better grades of ink. It has the property of absorbing oxygen, and when spread out in a thin film it forms a very smooth, hard coating which, after drying a few hours, will not rub off. The rosin varnishes, which do not dry so rapidly, are used in the cheaper grades of ink. They are intended for printing on softer paper which will easily absorb the ink.

Each ink manufacturer has his own secret formulas for the making of different inks, and for various purposes he adds to the pigment and varnish other ingredients, such as tallow, soap, castor oil, and beeswax.

147. Different kinds of inks. There are many kinds, or classes, of printing inks, differing with each other in composition in accordance with the particular service each is made to render. In ordinary letter-press printing we have news, book or cylinder, job, bond, halftone, and cover inks.

News ink is a cheap grade of ink for printing on rough, uncoated wood-fiber paper, such as news print. It has no drying properties, and it "sets" only by absorption into the paper. It is not suitable for the better classes of printing.

Inks for cylinder presswork vary in their properties in accordance with the nature of the paper stock upon which they are to be printed. For the harder finishes of paper, a mixture that will dry more rapidly is used, as there will be less of absorption into the stock. Cylinder inks, generally, are made with a lighter, finer body that is calculated to give good results on jobs that pass through the press rapidly.

Fig. 105. A modern printing ink cabinet

Job inks are made for the general lines of work on the platen presses. They are heavy and full of color, and are designed for best results with flat impressions of type on the paper. One class, known as bond inks, is particularly suitable for printing on bonds, ledgers, and other classes of writing papers, that do not permit penetration of ink.

Halftone inks are used principally on the hard, smooth surfaced papers, such as coated and enameled book stock. Halftone ink is of a high grade. It is soft and flowing, yet it has the property of drying quickly on the sheet, so that stock may be handled without undue smudging or offsetting.

Cover inks are made up in stiff varnish, and are very strong in color. As the name implies, they are for printing on cover stock, where heavy covering capacity is essential.

Because of the heavy body of cover ink, it cannot be used successfully in the printing of very small type, or of cuts with fine lines, as the ink will fill the counters.

148. **Driers.** It is occasionally necessary that driers be used in inks, as the drying quality of an ink is affected by temperature, and by atmospheric conditions. There are two kinds of driers, one that penetrates the stock, and one that dries by the action of the air. The former may be used on soft book papers, but the latter must be used on bonds and ledgers. Driers should be used wisely and sparingly.

149. **"Doping" inks.** Each grade of ink is prepared to give satisfaction with a particular grade of paper. It has been made in a laboratory of specialists, who have balanced its ingredients scientifically. If other materials are added, this balance may be upset, and the printing may be ruined. The promiscuous "doping" of inks is not to be encouraged. Experienced pressmen have developed certain methods for meeting troublesome situations involving ink, paper, and peculiar weather conditions, but for the beginner, it is safer to depend upon the ink manufacturer.

150. **Care of inks.** If a can of ink is left uncovered, a thick scum will form over the top of it, and there will be a needless waste of ink. For this reason, the lid should always be replaced at once whenever the can is used. This same rule should apply to inks in tubes. When a can of ink is placed on the shelf for an indefinite period, an oiled paper should be drawn across the top of the ink can and the cap pressed down over it, to further seal it. Some pressmen pour a film of oil over the top of the ink, or fill the can up with water, to prevent deterioration, and scumming.

In removing ink from the can, do not dig deeply into the can, but take it from the top without disturbing the lower mass of ink. Always leave the surface smooth, so that air cannot penetrate it. Do not leave the ink-knife in the ink.

151. **Mixing colored inks.** Colored inks are obtained, ready-mixed, from the manufacturers, but many special colors and tints must be made up as needed, in the press-room. Inks are mixed on a clean, smooth surface, with a spatula, or ink-knife. Ordinarily, a marble slab, a piece of thick glass, or a cardboard, is used as a mixing-board. Glass is best, as ink cannot penetrate it, and it is easily cleaned.

Fig. 106. Rotary newspaper press of the Milwaukee Journal

To avoid wasting, it is well to mix a small trial batch of ink, noting the proportion of each color. One should start with white, or the lightest color to be used, and then add other colors sparingly. If the lighter color should be added last, it would take much more ink to secure the proper proportions, and would result in an over-supply of the mixture.

The mixing-board and knives must be absolutely clean when mixing colors. If inks are mixed on glass, it is well to place a sheet of white paper under the glass as an aid in visualizing the color that is being made up.

In order to ascertain the exact color of the mixture, a very small quantity should be spread out thin on a white sheet, for examination, as the ink in the mass will appear slightly darker than the color will prove to be when it is printed on the sheet. If the ink is to be printed on colored paper, this test should also be made on a sheet of the stock that is to be used. When preparing a special color, do not put any of the ink on the press until the color is approved.

Varnishes, reducers, or driers are apt to affect the color of the lighter tints of inks, and due allowance for them is necessary, when they are to be used.

Fig. 107. A round end spatula, or ink-knife

SUGGESTIONS

Obtain a small sample of news, job, cover, and any other inks that are available in your shop. Spread them out with the spatula, and note their characteristics. Examine jobs that have been printed with each kind of ink. You will soon learn to know an ink by its body and consistency.

Practice mixing small quantities of different colors, starting with the weaker one, as suggested. Then test the colors out on white paper.

BIBLIOGRAPHY

Vol. 12, U. T. A. Typographic Technical Library
Modern Printing Inks—Seymour.   D. Van Nostrand Company
The Practice of Presswork—Spicher.   Published by the author
Inks: Their Composition and Manufacture—Mitchell and Hepworth.   The
    J. B. Lippincott Company

QUESTIONS

1. What are the two main ingredients in ink?
2. What can you tell about news ink?
3. What properties are necessary in cylinder press inks?
4. What kind of ink is suitable to general job press work?
5. How does cover ink differ from other inks?
6. What can you say about the care of inks?
7. How should ink be removed from the can?
8. What implements are needed for mixing ink?
9. What color should be used first in mixing?
10. How may a mixture be tested?

CHAPTER XVII

Composing Machines

THE BODY composition of newspapers, magazines, and books, and quite a large per cent of straight matter generally, is set by machine, as a more rapid and economical method. The two machines most extensively used for the production of mechanical composition are the Linotype and the Monotype. On the Linotype, individual matrices are assembled in the desired order, for each line of the matter, and a type-high metal slug, with the letters in relief, is cast in one piece. The Monotype, on the other hand, casts and assembles individual letters. The machine automatically operates a plate of assembled matrices, so that one character at a time is adjusted over the mold, and the types are

Fig. 108. The Linotype

cast and moved along into lines, automatically justified, and the lines in turn are assembled into columns, on the galley.

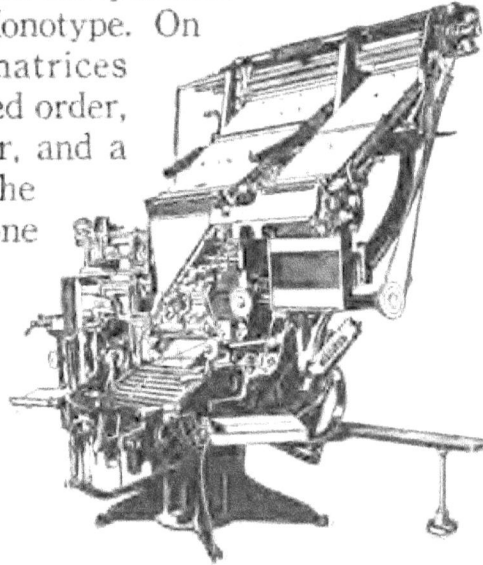

THE LINOTYPE

152. Matrix is unit of composition. The Linotype is not a type-setting machine. It composes with matrices, or small brass dies, which have the forms of the various characters indented in their sides. The matrices for each letter are held in separate channels of the magazine which rests in an inclined position above the keyboard. The pressing of each

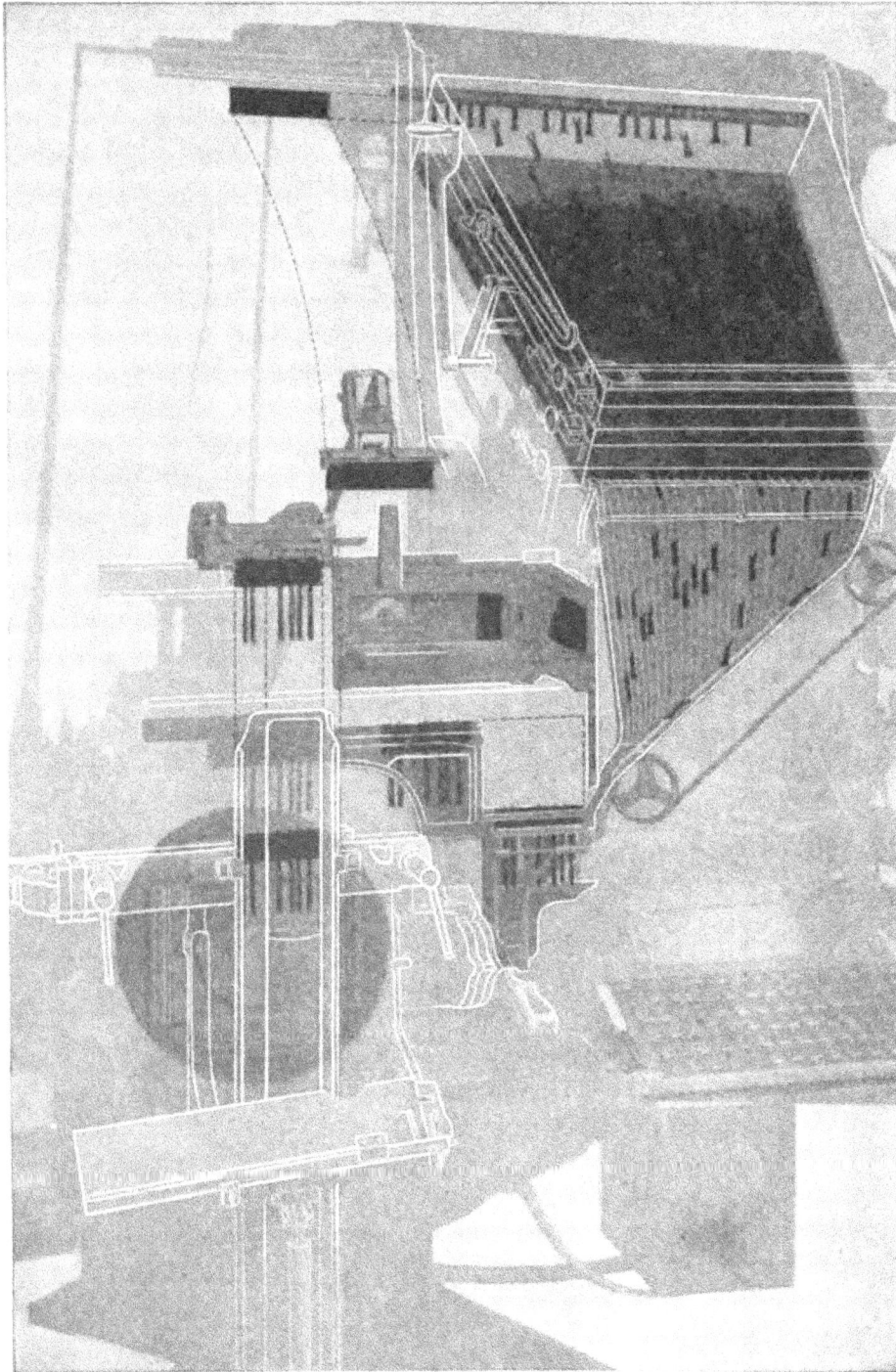

Fig. 109. Phantom view of the Linotype showing the successive stages in the journey of the matrices

key releases its corresponding matrix, and the matrix is then carried into the "stick," or assembling elevator, to take its place in the line. A matrix is illustrated in Fig. 111.

153. **Justification is by space-bands.** For spaces between words, the operator drops space-bands between matrices. They are wedge-shaped devices, capable of expanding when pressed up from the bottom. After a sufficient number of characters have been placed in the line, it is transferred to the casting position at the mold-wheel, and a rod from underneath presses the space-bands upward, thus uniformly increasing the intervals between words, until

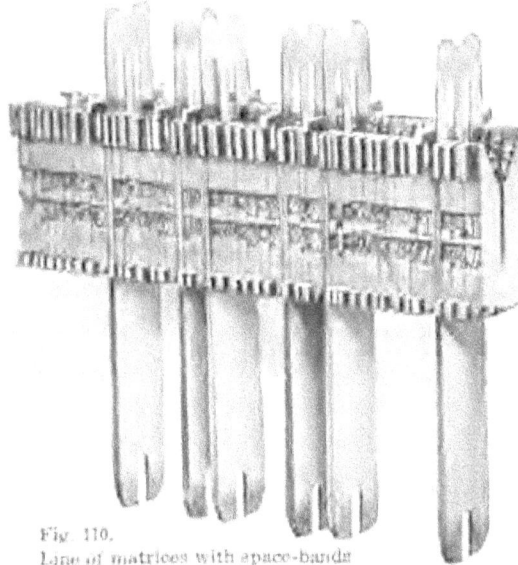

Fig. 110.
Line of matrices with space-bands

the line is firmly spaced to the full width of the measure. The justification, therefore, is entirely automatic.

Fig. 111. A matrix

154. **Slugs are cast automatically.** Behind the mold-wheel is the metal-pot, heated by electricity or gas, which contains molten lead. After the line is justified, a plunger in the metal-pot forces the metal into the mold and against the line of matrices, thus forming a slug with the letters in relief on one edge. The slug is then trimmed by knives that operate against the mold-wheel, and is pushed out on a galley, where it takes its place in the column. After the line has been cast, the matrices are lifted automatically and carried to the top of the magazine where they are distributed into their proper channels, ready for use again. (See Fig. 109).

The Monotype

The Monotype is a type-casting machine which produces individual types, set up in lines, and justified to any width. It consists of two parts—a keyboard, and a caster.

155. **The keyboard** punches a series of holes in a strip of paper which passes from one spool to another as the machine is operated. Punches, representing the various characters, are controlled by

Fig. 112. The Monotype keyboard

Fig. 113. The caster machine

pressing corresponding keys on the keyboard. When a job has been "set," it is recorded on the strip of perforated paper, somewhat similar to a music-roll. This strip of paper, called the *ribbon*, controls the action of the caster.

156. **The caster machine** holds a pot of molten metal, which connects with a stationary mold for the size of the type to be cast, and a matrix-plate. This matrix-plate, or assemblage of matrices, is about five inches square, and it contains molds for each of the type characters. The ribbon guides the movements of the matrix-plate, so that each required letter, in its turn, is adjusted exactly in place over the mold, into which the metal is forced. As soon as each letter is cast, it is moved into its proper place in the line. When the line is completed, it is moved out on the galley.

Justification of lines is automatic on the Monotype. In the casting of each line, the proper spaces are cast with it, the spacing needed to justify the line being indicated on the perforated record as it is being set at the keyboard.

Corrections in Linotype matter are made by resetting the slugs in which the errors occur, but in the Monotype forms, corrections are made from a case of the same style of letter, that has been previously cast for that purpose.

SUGGESTIONS

The operation of the Linotype or the Monotype is a separate phase of work, requiring special training. However, a thorough knowledge of the fundamentals of typography, as covered in this text, furnishes the necessary background for all successful composition, whether hand or machine. The learning of the keyboard is the smallest part of the training of a machine operator, if he expects to turn out an acceptable product.

It should be noted that, although the Monotype system of composition has proven quite satisfactory for the production of body matter, and of tariffs and other intricate tabular work, in which the type is mechanically composed, and then consigned to the melting pot without being distribu- ted, its individual types are not a satisfactory substitute for foundry type for the better grade of hand composition. The material is softer, and it will not stand the usage to which hand-set type is subjected, and it is not cast with the finish and individuality of the best foundry type. A few schools have made the mistake of filling their type cases with Monotype product, because of its lower cost, but such practice is to be discouraged. Best results cannot be had with this material in the cases. The foundry type is not only superior in quality, but is much cheaper in the long run.

Beginners sometimes wonder if machines will not eventually replace hand compositors. There is very little probability of this. The finest work will continue to be composed by hand, and, also, as machine composition advances, the industry becomes further developed, and the work of the hand compositor increases in volume and importance.

BIBLIOGRAPHY

History of Composing Machines—Thompson. The Inland Printer Co.
The Mechanism of the Linotype—Thompson. The Inland Printer Co.
Modern Book Composition—DeVinne. Oswald Publishing Co.
Vol. 23, U. T. A. Typographic Technical Library
Publications of the Mergenthaler Linotype Co. and Lanston Monotype Co.

CHAPTER XVIII

Brass Rules and Their Uses

BRASS RULES are cut from sheet brass which has been rolled down to thicknesses conforming to denominations of the point system, and planed to the standard height of type (.918 inch). Rules are furnished either in strips, two feet in length, or cut to sizes, and put in labor-saving fonts of one pound, and larger. A font of brass rule contains lengths from 1 to 10 picas, by nonpareil graduations, then by picas, up to 20 pica, or 36 pica, lengths, according to its weight.

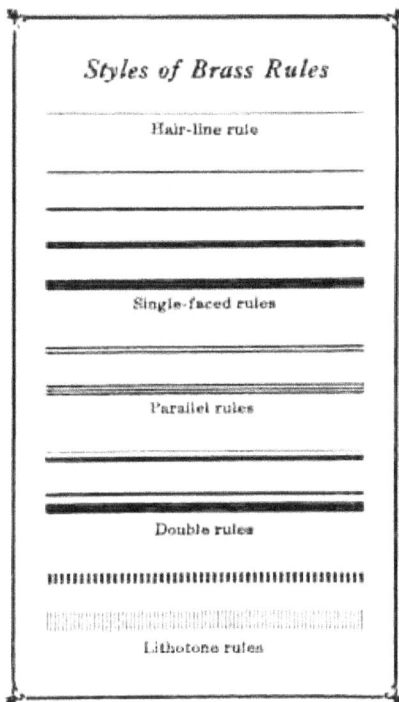

Styles of Brass Rules

Hair-line rule

Single-faced rules

Parallel rules

Double rules

Lithotone rules

Fig. 114

157. **Styles of rules.** There are a great many styles of brass rules, ranging from those that print a single line to rules with elaborate patterns. The usual classifications as to style are shown in Fig. 114. The plainer styles are used in most work.

158. **Construction of rules.** They are classified, also, with respect to the position of the face on the body. There are full-faced rules, which print a line the full width of the body; rules in which the face is centered on the body, leaving an equal shoulder on each

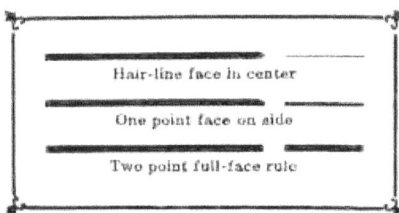

Hair-line face in center

One point face on side

Two point full-face rule

Fig. 115

side; and rules that have the face flush on one side, with a shoulder on the other. In Fig. 115, three two point rules are shown, illustrating the three different positions of the printing faces on the body of the rules.

Fig. 116. A full-size rule case

159. **Rule cases.** Brass rules are kept in cases specially designed for their use. They vary in size from a full-size case, as shown herewith, to a Midget Case, twelve of which will fit into a full-size blank case. The Compact Rule Case, quarter-size, is a popular case for smaller fonts of rule.

160. **Miters.** Mitered pieces are made for practically all rules, and are sold separately in fonts containing a few sets of right and left miters. Eight miters—four right and four left—make up the four corners of a panel. See Fig. 117.

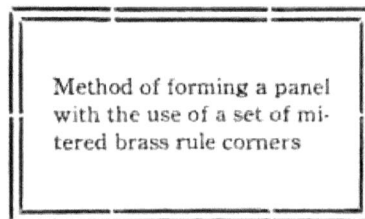

Method of forming a panel with the use of a set of mitered brass rule corners

Fig. 117

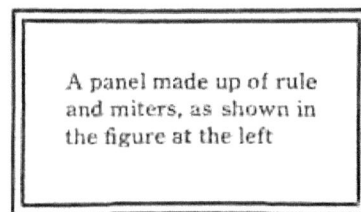

A panel made up of rule and miters, as shown in the figure at the left

Fig. 118

The mitered pieces ordinarily measure $2\frac{1}{2}$, 4, or 5 picas in length. Perfect joints may be made at the corners of borders and panels by the use of miters, especially when they are held in correct position with the aid of corner quads.

161. Butted Corners. Panels may be formed without the use of miters, with full-faced rule, or rule with the face on the side, in the manner illustrated in Fig. 119. If the latter kind of rule is used, the top and bottom pieces must be set with the face inside and shoulder out; and the side pieces with the face out. This brings the faces together properly.

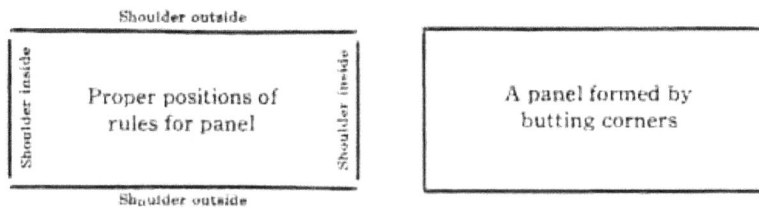

Fig. 119. Method of forming a panel with rules having the face on one side

Rules with the face in the center, double-faced, or patterned rules cannot be made up in panels without mitered corners, as the faces will not meet properly at the corners.

162. Using rules with type. Brass rules are sometimes used with type, in the printing of blanks, and similar work. When this is the case, the face of the rule should always be

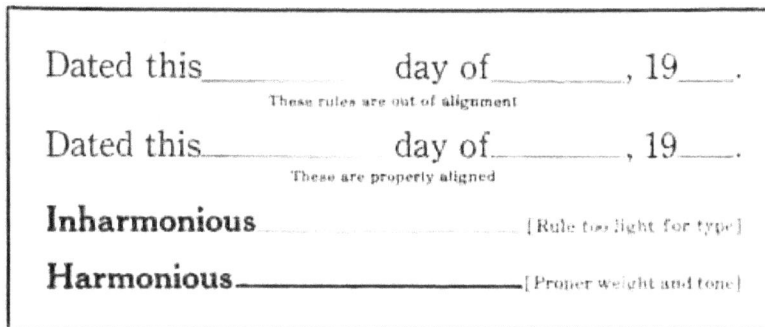

Fig. 120

aligned with the letters. It should also be the same weight, or tone, of the type, so that a pleasing effect will be had. In Fig. 120, correct and incorrect combinations are shown.

Instead of setting in a number of short rules between words, as above, some kinds of blank work will permit the use of full-length rules under the type lines, as in Fig. 121.

Although rules are often used with type in the manner just described, for ordinary blank work the use of leaders

Name	Birthday	19
No.	Street—Phone	
Parent's Name	Business	

Fig. 121

is preferred by many printers, as they are much easier to justify in the lines, and they are made to align perfectly with all standard lining type. This is illustrated in Fig. 122.

Name	Birthday	19
No.	Street—Phone	
Parent's Name	Business	

Dated this_____day of_____, 192__

Fig. 122

SUGGESTIONS

Learn all the styles of rule in your shop. Select one piece from each style, classify them, and make up a chart of rules, labelling each for style and size of body, as "2 point, hairline in center," "2 point body, 1 point face on side," etc. File a proof of this in your notebook.

Make up specimen panels of rule, both with mitered and butted corners, take proofs of them, and then distribute the forms carefully.

QUESTIONS

1. What are brass rules used for?
2. What constitutes a font of brass rule?
3. What are some of the common styles of rules?
4. Name three kinds as to construction.
5. How are mitered corners used?
6. Explain how to form a panel without miters.
7. What rules can be panelled without miters?
8. What kinds require miters at the corners?

CHAPTER XIX

Composition of Tabular Forms

TABULAR forms consist of type matter set in parallel columns, with successive items in alignment across the page. The columns usually are separated by vertical rules, although in some classes of work, intervals of spacing may serve the same purpose. The composition of tabular forms is precise work, requiring very accurate justification and spacing out of the columns. An error in spacing in one or more columns will interfere with lock-up, and may throw the whole form out of alignment. However, this work ought not to be difficult for the compositor who carefully plans his work, and gives proper attention to details.

163. **Casting up a table.** The laying out of the matter to be set, and computing the widths for the various columns, is known as *casting up* a table. The measure of width for the table is divided into the various columns, allowance being made for the combined width of the column rules. If it is possible, each of the columns will be set to multiples of nonpareils or picas, in order to use the standard lengths of rules and spacing material.* If, after allotting space to each column, and allowing for the column rules, odd points of space remain, thin leads must be inserted along the column rules, at opportune places, to make out the full measure. The matter inside the head and foot rules must always be built accurately to even picas both in width and length, or the form cannot be locked up satisfactorily for printing.

---

* In the ordinary job shop, it is customary to set the various columns to widths corresponding to the standard nonpareil and pica lengths of rules, leads, and slugs. This does not necessitate cutting the materials to odd lengths, for tabular work. Printing plants making a specialty of tabular and tariff work carry a full equipment of short leads, slugs, and rules, in many odd sizes, and find it easier to disregard pica widths.

164. **Construction.** There are a few general rules that govern the manner of construction of tables, that should be followed by the compositor. An outstanding rule is that the column rules should run full length, and the cross rules should be broken at the intersections. There are very few places where it is necessary or advisable to do otherwise.

RIGHT	METHOD

Fig. 123

WRONG	METHOD

Fig. 124

It is customary to place double rules at the head and the foot of a table. These should have face flush with the body so that perfect connections will be made with the ends of the column rules. Double column rules, or a heavier rule, may be used to indicate a more definite separation between certain columns, or sections, of a table. If the table is set only half the page width, and then is doubled upon itself, double rules should be placed between the two divisions.

THE VARIOUS CHARACTERISTICS OF STYLE IN TABLES

THIS SECTION OF THE TABLE IS CALLED THE STUB	USE OF MODERN AND OLDSTYLE FIGURES		En (Dot) Leaders Used as Decimals	Use of En Quads for Decimal Points	
	Modern Figures	Wordy Headings May Run This Way			
Leaders will be _____	123,456	1234	3.1416	$42	00
Set flush to the right ____	253,000	5678	2.	17	45
Of the column and _____	36,842	9000	7.5	2	50
Any necessary spacing __	1,000	2587	12.75	11	40
Will then be inserted____	22,750	4690	.12	1	00
Between type and leaders	319,640	1926	3.33+	10	00
Note use of dollar mark	756,688	25115		$84	35

Fig. 125

The first column usually contains the subject-matter of the table, and it is called the *stub*. Its items are connected with the figures or other matter in the remaining columns by lines of leaders, set flush to the right side of the stub.

Some columns may contain narrow figures, headed by larger groups of words. If necessary, to save space, such headings may be turned lengthwise in the columns, so that they will be read from the bottom up.

If the table is to accompany other type matter, it should harmonize with the general style of the matter. If possible, type of the same series should be used. Oldstyle figures should be used if they appear in the other matter; modern figures, if they are to accompany modern ones. Hair-line rules will be used with all ordinary body type, but if the table is set in a heavier display letter, then rules should be chosen that will fit the tone of the type, so that a pleasing effect will be had. The principles of good typography can be applied to tabular composition as well as to other work.

165. **Proportioning the space.** After ascertaining the narrowest possible width for each column, whatever space then remains should be divided up between the columns, to give an effect of even spacing to the whole table. Some space should be allowed on both sides of the figures in a column, whenever possible. An en quad, or even an em quad, is recommended when the space will permit. It will improve the appearance and legibility of the job. In Fig. 126 the minimum space is given the figure columns, while in Fig. 127 the space is equalized, greatly improving the job.

TABLE OF COMPARATIVE TYPE SIZES

1000 EMS	12	10	8	6
12 point	1000	1440	2250	4000
10 point	694	1000	1563	2778
8 point	444	640	1000	1778
6 point	250	360	563	1000

Fig. 126

TABLE OF COMPARATIVE TYPE SIZES

1000 EMS	12 pt.	10 pt.	8 pt.	6 pt.
12 point	1000	1440	2250	4000
10 point	694	1000	1563	2778
8 point	444	640	1000	1778
6 point	250	360	563	1000

Fig. 127

166. **Handling figures.** When figures are placed in the column, they should always be lined up at the right side, if they are whole numbers, or lined on the decimal points, if these are used. Instead of the period, the en (dot) leader is frequently used for the decimal point, as this keeps the column widths in multiples of the en of the type body. Its use is not at all necessary unless it simplifies justification.

10,000	$ .25	$20 00	100.00	2½
1,000	17.00	17 50	.037	17¼
100	480.00	8 50	1.18	¼
10	16.50	10 00	72.08	9½
11,110	$513.75	$56 00	173.197	29½

Fig. 128. Table showing proper alignments of figures in columns

When amounts of money are expressed, the dollar mark will always appear with the first figure, and again with the total, but not with the other figures. Its position is at the left of the widest figure in the column, and this sometimes necessitates the insertion of space between it and the first figure, as in the second column of Fig. 128. En quads are occasionally used to divide dollars and cents, in the place of periods, as illustrated in the third column of this figure.

167. **Making columns self-spacing.** In setting columns of figures, the work is greatly simplified by planning for the use of such materials as will make the lines come out to even points with standard spaces. The figures and the dollar mark are cast on the en body, in nearly all fonts. If en quads or en leaders are used for decimal points, all the characters of each line will be of the en width. Spaces are now made point-set, i.e., cast in point widths, and combinations may be made that will automatically justify the lines of any width column to exact points.

STANDARD WIDTHS
POINT-SET SPACES

Body	3-em	4-em	5-em
6	2	1½	1¼
8	3	2	1½
10	3½	2½	2
12	4	3	2½

Fig. 129

To illustrate this method of spacing, tables are given below for some of the possible combinations in 8 point and 10 point type, which provide for automatic justification of lines to a few standard widths. A study of these schemes will make this method of spacing clear to the student.

Width of Column, Points	SPACE PRECEDING FIGURES		TOTAL NUMBER OF EN WIDTHS OR FIGURES TO LINE OF 8 POINT TYPE	SPACE FOLLOWING FIGURES		Width of Column, Points	SPACE PRECEDING FIGURES		TOTAL NUMBER OF EN WIDTHS OR FIGURES TO LINE OF 10 POINT TYPE	SPACE FOLLOWING FIGURES	
	Denominations of Spaces	Total Points		Denominations of Spaces	Total Points		Denominations of Spaces	Total Points		Denominations of Spaces	Total Points
18	4-em	2	4 en widths	....	....	30	....	....	6 en widths	....	....
24	....	....	6 en widths	....	....	36	4, 4	5	5 en widths	3, 4	6
30	3-em	3	6 en widths	3-em	3	42	3-em	3½	7 en widths	3-em	3½
36	....	....	9 en widths	....	....	48	3, 3	7	7 en widths	3, 4	6
42	3-em	3	9 en widths	3-em	3	48	5, 5	4	8 en widths	5, 5	4
48	....	....	12 en widths	....	....	60	....	....	12 en widths	....	....
Example: 42 points — $500.00						Example: 48 points — $125 87					

Fig. 130

168. Spacing out columns. The length of a column will always be a multiple of picas, or nonpareils, in order that standard lengths of rules may be used between columns. In spacing out the length, some allowance must be made for "type squeeze," for a long column consisting of many small pieces of material will be compressed slightly under pressure of quoins. No definite rule can be given for this, but a little experience will help in making this allowance.

The amount of space between the matter in the column and the cross-rules above and below it is usually about one half the thickness of the type body used. In an 8 point table, about 4 points of white space will be allowed above and below the matter, and for 10 point or 12 point type, a nonpareil slug is customary. These spaces may be varied at times to bring the column to an even measure in length.

169. Multiple justification. Some tables may be set full width in the stick, each line across the various columns being justified in a single measure. This is especially true of matter in parallel columns, with no column rules. A simple form of this kind is shown below. After the plan of spacing for the lines has been worked out, all the columns of figures are self-spacing, and the only justification that is required for the entire width is between the matter in the stub and the first column of figures. Study Fig. 131.

Timothy [Justification here only]	36	.20	1.75	15.00
Orchard Grass	14	.45	4.00	35.00
Bermuda Grass	36	.60	5.50	50.00
Sweet Vernal (extra hardy)	10	1.00	9.50	90.00

Fig. 131. A style of tabular composition easily set in one measure

This method of multiple justification may be followed, also, with tables of figures containing vertical rules, if the blanks between the columns are divided up properly, so that each column may be separated from its neighbor, and the rules inserted after the table is set. Allowance must be made for the column rules, when the line is justified. This is done by placing the necessary number of rules in the left side of the stick, then setting the line firmly against them. This method of composition is shown in Fig. 132.

Fig. 132. Method of setting a number of self-spacing columns in one measure

After the matter has been set in this manner, the galley containing it may be turned carefully about, with the head down, and the spaces between the columns may then be opened with a knife blade, or a rule, and the column rules inserted. This is a convenient way to set forms containing a number of very narrow columns of figures which can be made self-spacing, but it should not be attempted at first.

When individual justification is necessary in more than one column, the job may be set in a single measure, across the full width of the form, by the following method.

Apportion the necessary width for each column, and provide accurate pieces of nonpareil or pica brass rule, one the width of the last column, another the width of the last two columns, and so on until the first column is approached, but not included. Place the longest piece of rule in the right side of the stick, and set and justify the first column accurately to the rule. Then remove the rule, and substitute the one next in length. Justify the second column to this rule. Continue this process until the line is complete, and set all other lines in the same manner. An example of this method, showing the various steps, appears below.

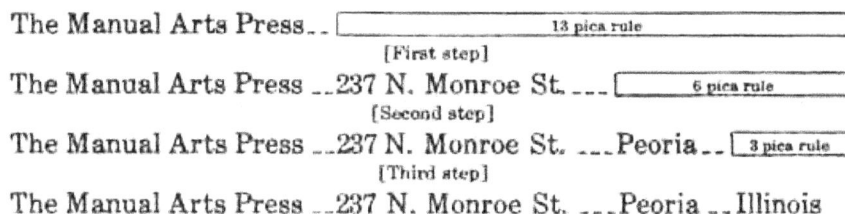

The Manual Arts Press __ [_____ 13 pica rule _____]
[First step]

The Manual Arts Press __237 N. Monroe St. ___ [_____ 6 pica rule _____]
[Second step]

The Manual Arts Press __237 N. Monroe St. ___Peoria __ [3 pica rule]
[Third step]

The Manual Arts Press __237 N. Monroe St. ___Peoria __Illinois

Fig. 133. A method of multiple justification

If vertical rules are to be used in the job, allowance will be made for them in the stick before the work is started.

170. **Setting columns to odd measures.** Sometimes it is necessary to set columns to odd measures, in order to bring all the material within a given space. When this is done, the columns are usually laid out in multiples of ens of the type used. A column of 8 point may be 28 points wide, or 32 points wide, etc. Usually, such a table will be set solid, and the only spacing will be at the head and foot of the matter. Leads and slugs of the same width must be provided for the job, or point-set spaces may be used.

171. **Use of point-set spaces.** Point-set spaces sometimes are used in place of leads in columns of odd measures. The student will note, by consulting the table of widths on page 135, that the 6 point 4-em space and the 8 point 5-em space are 1½ points wide; that the 6 point 3-em space, the 8 point 4-em space, and the 10 point 5-em space are 2 points wide; that the 10 point 4-em space and the 12 point 5-em space are 2½ points wide; and that the 6 point en quad, 8 point 3-em space, and 12 point 4-em space are 3 points wide. By making the proper combinations of these spaces, almost any necessary width and length of spacing may be made.

Although this matching of spaces is often necessary and it affords valuable practice for the student, he will find that in many shops leads would be cut to the measure, as the saving of time would justify the cutting of leads to the odd length. Such material need not be considered as a loss, for it may be labelled and stored for use again on like jobs, or trimmed to the next lower standard measure, after the job has been distributed. The student will not cut material to odd lengths without the approval of his instructor.

172. **Work-and-twist jobs.** Some jobs, containing a number of narrow columns, should be made up into two forms which will print one upon the other, to make the finished table. This simplifies the composition, and makes a neater job, as there are fewer breaks in the cross-rules. When this method is followed, the two forms are locked up together, head to head, or side to side, and printed on stock cut twice the size of the finished job. The sheet is printed once, and then turned about so that each form will strike the other in the proper place, at the second impression. After this, the stock is cut in two, and each sheet makes two complete copies. This method is known as work-and-twist, or work-and-whirl, printing. It differs from work-and-turn printing, as the sheet is not turned over, but is printed twice on the same side. A work-and-twist form is shown on next page.

	Enrolled			No. Belonging	Days Present	No. Absent	Tardy		Admitted				Withdrawn				Not Absent	Non-residents	No. Visitors
	Boys	Girls	Total				Boys	Girls	Enrolled	Transfer	Reentered	Reinstated	Leaving	Transfer	Absence	Discipline			

Fig. 134. The register form of a work-and-twist job, containing the head and foot rules

1st Month
2nd Month
3rd Month
4th Month
5th Month
6th Month
7th Month
8th Month
9th Month

Fig. 135. The second form, containing the cross-rules

	Enrolled			No. Belonging	Days Present	No. Absent	Tardy		Admitted				Withdrawn				Not Absent	Non-residents	No. Visitors
	Boys	Girls	Total				Boys	Girls	Enrolled	Transfer	Reentered	Reinstated	Leaving	Transfer	Absence	Discipline			
1st Month																			
2nd Month																			
3rd Month																			
4th Month																			
5th Month																			
6th Month																			
7th Month																			
8th Month																			
9th Month																			

Fig. 136. The completed job

In the composition of work-and-twist forms, it is well to divide the matter in such a way that the two sections will easily fit into one another, and that a slight variation in the register at the guides, at either printing, will not be very noticeable. Tabular forms necessitating a hair-line register present very trying problems to the pressfeeder.

173. **Typotabular Squares.** For the composition of ruled blanks, type-metal pieces, known as Typotabular Squares,

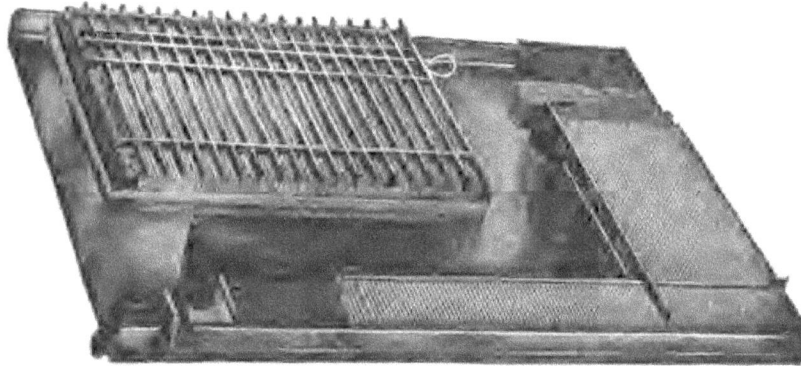

Fig. 137. An outfit of Typotabular Squares

are sometimes used. These are cast on the em 6 point body. The tops of the squares are shaped as four-sided pyramids, and when they are assembled in masses, V-shaped channels are automatically formed, running at right angles 6 points apart, into which rules may be inserted as desired. The advantage of this device is that blank forms may be set by merely selecting and inserting the rules. After printing, the form may be taken back on the galley, the rules taken out, and the squares will be ready for the next job.

Another scheme for the setting of ruled blanks is the use of Tabular Quadrules, which are in the form of quads of 12, 18, and 24 point sizes, with a rule face running across the top. When assembled into columns of desired width, they print the cross-rules of the table, while brass rules, inserted between them, print the column rules.

174. **Protection for rollers.** Ink rollers may be damaged
by striking the sharp ends of rules placed horizontally in
the chase. If such rules are to be printed to the extreme
edge of the paper, cutting of the rollers may be avoided by
placing extra horizontal rules at the ends of the vertical
ones, letting them strike the tympan just off the sheet. An
example of this method of protection follows.

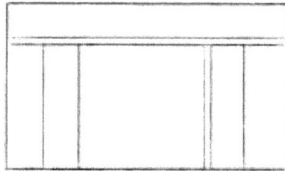

Fig. 138. As printed on the sheet   Fig. 139. Showing rule guards

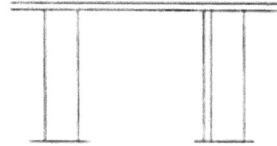

175. **Machine-set tabular work.** The modern tendency
is to set intricate tables by machine, whenever possible, as
an economy of time and expense. There are a number of
methods for the production of tabular composition.

The Monotype is much used for setting tables. On this
machine, the operator may "set" each line of copy across
the entire width of the table, no matter how intricate, and
then the column rules may be inserted on the galley, as in
the case of multiple justification by hand. Tariffs, time-
tables, and other matter which contain many very narrow
columns are frequently set on the Monotype.

Ruled blank forms can be set on the Ludlow Typograph,
or on the Linotype, by the use of leader matrices punched
vertically (⋮) instead of horizontally (....). After the exact
spacing between the horizontal lines is determined, a single
line of vertical leaders is set, the machine is locked, and a
sufficient number of slugs is cast. By assembling the slugs
longitudinally on the galley, the leaders will form the horizontal lines. Then type-high brass rule can be inserted as
desired, to form the column rules. Fig. 140 shows a form
made up from vertical leader slugs cast on the Typograph.

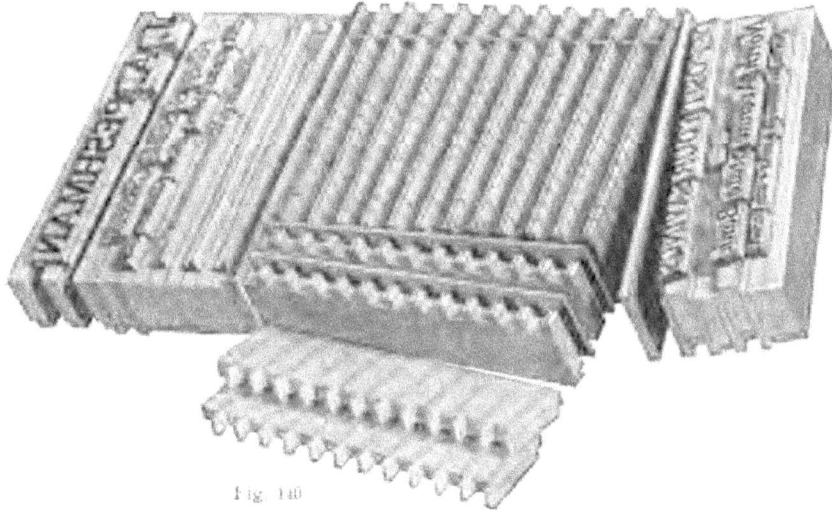

Fig. 140

SUGGESTIONS

The student must realize that perfect justification of all the units of a table is necessary, if he expects the form to be safely locked up for the press. The body must always measure to even picas in length and width.

In setting a table, the first column should be completed first, and be fully spaced out in finished form, with its head to the head of the galley. The column rule at its right should be placed in position, and then the second column should be assembled upon it. In this manner, the form is solid and stable at all times, and also, the first column serves as a guide for the spacing of the other columns. If there are a number of headings to be set the same width, it is well to set all of them at once, and place them on another galley, so that each may be lifted to the form in its turn.

The beginner should not attempt multiple justification until he has had some experience in setting up tables by individual columns, and has gained a fair knowledge of the proper formations of tables.

QUESTIONS

1. What is meant by casting up a table?
2. Why must the body be filled out to even picas both ways?
3. What is the stub of a table?
4. How may columns of figures be made self-spacing?
5. How much space should be at the head and foot of columns?
6. How do point-set spaces aid in tabular composition?
7. Explain the principle of multiple justification.
8. What is a work-and-twist job?
9. What can you tell about machine-set tabular work?

CHAPTER XX

The Use of Lay-Outs

PRELIMINARY plans, or sketches, should be made for the better class of printed jobs, before actual composition is started. This helps the compositor to have a clear, definite idea of each job, and to make sure that all parts of the printed design will be in harmony, and appropriate. It also saves time and labor, for it is considerably easier to change the specifications on paper than in the galley. These preliminary sketches are known as lay-outs.

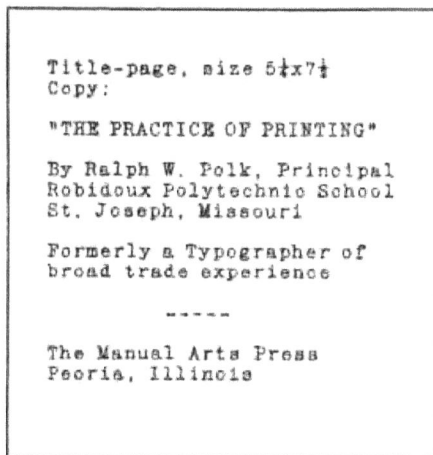

```
Title-page, size 5¼x7½
Copy:

"THE PRACTICE OF PRINTING"

By Ralph W. Polk, Principal
Robidoux Polytechnic School
St. Joseph, Missouri

Formerly a Typographer of
broad trade experience

- - - - -

The Manual Arts Press
Peoria, Illinois
```

Fig. 141. Copy for title-page

In most of the large printing plants, special lay-out men are employed to make sketches, and to arrange detailed specifications, for the various jobs. In the smaller plants, this work is usually done by the foreman. Any compositor should be able to make lay-outs, when necessary.

176. **Lay-out blanks.** Lay-outs are prepared on blanks ruled in pica squares and numbered at the top and left edges, and the designs are drawn to actual size as indicated by these pica measurements. The lay-out blanks may be printed from electrotypes of dotted-rule forms that have been prepared for the use of printers generally, or they may be made by building forms of rules in pica columns, and printing them both ways of the sheet, so as to make squares. The ordinary size of the sheet is 8½ x 11 inches.

Fig. 142. A lay-out for the copy
on the opposite page, and the
form set from the lay-out

177. Lay-out should be detailed. The lay-out should be sketched sufficiently in detail to serve as a guide to any compositor who might be assigned to the work. Groups of body matter may be indicated by outlines defining the area to be covered, as indicated in the figure here shown. Full detailed specification of sizes and styles of the type, ornaments, and borders to be used should be listed on the sheet, at the right of the sketch.

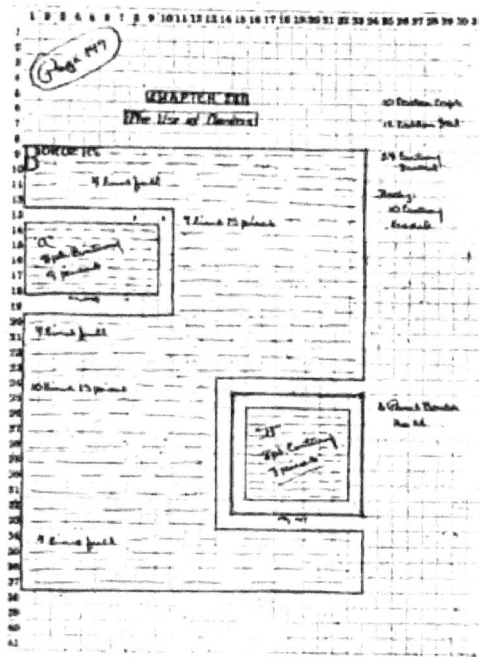

Fig. 143. Lay-out for opposite page

SUGGESTIONS

It will be well for the student to begin lay-out work by drawing sketches of simple jobs that are already printed. He should give particular attention to the proper spacing, and to indicating the sizes of type lines. After a little practice of this nature, he may proceed with original work.

It does not require an artist to make a printers' lay-out. Previous training in sketching or lettering is not necessary. Any student, who will study the details of type designs, can, after a little practice, indicate his plans in a clear and simple manner on the ruled lay-out sheets. Exactness in the letter formations need not be attempted, especially at the first, but accuracy in the sizes and positions of the groups should be stressed.

Form the habit of making lay-outs for all your jobs, and carry this practice on through your course. Compare your lay-outs with the printed jobs, and note your weak points, that special attention may be given them.

QUESTIONS

1. What is a lay-out? What is its purpose?
2. How do lay-outs save time and labor?
3. In commercial plants, by whom are lay-outs usually made?
4. Describe a lay-out blank.
5. Why should lay-outs contain full specifications?

CHAPTER XXI

The Use of Borders

BORDERS are considered a necessary part of a very large per cent of good printing. They may be made of brass rules, of type border units, of Linotype slugs, or of some combination of the various kinds of border material.

This is an unbordered paragraph. While this is set off from the main body matter of the page by the ordinary margins, it does not stand out very well, without a border.

Fig. 144

178. **Purpose of borders.** The purpose of the border is to hold the job together, and to separate it from other matter, if it appears on the page with other groups. It serves to focus the attention of the reader within the area of the printed page, and, as a decorative element, it adds interest and attractiveness to the piece of printing. It may be considered as the frame for the typographic picture, or group, around which it is assembled, and which it is to emphasize.

179. **Use of rules as borders.** Brass rules that match the type form make neat borders. They are particularly appropriate for use in printing of a formal nature. As has been noted in an earlier chapter, some rule borders may be built up by butting the corners, the top and bottom pieces extending full width and the side pieces coming within them, while other styles of rule require the

The panel border that is placed around this paragraph sets it apart from the main body of the page, and helps to attract and to hold the attention of the reader.

Fig. 145

mitered corner pieces. The corners of a border should be made to join nicely, as any weakness at the corners will greatly detract from the effectiveness of the whole design.

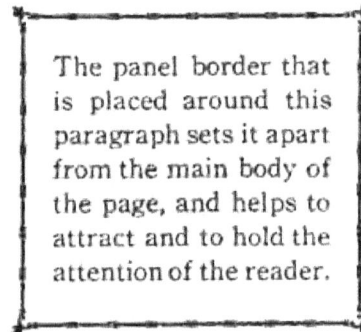

Sometimes old rules must be used to form borders. When this is the case, unsightly corners may be avoided by using the corner pieces of type borders with them, as below.

Fig. 146. Corner pieces used with brass rules

180. **Panel borders** make good substitutes for rule borders. They may be assembled rapidly, and although simple in design, they have sufficient individuality to add interest to the job. A few panel borders follow.

Fig. 147. A few representative panel borders

More ornamented type borders are made for use in general display printing. There are a great many varieties of type borders, ranging from 2 to 48 points in size. They should be selected with judgment, for they should be of suitable size to match the type form, and the size of the page, and also, they should match the style of the type used. If possible, they should suggest the spirit of the message expressed in the type. Certainly they should never be out of harmony with it.

THIS BORDER IS MADE UP OF 6 POINT PANEL BORDER AND 3 POINT PARALLEL RULES

Just as one selects a frame that will harmonize with the picture and add to its beauty, one should select an appropriate border, in keeping with the type.

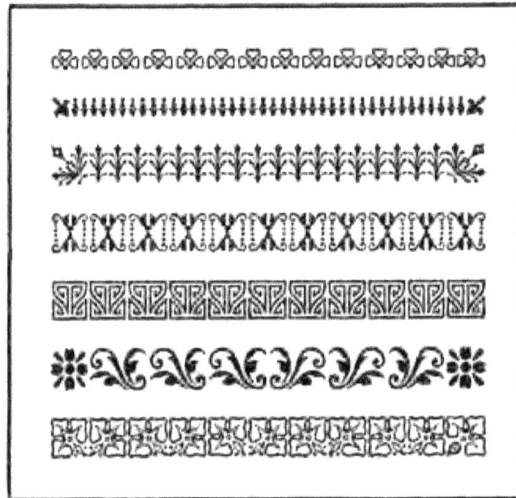

Fig. 148. A few decorative borders

181. **How to build a border.** In the composition of display advertising, it is customary to assemble the border and the marginal spacing material into position before putting in the body of the ad. This practice is also followed in the setting of many bordered jobs. This portion, exclusive of the body, or type section, is the *skeleton* of the ad.

THIS BORDER IS A COMBINATION OF BRASS RULES WITH 12 POINT OLD ENGLISH BORDER

Fig. 149. Proper construction of skeleton, with head to the right

Slugs the full width of the border will always be placed at the head and foot of the form. As the border is built up, slugs, representing the side margins between the type and border, will be inserted inside the border, and these will be separated and held in place by other slugs the width of the measure of the type matter, which will serve as margins above and below the type. The side slugs will *always* run full length inside the border, and the slugs at the head and foot of the type matter will go *inside* the side slugs. This is not only the simplest manner of building up a skeleton, but the material thus assembled will stand securely in its position on the galley until the type matter is inserted.

When nonpareil or pica borders are used, the side margins will be built up of slugs, or metal furniture, in multiples of nonpareils. If a 2 point rule border is used, the spacing material on each side must include two leads, to build the rule out to nonpareil thickness. Whenever the thickness of the border is in odd points, proper spacing must be added to bring it to an even measure, in multiples of nonpareils.

182. **Machine-cast borders.** Borders and rules, in strip form, are cast on the composing machines. The strips are cut to size for the individual job, and are mitered for the corner connections. Those made by the Linotype are in the form of 30 pica slugs, while Monotype rules are about 24 inches in length. Linotype borders are sometimes cast with the corner pieces at the end of the slug. When this is the case, four pieces containing corners will be cut to size and placed about the form. This method of building up a border is demonstrated in the accompanying figure.

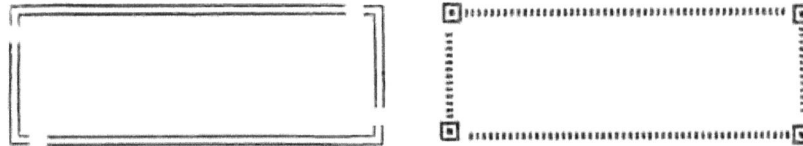

Fig. 150

SUGGESTIONS

In Chapter XVIII, you were asked to make a chart of the brass rules to be found in your shop, for your notebook. Set up a line of each of the borders available, 30 picas wide, label them as to style and size of body, and file a proof of this with the chart of rules, for future reference.

Be sure to learn the proper method of constructing the skeleton for a bordered job, and to follow it in the setting of all work requiring borders. When you have figured out the necessary amount of spacing on each side between the type and the side border strips, set this in the full length of the area inside the border. Then the center section of the job, which will always be the width of the type matter, will include all the spacing above and below the type, and will be built out to full length inside the border.

Practice the building of skeletons to various dimensions, beginning with nonpareil and pica borders, then with 2, 3, and 4 point rules.

QUESTIONS

1. What are some of the purposes of borders?
2. How may a border be compared to a picture frame?
3. How may good corners be made for worn rules?
4. What considerations should govern the choice of a border?
5. What material comprises the skeleton of a bordered job?
6. Explain how a skeleton is built up.
7. What is done when a border of odd points in width is used?
8. What can you tell of machine-cast borders?

CHAPTER XXII

Classification of Type Faces

THERE are many different styles of lettering in modern typography, and one is apt to become confused in his choice of types unless he analyzes them into logical groups. Generally speaking, all type faces may be listed under five classifications, as follows: Roman, Italic, Text, "Gothic," or Block-letter, and Script.

Roman

Italic

𝕿𝖊𝖝𝖙

"GOTHIC"

Script

Fig. 151

ROMAN TYPES

183. **Roman most important group.** The Roman faces comprise by far the largest and most important group. The capitals were evolved from the Greek, and were used by the Latin scribes (in Uncial form) in the lettering of earlier manuscripts, and by the stonecutters (in a more rigid and angular form) in their inscriptions. For a long period, the capitals were used alone. Lower-case letters came into use in the eighth century, but they were not developed into any finished form until the early typographers gave them the grace and beauty they now possess.

The Roman group alone includes a vast number of individual styles of letter-

Fig. 152. Roman capitals in ancient inscription

ing, which have been produced periodically, by printers of many countries, from the days of Aldus and Jenson, to the

Table of Alphabets and Lettering

	Earlier Characters					Styles of Lettering									
Hebrew Letters	Phenician Object and Name	Ancient Phenician	Ancient Greek	Greek Letter Names	Classic Greek	Lapidary Roman	Uncial	Typical Early Black-letter	Old-style Italic	French Old style (Modernised)	Early English Lettering (Caslon)	Modern face Roman	Modern face Italic	Modern Gothic Letter	Black letter
א	Ox · Aleph	ꝳꝲ	Δ	Alpha	Aα	A	A	Ka	Aa	Aa	Aa	Aa	Aa	Aa	A
ב	House · Beth	ꝱ	ꞵ	Beta	Bβ	B	Θ	Bb	Bb	Bb	Bb	Bb	Bb	Bb	B
ג	Camel · Gimel	7	Γ	Gamma	Γγ	C	C	Cc	Cc	Cc	Cc	Cc	Cc	Cc	C
						G	G	Gg	Gg	Gg	Gg	Gg	Gg	Gg	G
ד	Door · Daleth	Δ	Δ	Delta	Δδ	D	D	Dd	Dd	Dd	Dd	Dd	Dd	Dd	D
ה	Window · He	Ⅎ	E	Epsilon	Eε	E	G	Ee	Ee	Ee	Ee	Ee	Ee	Ee	E
ו	Hook · Vav	Ⴤ	Y	Digamma)		F	A	Ff	Ff	Ff	Ff	Ff	Ff	Ff	F
ז	Dagger · Zayin	ⱬ	Z	Zeta	Zζ	Z	Ꝫ	Zz	Zz	Zz	Zz	Zz	Zz	Zz	Z
ח	Fence · Cheth	目	Θ	Eta	Hη	H	Ꜧ	Hh	Hh	Hh	Hh	Hh	Hh	Hh	H
ט	Basket · Teth	⊕	Θ	Theta	Θθ	(t.h)									
י	Jot · Yodh	⌐	I	Iota	Iι	I	I	Ii	Ii	Ii	Ii	Ii	Ii	Ii	I
							J	Jj	Jj	Jj	Jj	Jj	Jj	Jj	J
כ	Hand · Kaph	Ꝁ	K	Kappa	Kκ	K	Ꝃ	Kk	Kk	Kk	Kk	Kk	Kk	Kk	K
ל	Goad · Lamedh	⌐⌐	Λ	Lambda	Λλ	L	L	Ll	Ll	Ll	Ll	Ll	Ll	Ll	L
מ	Waters · Mem	ᒲ	Μ	Mu	Mμ	M	Ⱉ	Mm	Mm	Mm	Mm	Mm	Mm	Mm	M
נ	Fish · Nun	Ꞁ	Ν	Nu	Nν	N	Ⱂ	Nn	Nn	Nn	Nn	Nn	Nn	Nn	N
ס	Post · Samekh	⧻	Ξ	Xi	Ξξ	X	Ⱬ	Xx	Xx	Xx	Xx	Xx	Xx	Xx	X
ע	Eye · Ayin	⊙O	O	Omicron	Oo	O	O	Oo	Oo	Oo	Oo	Oo	Oo	Oo	O
פ	Mouth · Pe	?	Γ	Pi	Ππ	P	Ⱂ	Pp	Pp	Pp	Pp	Pp	Pp	Pp	P
צ	Scythe · Tsade	⌐				(ts)									
ק	Knot · Qoph	φ	φ	(Koppa)		Q	Q	Qq	Qq	Qq	Qq	Qq	Qq	Qq	Q
ר	Head · Resh	ꝺ	P	Rho	Pρ	R	R	Rr	Rr	Rr	Rr	Rr	Rr	Rr	R
ש	Teeth · Shin	wꟄ	Ξ	Sigma	Σσς	S	Ꞩ	Ss	Ss	Ss	Ss	Ss	Ss	Ss	S
ת	Cross · Tau	†	Τ	Tau	Ττ	T	Ⱅ	Tt	Tt	Tt	Tt	Tt	Tt	Tt	T
							U	Uu	Uu	Uu	Uu	Uu	Uu	Uu	U
		Υ		Upsilon	Yυ	V	V	Vv	Vv	Vv	Vv	Vv	Vv	Vv	V
						Y	Y	Yy	Yy	Yy	Yy	Yy	Yy	Yy	Y
		Φ		Phi	Φφ	(p·h)									
		Χ		Chi	Χχ	(k·h)									
		Ψ		Psi	Ψψ	(ps)									
		ω		Omega	Ωω	—Form only—	W	Ww	Ww	Ww	Ww	Ww	Ww	Ww	W
1	2	3	4	5	6	7	8	9	10	11	12	13	14	15	16

Fig. 153. Table showing derivations of the letters, and a few characteristic styles of lettering

present. Many of these styles came into being through an effort to improve the legibility, or the beauty, of the printed page; some were designed to express a certain feeling or tendency in the art of a period; some were originated to establish distinctiveness or individuality in the product of a great printing-house; some to express the personality, or the whim, of the designer; and not a few—we fear—must have been created merely for the purpose of bringing out "something different." Naturally, in this great array of type faces, we find those that are good, bad, and indifferent. The student of printing must learn, therefore, to classify type faces, and to judge as to their quality, and their fitness for the various classes of printed work.

The characteristics of Roman letters are heavy strokes, or elements, forming the main lines of the letters, lighter strokes as connecting lines, and serifs at the terminations of the elements. There are no fixed rules for the relative widths of light and heavy elements. In fact, the variations in these relative widths, or weight, of the strokes, together with the formation of the serifs, are the main features that distinguish one Roman type face from another.

184. **Serifs.** It is generally considered that serifs were first attached to the letters by ancient stonecutters, for the purpose of more clearly defining the limits of the strokes of the letters, as they were chiseled in the stone. In adding this line, or serif, small bits of stone were broken out at the sharp intersections, producing an angled or rounded effect.

As a rule, type faces with relatively thin light elements will also have thin, light-weight serifs, while the faces with bolder light elements will have correspondingly bold serifs. The weight and the manner of formation of the serif has much to do with the individuality and beauty of a letter.

Roman types may be divided into three classes: oldstyle, modern-face, and a third class comprising faces which are a mixture of the first two, known as modernized oldstyle.

HEAVY, uniform body elements and angular serifs are the chief characteristics of early Italian letters, and most of our oldstyle types are based on them

Cloister Oldstyle, patterned after the early Italian types

HERE is the Caslon Oldstyle type, originated by the celebrated early English typefounder, William Caslon. It is beautiful and legible

Caslon Oldstyle, an early English face, of lighter proportions

HAIR-LINES and thin, straight serifs are the characteristics of modern-face types. They are more formal and precise than oldstyles

Bodoni type. A good example of modern-face letter

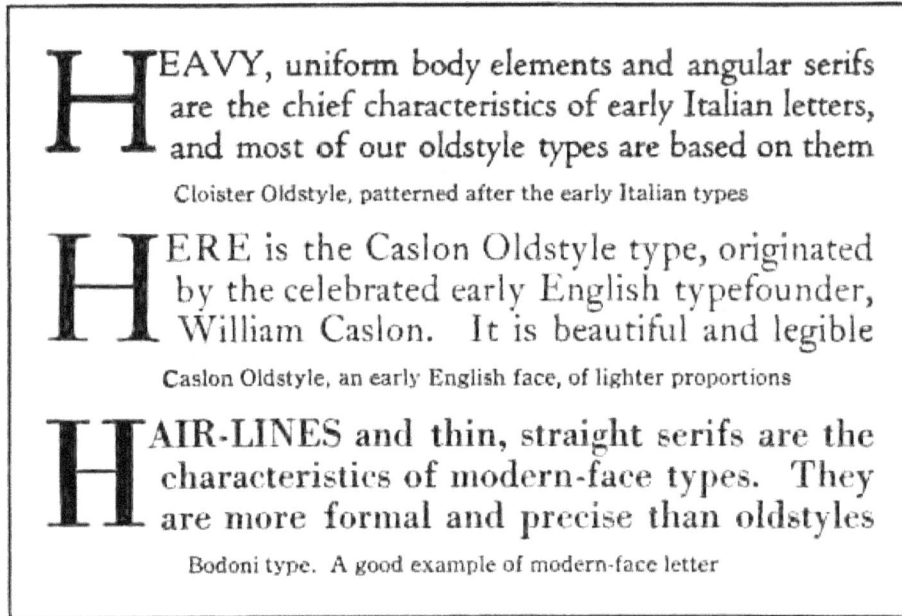

Fig. 154. Examples of oldstyle and modern-face types

185. Oldstyle types. Naturally, the pure oldstyle types are those patterned after letter forms of the early master printers. The chief characteristics of this style are a comparative roundness of form and nearly uniform thickness of lines, long descenders and ascenders, with short, angular serifs. A pleasingly rugged, substantial effect is had, free from stiffness or mechanical restraint and precision. The Cloister Oldstyle face in Fig. 154 represents this style.

Another form of oldstyle is exemplified in the original Caslon Oldstyle, a letter somewhat lighter in tone than the early Italian types, more delicately modeled, with interesting irregularities of construction, yet well proportioned and of humble dignity. It has an exquisite charm, and a free, flowing manner, that has made it the world's most popular type face, and a pattern for practically all of the ordinary body types that are in use in modern printing.

Oldstyle types are generally more legible than modern-face. The soft, flowing effect of the letters, the even tone of the type in the mass, with the freedom from the sharp contrasts between elements of the letters, make this type more friendly to the eye, and easier to read in body form. The modern-face types are at their best in display work.

186. **Modern-face types** differ from oldstyle in that they are more symmetrical, more regular and even, and in that their serifs are less angular and heavy, meeting the stems at sharp angles. The light elements are usually quite thin,

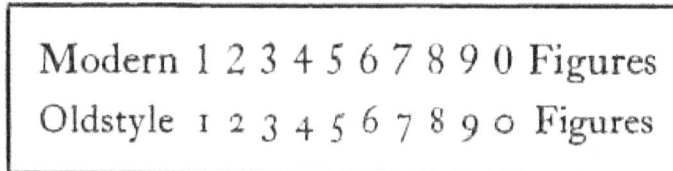

Modern 1 2 3 4 5 6 7 8 9 0 Figures
Oldstyle 1 2 3 4 5 6 7 8 9 0 Figures

Fig. 155. Comparison of the oldstyle and modern forms of figures

often consisting of hair-lines, which are in strong contrast with the heavy elements. The construction is precise, and has the appearance of being mechanically exact and rigid.

Giambattista Bodoni, of Parma, originated this modern style of letter, at the close of the eighteenth century. The best example of modern-face type in use today is a revival of Bodoni's style of lettering which bears his name.

187. **Transitionary forms.** Many of our types today are mixtures of oldstyle and modern-face. The tendency is toward the use of oldstyle types for most of our printing, but a great many of the so-called oldstyle types now in use —such as Century Oldstyle in which this book is printed— show considerable influence of the modern-face, and are in reality modernized oldstyle types. Century Oldstyle owes its charm and popularity to the fact that it has some of the softness and the flowing qualities of the oldstyle, combined with an air of orderliness and regularity of the modern-face. Also, it has no eccentricities of construction to confuse the reader. A number of other mixed, or hybrid, types possess these good qualities, while some are not so fortunate.

188. Oldstyle and modern figures. Modern figures are uniform in height; oldstyle figures follow the ancient forms of the characters, some of them (1, 2, 0) being the height of the lower-case letters, some (6, 8) ascending to the full height, and others (3, 4, 5, 7, 9) descending below the base line of the letters. Originally, all the oldstyle fonts contained oldstyle figures, and the fonts of modern-face type contained modern figures, but since modern figures are generally preferred in printing, some oldstyles are supplied with both oldstyle and modern figures.

189. Types in families. Many of our most popular type faces are grouped in families. Italic, and then bold face, with its Italic, have been added to the regular Roman series. So far, the development is a distinct advantage in the ordinary run of printing, as it provides both display and body type of common design which makes for a pleasing harmony on the page. But, in addition, extended, condensed, extra condensed, and many other variations of what one author calls "distorted" types have been added to many of these family groups. Undoubtedly, some of these

Cheltenham Oldstyle

Cheltenham Wide

Cheltenham Medium

Cheltenham Bold

Cheltenham Bold Condensed

Cheltenham Bold Extra Condensed

Cheltenham Bold Outline

Cheltenham Oldstyle Condensed

Cheltenham Italic

Cheltenham Medium Italic

Cheltenham Bold Italic

Cheltenham Bold Condensed Italic

CHELTENHAM BOLD EXTRA CONDENSED TITLE

Cheltenham Bold Extended

Cheltenham Extrabold

Fig. 156. Some members of the Cheltenham family

special types have occasional legitimate uses, but the real necessity for faces other than of normal proportions seems very limited. At any rate, wide and narrow faces should never be used together, indiscriminately, in one form.

ITALIC TYPES

Italic type was first used by Aldus Manutius in 1501, as a condensed, close-fitting letter that would admit of more words to a given page. He made only lower-case letters and and used them with the Roman capitals, but a little later, other printers who copied his style of lettering added slanting capitals.

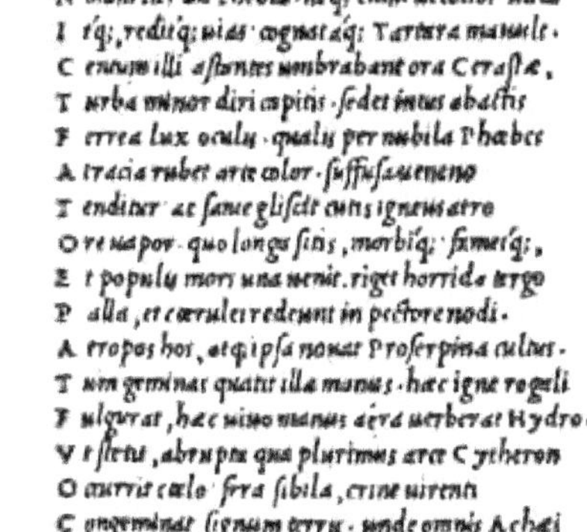
L uminis turbauit equos · procul arduus Atlas
H orruit · et dubia caelum ceruice remisit ·
A rripit extemplo Maleæ de ualle resurgens ·
N otum iter ad Thebas · neq; enim uelocior ullas
I tq;, reditq; uias · cognataq; Tartara mauult ·
C entum illi astantes umbrabant ora Cerastæ,
T urba minor diri capitis · sedet intus abactis
F errea lux oculis · qualis per nubila Phœbes
A tracia rubet arte color · suffusa ueneno
T enditur · ac sanie gliscit cutis igneus atro
O re uapor · quo longa sitis, morbiq; · fameq;,
E t populis mors una uenit. riget horrida tergo
P alla, et cærulei redeunt in pectore nodi ·
A tropos hos, atq; ipsa nouat Proserpina cultus ·
T um geminas quatit illa manus · hæc igne rogali
F ulgurat, hæc uiuo manus aëra uerberat Hydro ·
V t stetit, abrupta qua plurimus arce Cytheron
O currit cælo · fera sibila, crine uirenti
C ongeminat signum terris · unde omnis Achæi
O ra maris late, Pelopeiaq; regna resultant,

Fig. 157. Portion of page by Aldus, 1502, [reduced], showing use of first Italic

Although Italic was originally cast as a body type, it is seldom used now for that purpose, but it is used rather sparingly, in small groups, or in single words, for emphasis, or for differentiation, in connection with Roman. Nearly all standard Roman types have their corresponding Italics which harmonize in their general form and style. When Roman and Italic are used together, they should be of the same type series, as Bodoni Italic with Bodoni, or Packard Italic with Packard.

In display printing, Italic is used to introduce pleasing contrasts in the letter forms, and to relieve the monotony of one style of letter. Properly used, it may add liveliness and interest to the page. There is also an element of decoration in the use of Italic, especially when used sparingly, in the larger sizes, in contrast with the Roman letters.

190. **Italic usually kerned.** Most fonts of Italic contain kerned letters, to allow for close fitting, and they must be handled carefully in composition, proofing, and distribution.

191. **Swash letters.** Most of the fonts of oldstyle Italic include swash characters, more extended than the regular ones, and ending in an ornamental flourish. The Cloister Oldstyle Italic, for example, includes the swash characters shown in Fig. 158, in addition to all the regular letter forms. Swash characters add a graceful and informal touch to the form, but they must be used judiciously, and with restraint. Ordinarily, they will be placed at the outsides of the words, or groups, and not in the middle of a word. Right and wrong uses of these letters are shown in the accompanying figure.

Recently, the type founders have designed sets of capitals, known as Cursives, for some of the most popular oldstyle Italic faces. The alphabet of Cloister Cursives also appears herewith. In formal printing, the regular capitals are more appropriate, but these give a distinctive air to some informal work. Like swash letters, they are most effective when used sparingly.

ANNUAL RECITAL
RIGHT · WRONG
Right: withdrawn, solve
Wrong: withdrawn, solve

Right and wrong use of
swash characters

A B C D E G H J M N
P Q R T V Y k v w

Regular capitals

A B C D E G J M N
P Qu R T U Y k v w

Swash characters

A B C D E F G H
I J K L M N O
P Q R S T U V
W X Y Z

Cloister Cursive capitals

Fig. 158

192. **Italic capitals.** Many of our leading typographers maintain that lines of copy should not be composed in all Italic capitals. Traditionally, Italic was first cast and used in lower-case only, and even when capitals were cut, they were never used separately by the early printers. Roman was always used for lines of capitals. Structurally, Italic capitals are weak, especially in the lighter faces, and this,

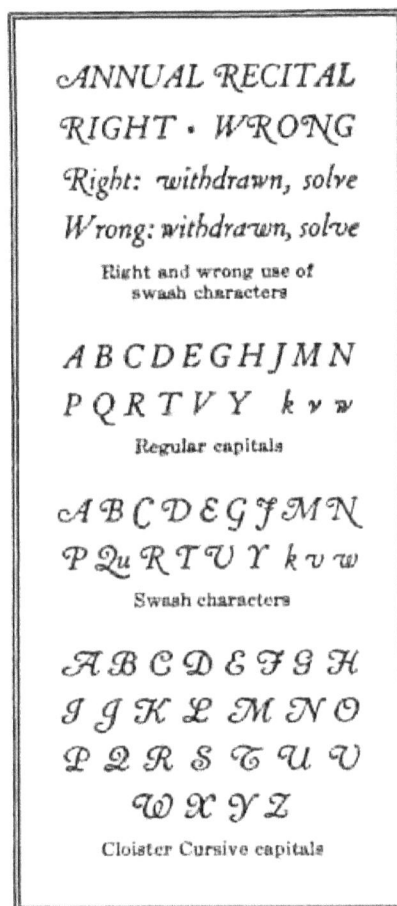

WEAK AND AWKWARD	STRONG, PLEASING LINE
Better Use of the Italic	Beautiful and Legible

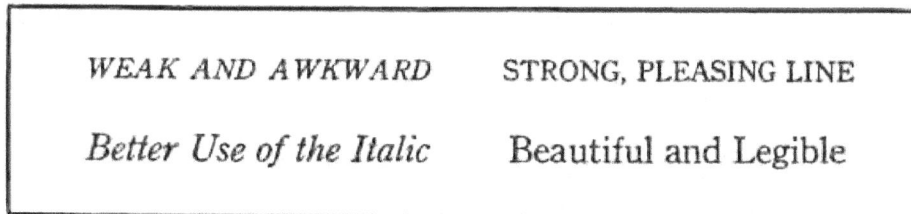

Fig. 159. A line of Italic capitals compared with lines of other letters

combined with the slant of the letters, gives an effect of awkwardness and instability to a line of Italic capitals. For these reasons, it seems that the practice should be avoided.

The author has never seen a design containing lines of Italic capitals which he thinks would not be improved by the substitution of lines of Roman capitals, or of upper- and lower-case Italic letters of suitable size.

TEXT TYPES

Text-letter, known by many printers as Old English, and sometimes as Black-letter, or Gothic, had its origin in the style of handwriting of the makers of manuscript books. Originally, it was a black, angular letter, quite condensed and closely spaced on the page, for paper could not be wasted by extended letters, or by unprinted spaces. Printers in northern Europe fashioned their types in close imitation of this style of letter, and thus perpetuated the Gothic lettering of the scribes, although those of Italy and western Europe eventually discarded Text for the plainer Roman.

A Few Text Types

Good Printing

A Light Weight

Early Black-Letter

Missal Letters

ABCST

First Church

Fig. 160

193. **Use of text types.** Text types exist today in a number of beautiful forms. The lighter faces, such as Wedding Text, and Plate Text, are used almost exclusively for society printing, in the form of cards, invitations, announcements, etc. The bolder

faces, including Engravers Old English, Caslon Text, and others, are used largely on church and holiday printing, or to lend variety and interest to general commercial work.

When Text type is to appear in display work, it must be used judiciously, and sparingly. It is better to use it only in the larger sizes, and to let a few words in Text stand out in contrast with a larger proportion of Roman. It should be remembered that this is an oldstyle letter, and that only oldstyle types should be associated with it, on the page.

Text should never be letter-spaced, nor should there be wide spacing between words, as this is not in keeping with the traditional use of the letter, or with its bold, condensed form. Also, this style of letter should never be set in all capitals, as it is unsightly, and 𝔇𝔌𝔉𝔉𝔌𝔠𝔘𝔏𝔗 𝔗𝔒 𝔎𝔈𝔄𝔇.

194. **The real Gothic letter.** This style of lettering, born in the early Church, and suggesting, by its form and characteristics, the cathedral spires and other forms of early ecclesiastical imagery, is as truly Gothic as is other Gothic art and architecture, and it should be so classified among printers. It is unfortunate that the term Gothic should ever have been applied to a type face so unlike this one.

195. **Missal letters,** sometimes used as initials, or as capitals for Text lines in display, should be classed with Text types, as they also have their origin in early manuscripts. They are particularly appropriate in religious printing.

BLOCK-LETTER, OR "GOTHIC"

Plain, square types without serifs or hair-lines are listed in the type catalogs as "Gothics," although the name is very misleading, and is without any logical foundation. They are known to some as Block-Letter, and in Europe names such as Sans-Serif, Antique, and Grotesque are given them.

"Gothics" in smaller sizes are used occasionally in the setting of formal business cards and professional stationery. Condensed bold "Gothics" constitute the headlines of some newspapers. This letter also invades other display printing occasionally, although this seems quite unnecessary, with all the beautiful and effective display types now available.

SCRIPT TYPE

Script type includes such faces as are patterned after modern handwriting. Script is very seldom used, and it is permissible only in social forms, where it is used in imitation of copperplate engraving. This type is too delicate for general use, and must be handled very carefully in order that the hair-lines and kerned portions may not be ruined.

SUGGESTIONS

The student should give special attention to oldstyle and modern-face letters, and be ready to classify any types encountered. A study of type specimen books is one of the best ways to get acquainted with type faces.

The various type faces in your shop should be especially studied. It would be well to make up proofs of the different styles for the notebook.

Also form the habit of analyzing the display pages of magazines, and other printed matter, in the attempt to identify the types used. You will be surprised how soon you will become acquainted with a large number of the standard display types, and this will be very helpful to you.

BIBLIOGRAPHY

Printing Types: Their History, Forms and Uses—Updike. The Harvard University Press
Type Lore—Frazier. The Inland Printer Company
The Alphabet—Goudy. Mitchell Kennerley
American Type Design in the 20th Century—McMurtrie. Robert O. Ballou

QUESTIONS

1. What are the five general classes of type faces?
2. How did serifs originate, and why are they important?
3. Name the three general subdivisions of Roman types.
4. What are the distinguishing characteristics of oldstyle letters?
5. How do modern-face types differ from oldstyle?
6. Name the leading type faces in your shop, and classify each of them.
7. Tell what you can about type families.
8. Why should Italic letters not be set in cap lines?
9. What are swash letters? How should they be used?
10. What can you say about the uses of Text type?

CHAPTER XXIII
Legibility of Type Faces

THE chief function of type is to get itself read. It may be beautiful, or artistic, and these are elements to be desired, but these and all other qualities that letters may possess must necessarily be built around legibility, and should support, and surely never interfere with, the ease with which the type may be read. According to Benjamin Sherbow, "Type was made to read . . . consequently type is nothing at all when it is not easy to read."

196. **Conditions affecting legibility.** Among other things, the legibility of printed matter may depend upon (a) the size and style of the type used, (b) the paper upon which it is printed, (c) the width of the measure in which the type is set, (d) the spacing between lines, and (e) the margins, or white space, around the matter. These elements which affect legibilty will be dealt with briefly in this chapter.

LETTER STYLES

Some types are more legible than others, as a comparison of specimens will readily prove, and those which are easiest to read are the lower-case types of the conventional Roman style, with which the eye is most familiar. These have no marked eccentricities or peculiarities of construction that would distract the reader. For this reason, the various oldstyle Romans are most popular for book work and general body composition. We are most accustomed to their letter forms, and therefore they are "more friendly to the eye." Any variation in the shape or construction of a letter, to which the eye is not accustomed, interferes with comfortable, easy reading of the matter in which it appears.

As has been observed in the preceding chapter, the more graceful, flowing oldstyle types are more legible than the stiffer, and rather mechanical, modern type faces.

197. Capitals not as legible as lower-case. The Roman capitals are often quite beautiful, and their stateliness and uniformity of shape make them very attractive, but it prevents them from being read with ease.* In some kinds of formal or classical printing, capitals are rather effective, as in Fig. 161, but they should be avoided when the copy is heavy. Italic must also be used sparingly, as it, too, is a less familiar, and therefore less legible form of letter, for body use.

THE AMERICAN INSTITUTE OF
GRAPHIC ARTS

THE OBJECTS OF THE INSTITUTE ARE TO STIMULATE AND ENCOURAGE THOSE ENGAGED IN THE GRAPHIC ARTS · TO FORM A CENTER FOR INTERCOURSE AND FOR EX-CHANGE OF VIEWS OF ALL INTERESTED IN THESE ARTS · TO PUBLISH BOOKS AND PERI-ODICALS · TO HOLD EXHIBITIONS IN THE UNITED STATES & TO PARTICIPATE AS FAR AS POSSIBLE IN THE EXHIBITIONS HELD IN FOREIGN COUNTRIES RELATING TO THE GRAPHIC ARTS · TO INVITE EXHIBITS OF FOREIGN WORK · TO STIMULATE THE PUB-LIC TASTE BY SCHOOLS · EXHIBITIONS · LEC-TURES AND PRINTED MATTER · PROMOTE THE HIGHER EDUCATION IN THESE ARTS & GENERALLY TO DO ALL THINGS WHICH WILL RAISE THE STANDARD & AID THE EX-TENSION AND DEVELOPMENT TOWARD PERFECTION OF THE GRAPHIC ARTS IN THE UNITED STATES

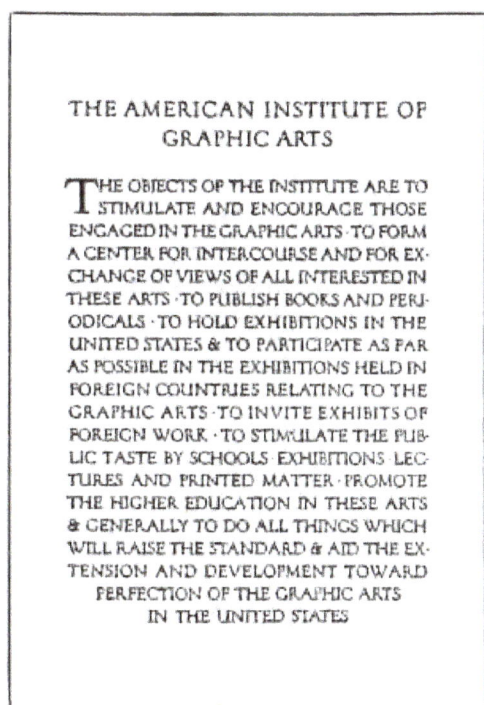

Fig. 161. Announcement set all capitals. The type is Forum Title, designed by Frederick W. Goudy

198. Text is not legible. Text, or Old English, letters are beautiful, and for some classes of work they are very appropriate, but they cannot be said to be legible. The letter forms are quite unfamiliar to the eye, as people are not accustomed to seeing this earlier style of lettering. The average reader scans work printed in Text types with much difficulty, especially in the smaller sizes.

* Most of our reading is done by the perception of "word forms" rather than by a putting together of the separate letters of the word. The general shape and appearance of the word enables us to recognize it even when it is so far away that the separate letters cannot be seen at all. For this reason, the lower-case letters are much more legible than capital letters. Capitals do not permit of reading by word form, since all words made up of capitals have the same rectangular shape, differing only in length. But when the lower-case letters are used each word has its own characteristic appearance.—*Advertising: Its Principles and Practice*, Ronald Press Company.

199. **Shaded letters** are always difficult to read. They do not lie flat on the paper, and some styles even seem not to lie still as one scans them. They have come into being as a substitute for the shaded effect in copperplate engraving. Shaded letters are "pretty," but one should have a stronger excuse for the selection of a type. In the interest of legibility, at least, it seems best to avoid use of them.

200. **Avoid bold type in mass.** Bold types are designed for open display, in which they may appear in broken lines, or balanced groups, surrounded by a suitable amount of white space. They prove tiring to the eye when they are set in close body form.

On page 166 are shown a few representative type faces of the plainer sort, which are always safe to use where legibility is to be emphasized. A group

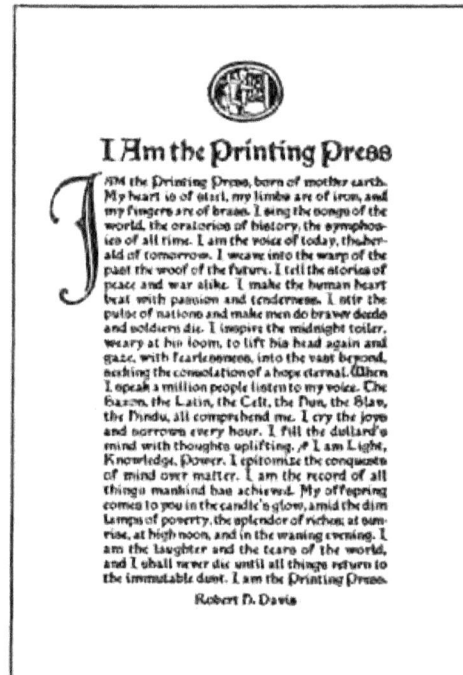

Fig. 162. Design set in the early English form of Text.
Very rich in color, but not as legible as Roman

of faces in which marked individual beauty and legibility are happily combined, appears on page 167. These types, most of them based on examples of the best early Italian letters, are some of the most popu-

Shaded types are low in legibility. They seem not to lie flat on the sheet, as the other type faces do.

Fig. 163

lar, as well as the most beautiful, body types that are in use today.

Fig. 166 shows a page of very attractive type faces, admirable for special classes of printing, but which are not so suitable for use in masses, because of their noticeable individuality.

In the oldstyle types the hair-lines are thick and short; the stem protracted to great length before it tapers to hair-lines; serifs are short and angular

Caslon Oldstyle

The old cutter put readability first; making his types graceful if he could, but he must first of all make them distinct and readable in a mass

Scotch Roman

The capitals and lower-case letters were first made in type in the year 1465 by two early printers, Sweinheim and Pannartz, at Subiaco

Century Oldstyle

The chief merits of the conventional Roman letter are its simplicity and perspicuity; it has no useless or meanlingess lines and is very simple and legible

Bodoni Book

Roman lettering has been the object of much experimentation for over four centuries. Many faces that were once popular are now forgotten

French Oldstyle

Small capitals and italic were first made in type form for Aldus Manutius of Venice, and were first shown by him in his noted octavo edition of Virgil issued in 1501

Cheltenham

Roman capitals as they are now made by the type founders are in imitation of the lapidary characters used by the early Roman sculptors

Bookman Oldstyle

Fig. 164

The Roman form of type is subdivided by printers and
founders into the two classes of oldstyle and modern,
and several different varieties of each style are founded
Cloister Oldstyle

The modern punch-cutter thinks it is his first duty
to make every letter of graceful shape, but his notion
of gracefulness is very largely formal and mechanical
Garamond

Lines of all capital letters should always be leaded
and spaced wider than the letters of the lower-case
for the sake of greater legibility and attractiveness
National Oldstyle

Types that have marked peculiarities of formation
are always more difficult to read in the group than
are those which are not so distinctively individual
Kennerley

For small booklets and catalogs that do not carry
large pages of descriptive matter, no better styles
may be found than the letters shown on this page
Venetian

Each of these type styles has strong individual
beauty and originality of design, and yet each
is quite legible and pleasing in smaller groups
Artcraft

Choice of a particular letter for a job of printing
should be governed by the appropriateness of the
letter style, and its ability to do its necessary work
Goudy Oldstyle

Fig. 165

The leading out of lines of type calls for as
much care as the spacing of words since the
improper spacing would detract from the job

Bullfinch

*Handlettered effects are
seldom attempted in type
but the designer of this
face was very successful*

Colwell Handletter Italic

Harmony of type
and paper makes
possible the best
results in the job

Motto

Blanking out should never be done with
leads as a column or page so treated is
spongy and liable to bow in locking up

Invitation

Titles of a few words may be properly set without
a plan, but the arrangement of intricate title matter
cannot be accurately developed during composition

Cromwell

In narrow measures
even spacing is very
difficult, especially
so in the very short
lines of text types
which are set down
around and on the
side of illustrations.
Single letter spacing
is quite often used

Packard

Job faces require some
boldness, to attract the
attention, and also some
beauty in construction

Drew

Interest and beauty are
found in this type face
when it is used in small
groups of display work

Strathmore

Fig. 166

In selecting type for any specific use, choose one which seems most fitting for the occasion, and that will assist in creating the proper effect, or atmosphere, for the thought of the text. Do not select types merely for prettiness, or novelty of design, but if the message can be as effectively clothed in a beautiful type, use it. It is well to remember, however, that the bulk of the work of the typographic world must be borne by the humble and unpretentious, but most dependable workers—the conventional Roman faces.

SIZES OF TYPE

The small sizes of body type are not as legible as larger ones. This paragraph is set in 6 point type, and it is far too small for ordinary reading matter, for it causes undue eye strain to make out the letter forms. Many of the ads now appearing in newspapers and periodicals contain types no larger than this and some are even harder to read than this paragraph is. Whenever possible, the use of such type should be avoided.

This paragraph appears in 8 point, and as you read it you are impressed with the greater ease with which it may be read. One may read it faster than the 6 point and with much less eye strain. However, it is still somewhat small for perfect ease in reading, as will be seen by a comparison with succeeding sizes.

When we get into 10 point type, we begin to get a sense of more comfortable, easy reading. The letters now are large enough that the eye can take them in at a rapid glance, without any strain or tension. This is a size of type found in many books and other reading matter, and we are quite familiar with it. Consequently, we read it with ease and speed. Ten point, leaded, is used for the body of this book.

We come to the highest degree of legibility when we consider the 12 point size of body type. A number of best authorities designate this size of type, leaded adequately, as offering the maximum of legibility in the mass, and being the most inviting to the eye of the reader. At any rate, the range of sizes for most satisfactory reading is around 10 and 12 point type.

LENGTH OF LINES OF TYPE

The width of a column of matter influences its legibility. The ideal width for any piece of composition is based on the breadth of focus of the eye upon the page. For small types the focus will be narrow, and it will widen out as the type faces increase in size. If the column is set in too wide a measure, as is the case with this paragraph, the lines will be scanned with somewhat of effort, and it will be found harder to "keep one's place" as he reads. Also, it will require some effort to locate the starting point of each new line. A large amount of matter set like this would be tedious to read.

On the other hand, if the column is too narrow, fewer words may be grasped at a time, and thus, too frequent adjustments must be made for the numerous short lines of the type, seriously hindering the steady, even flow of the message. In addition, a greater proportion of words must be divided at the ends of the lines, and the spacing of the lines is necessarily uneven and awkward, also affecting the legibility.

This group is set the proper width for the comfortable, easy reading of 8 point type. The eye may easily take in a line at a time, and in this way the message may be read without any mechanical encumbrances. Larger types set to this width will present the same difficulties to the reader that are experienced in the 8 point example, set in the narrow measure, above. There is a suitable width for each size and style of type.

201. **A popular theory.** It has been found that the most effective width for any piece of body composition is that which is equal to one and one-half times the length of the lower-case alphabet of the size and style of the type used. Applying this principle to the type face we are now using we find the ideal width for 10 point Century is as follows:

abcdefghijklmnopqrstuvwxyzabcdefghijklm
The width for greatest legibility is 17 picas

According to this theory, types of wider design require a wider measure than normal letters, and condensed types take a narrower measure, as these alphabets show:

abcdefghijklmnopqrstuvwxyzabcdefghijklm
abcdefghijklmnopqrstuvwxyzabcdefghijklm

abcdefghijklmnopqrstuvwxyzabcdefghijklm

It is an established fact that a shorter line of type is much easier to read than a long one, and the smaller the type the shorter should be its maximum length of line, for legibility

abcdefghijklmnopqrstuvwxyzabcdefghijklm

In ordinary practice, we often set our type lines too long to be read easily. Inspection of the advertising columns of our modern newspapers and magazines will reveal this fact that much of the type is set too wide

Narrow types are best in short lines

abcdefghijklmnopqrstuvwxyzabcdefghijklm

Proper spacing between the lines has much to do with the ease with which the printed matter is read, and the word forms scanned

Each type face has its ideal length

abcdefghijklmnopqrstuvwxyzabcdefghijklm

The actual necessity for such a condensed letter is rather questionable, but if used, it should follow this principle of width of line

abcdefghijklmnopqrstuvwxyzabcdefghijklm

On the following page is a table for widths of lines, which covers the matter sufficiently for most of the ordinary work. It serves as a practical guide for the young compositor

Fig. 167

202. **Sherbow's table.** Benjamin Sherbow, an outstanding expert in the effective handling of type, has made a table of column widths for different sizes of type. It does not make allowances for individual type styles, but is flexible enough to cover them. Generally speaking, it coincides with the foregoing theory. The table of widths follows.

6 point_____ 8 to 10 picas	12 point_____14 to 21 picas
8 point_____ 9 to 13 picas	14 point_____18 to 24 picas
10 point_____13 to 16 picas	18 point_____24 to 30 picas

SPACING AND MARGINS

203. **Solid matter hard to read.** Types that are set solid are not as easy to read as those that are leaded. In solid matter there is not enough room between the lines of type to let the individual word forms stand out clearly as the lines are rapidly scanned. This is particularly true of many of our modern types cast on standard line, having rather full-faced letters, with short descenders. Some oldstyles, cast on script line, or art line, with a wide shoulder and long descenders, are exceptions, for they are quite legible, and make a very pleasing appearance, in the solid mass.

204. **Leaded matter is more legible.** This paragraph is leaded with two point leads, and it is much easier to read. The words are surrounded by sufficient white space to allow the eye to grasp their forms readily and without an effort. Ten point type may take as much as three points between lines with good effect. Twelve point type should be leaded from two to four points, for maximum legibility.

On the other hand, if matter is leaded too widely, the legibility will be interfered with. The lines will then appear as disconnected bands of color, running across the page, and the copy will be followed with some effort.

Suitable margins of white space around a group or page of type matter add to the ease and comfort with which the matter may be read. Margins isolate the group from other

Fig. 168. View in the stoneroom of Saults & Pollard, Winnipeg, Canada

elements that might diffuse the attention, and make it easy for the eye to focus on the matter. They also make a sharp contrast that is necessary to attract and hold the attention of the reader within the space. Crowded matter is quite uninteresting, oppressive, and fatiguing to read.

PAPER AND LEGIBILITY

205. **Glossy paper hinders reader.** The paper on which the type is printed has much to do with the legibility of the matter. The hard, glossy finishes of papers are not only a hindrance to legibility, but are also hard on the eye. Some very rough papers, printed with a grayish impression, may also cause strain on the eye. Both these kinds of paper have beautiful finishes, and are very appropriate for many kinds of work, but not for printing large groups of body matter. Dull finish papers, of fairly smooth surface, are better.

206. Smooth paper with modern-face type. Smooth-finish papers are more suitable for use with modern-face types. The light strokes of the letters do not print well on rough paper, and also, they wear out prematurely. The formal, precise style of the modern-face appears to best advantage on a paper that is uniformly smooth, brilliant and conventional, and this suggests the use of modern-face types on coated and enameled book, and other smooth papers.

207. Antique paper with oldstyle. Oldstyle types are most legible, and pleasing, when printed on soft papers. The angular, uneven strokes of the letters harmonize with the roughness and unevenness of the soft-finish paper, and both receive an added charm by the harmonious combination. Hard-finish papers are likely to accentuate the cruder details in the construction of oldstyle letters, and to make them appear unpolished and awkward. Traditionally, the oldstyle letters have always been associated with antique papers, and it is most fitting that they be used together.

SUGGESTIONS

Study these principles of legibility, and apply them in your daily work in the shop. Also look for the practical applications of these principles in the miscellaneous printed matter you see about you. All good printing will be found to be patterned in conformity with the foregoing rules.

BIBLIOGRAPHY

Effective Type-use for Advertising—Sherbow. Published by the Author
Making Type Work—Sherbow. Published by the Author
Principles of Advertising—Parsons. The Prang Company
Advertising: Its Principles and Practice. Ronald Press Company

QUESTIONS

1. What are some conditions that affect legibility of type matter?
2. Why are conventional Roman lower-case letters most legible?
3. How do the sizes of type used affect legibility?
4. What sizes of letters are most legible?
5. Discuss the matter of the length of type lines and legibility.
6. How does the leading out of matter affect its legibility?
7. What is the advantage of margins around a type group?
8. Discuss the matter of paper and legibility.

CHAPTER XXIV

Fundamental Principles of Display—Fitness

ALL successful printing is based on a few general principles which govern the details of its construction and arrangement. These principles are quite simple, and easy to apply, and when they have become a part of the working knowledge of the printer, he should be able to make every job a piece of good typography. Although they may seem somewhat rigid and mechanical at first, their practice soon gives the printer a "sense of design," that will prove to be a dependable guide in his typographic efforts.*

The workman who is trained to apply these principles naturally in his everyday work will produce good printing just as economically as inferior printing, as it is not more difficult to set and print well designed jobs than poor ones.

Occasionally, good designs are produced which seem to violate the rules formulated for the guidance of the beginner. This fact, however, does not weaken the rules, for a typographer must understand the fundamental principles

---

*Although the rules for designing suitable printing may seem unsubstantial and difficult to convey in words, it is still true that they are seen and felt in the mind of the worker. They are illusive rules, and yet none the less a man works from them with as much certainty as if they were set down on paper. It is because they are so illusive that many persons believe that, in designing printing there are no rules at all; because they commonly think of rules as matters of precise measurement, and definite proportion. As a matter of fact, the best rules for planning work are general rules and rules for the mind rather than for the hand—no less real because applying to what may be called, in a sense, a spiritual matter. So in properly laying out printing it is necessary to have a certain mental equipment, which is to tell the truth, where most designers of printing fail. . . .

"The prophetic eye of taste" (wrote the poet Gray), "when it plants a seedling, already sits under the shadow of it, and enjoys the effect it will have from every point of view that lies in the prospect." So it must be with the designer of printing: he should be able to visualize the effect of his work in its finished form before a single type is set. — Updike's *In the Day's Work.*

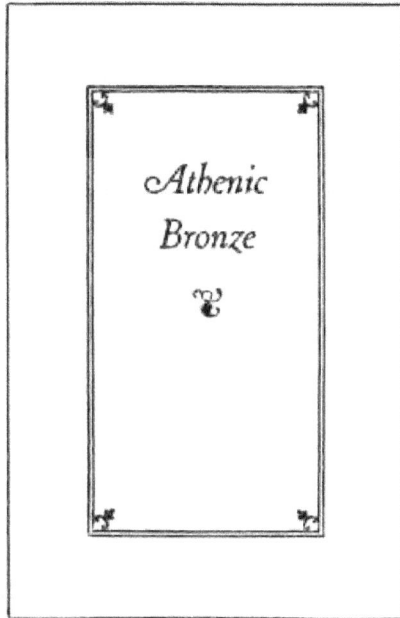

Fig. 169. Fitness: a jewelry announcement
should be attractive, dainty and refined

Fig. 170. Fitness: religious work is appropriately set in the traditional Text-letter

exceptionally well before he can successfully modify them.
The student will do well to follow these rules faithfully in
his work, and through them to develop his sense of design.

The five fundamental principles of display are (1) fitness,
(2) balance, (3) proportion, (4) shape harmony, and (5) tone
harmony. These are discussed on the following pages.

THE PRINCIPLE OF FITNESS

Fitness implies that the general plan of the job, as well
as its various details, shall be intelligently arranged, and in
close harmony with the nature of the work at hand. Before
planning a job, the question should be asked, "What is the
nature of the proposed job, and how will it best accomplish
its purpose?" The plan adopted should be a fitting answer.

208. **Simplicity.** One of the chief considerations of fitness is the matter of simplicity. There should be a simple
and orderly arrangement of the design, and no intricacies

Marshal Gasoline Engines

NET LIST
FOR 1927

Please destroy all
previous lists

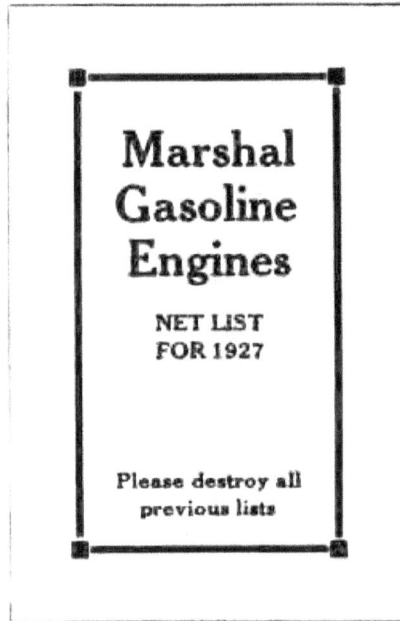

Fig. 171. Fitness: Type and border expressing strength and stability

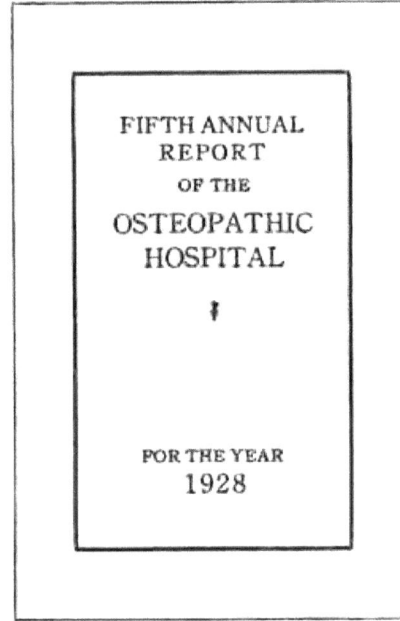

FIFTH ANNUAL
REPORT
OF THE
OSTEOPATHIC
HOSPITAL

FOR THE YEAR
1928

Fig. 172. Fitness: Quiet dignity and formal
arrangement appropriate in this form

or elaborations should enter into it unless the nature of the
copy particularly requires, or at least justifies, it. Few type
faces should be used, in as few sizes as possible, and they
should be kept in series. Decoration should be used quite
sparingly, and used appropriately. In short, there should
be a definite sense of fitness and order in the arrangement
of the design, and it should have no meaningless material.*

209. **General specifications.** Fitness suggests the choice
of a suitable style of type that will create the proper effect
for the message, and the use of this type in proper sizes.
Appropriate borders must be chosen, and if any ornaments
or illustrations are thought necessary, they must also pass
the test of special fitness for the individual job. The size

*The young compositor is often tempted
to try unusual arrangements in an effort to
produce something original. It may be well
that some thought be given to originality,
but simplicity, and soundness of design,
must never be sacrificed. One should not
do "stunts" for the sake of originality, or
novelty. Type was never intended for the
purpose of producing stunts or novelties.
Remember that "type was made to read."

and shape of the page or sheet, and even the kind of paper to be used for the job, will be determined as to fitness.

Naturally, some jobs will be perfectly plain, while others will be ornamented; some will be dignified and formal, and others will be given informal or unconventional treatment. Some typographers designate the principle of fitness as the "exercise of good common sense" with regard to the planning of individual jobs of printing, and indeed, it is at this point that the young printer may particularly prove his ability in the exercise of this function.

210. **Breaking up the copy.** Fitness also suggests that the copy be so handled that the wording will be broken up in lines of logical units which may be read and understood at a glance. The more important items in the copy should be sufficiently emphasized, and each group should be displayed, or "brought out," in proportion to its importance.

Not only does fitness imply the importance of knowing what to put into the job, but also the equal importance of knowing what to leave out of it. With the abundance of typographic material at hand today, great discrimination is necessary in its use, and fitness must be especially stressed.

SOME HELPFUL BOOKS ON DESIGN

Modern Type Display—Frazier.   The Inland Printer Company
Design and Color in Printing—Trezise.   The Inland Printer Company
Art and Practice of Typography—Gress.   Oswald Publishing Company
In the Day's Work—Updike.   Harvard University Press
The School Print Shop—Stillwell.   Rand McNally & Company
Group XIV, Design for Printers.   Standard Apprenticeship Lessons.   The
    United Typothetae of America

QUESTIONS

1. Name the five fundamental principles of display?
2. What question should be asked before starting a job?
3. What can you say about simplicity in the planning of printing?
4. How does fitness affect the simplicity of a job?
5. What suggestions are made about breaking up the copy?

CHAPTER XXV

The Principle of Balance

IN ORDER to produce correct display printing, the words or groups which comprise the copy must be balanced on the page or sheet. By the term "balanced" we do not mean "centered," as the optical center, or center of attraction, is not identical with the mathematical center of the page.

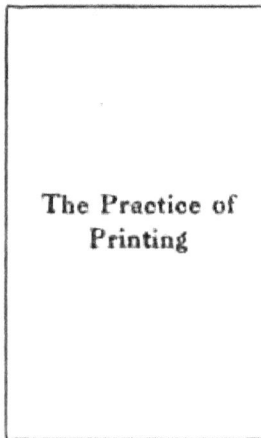

Fig. 173. Group centered on the page, vertically   Fig. 174. Page panelled in the proportion of 3 to 5 : 5 to 8   Fig. 175. Group at the optical center of the page

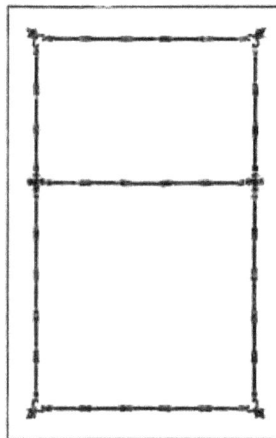

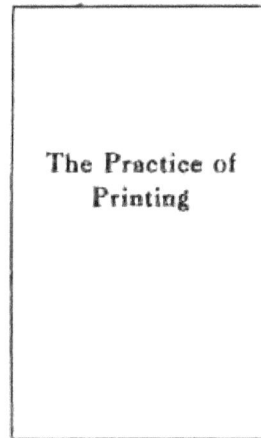

211. An optical illusion. To persons of normal vision, a perfect square will appear to be slightly flattened. Also, a point located in the exact center of a rectangle will appear to be below the center. Type designers recognize this fact and place the cross strokes on such letters as B, E, H, and S slightly above the center of the letters. In printing, allowance is made for this illusion, and the center of attraction, or center of balance, is considered to be slightly above the mathematical center of the page. A comparison of Figs. 173 and 175 demonstrates the superiority of the balanced page.

212. **The center of balance.** A popular method of finding the center of balance on the page is to divide the page into two parts, vertically, in accordance with the well-known rule of proportion, that "the smaller part is to the larger part as the latter is to the whole." Balance, then, is determined by so dividing a page that the upper panel will bear

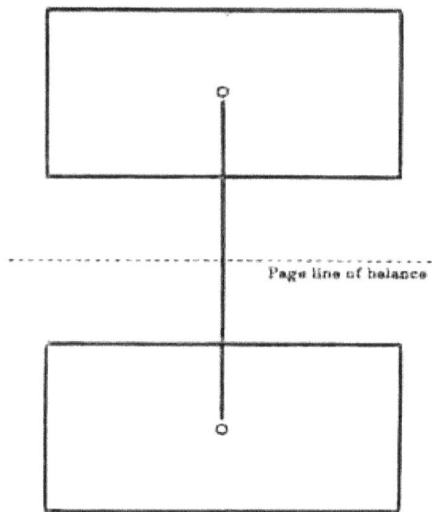

Fig. 176. Two groups of equal size in the proper position

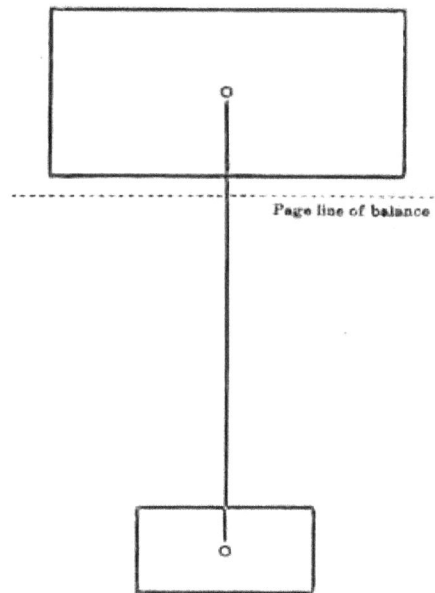

Fig. 177. Groups of unequal size properly balanced

the same relation to the lower panel that the lower one does to the entire page. Therefore, if a page is divided into eight equal parts, the point located three units from the top and five units from the bottom is the center of balance on the page. Fig. 174, on the preceding page, illustrates this.

If a single line of type is placed on the page, it should be placed on this line of balance. When a group, or mass, of matter appears, the center of the group should be located at the point of this three-to-five balance on the page.

If two or more groups are to be placed on the page, they should be placed in such positions that the center of balance between the groups will fall on the page center of balance.

213. **To find the balance between groups.** The different groups of words on the page attract the eye in proportion to their relative sizes, and boldness of tone. Accordingly, two groups of the same size and tone will balance each other, and should be placed on the page in such a way that their centers will be equidistant from the line of balance.

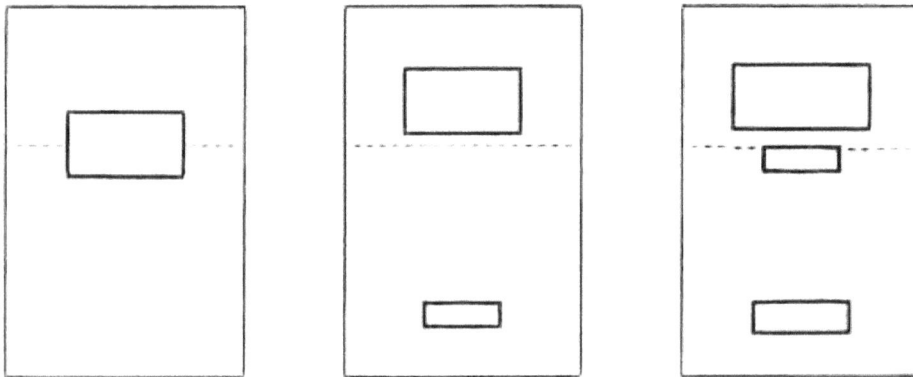

Fig. 178. Balance in forms consisting of one, two, and three groups

In nearly all good typography, the groups will be of un-equal sizes.   To find the center of balance between two such groups, a line should be drawn from the center of one group to the center of the other, and then the line should be divided at such point as will give each group a distance on the line that is in inverse ratio to the size of the group. The point thus determined is the point of balance between the groups. When they are placed on the page, this point should coincide with the line of balance of the page.

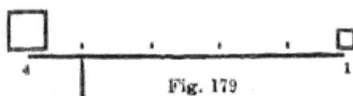

Fig. 179

This principle of balancing type groups is precisely the same as that of the balance scale, or of the more familiar teeter-board. The law of inverse ratio dictates that the heavier the boy, the nearer he must sit toward the center of balance. In Fig. 179, two weights bearing a ratio of 4 to 1 are balanced. The principle is the same as in Fig. 177.

When a third group is used on the page, one finds the common center between two of them, and then balances them with the third, in this same manner. The values of the first two will be added together, of course, in establishing the proper proportion with the third group.

214. **Margins affect spacing between groups.** The space between balanced groups may vary in accordance with the dictates of good taste, and the considerations of the proper margins around the groups. They may be placed either close to the center of balance, or far from it, and still be in proper balance, so the problem of margins is always to be considered along with the problem of balance.

No definite rule can be given for allowance for margins around the groups, as their widths and shapes must be considered. If the upper group is wide, leaving narrow side margins, it should be placed closer to the top of the page than would be fitting if it were set in a narrower measure. As this group is raised or lowered to allow proper margins, the lower group will be raised or lowered proportionately.

215. **Out-of-center balance.** When matter is balanced on the page horizontally as well as vertically, it is known as an out-of-center balance. This style is occasionally used on cover pages, and similar work, in which a small form is placed on a large page. One should not attempt out-of-center forms until his general sense of balance is well developed.

SUGGESTIONS

These rules are purely mathematical, and are given to develop a sense of balance. Practice them until the placing of groups comes naturally.

PROBLEMS

1. Using lay-out paper, indicate a page 6x9 inches, and locate the center of balance on the page. Find the center of balance on a page 4x6 inches; on one 5x7½ inches.
2. Outline two groups of equal size, and indicate the center of balance as done in Fig. 176.
3. Draw two groups with ratios of 3 to 1, and find their center.
4. Outline a page 4x6 inches, and properly locate one group 8x5 picas.
5. Add a second group 5x3 picas, and show the proper balance.
6. Balance three groups bearing ratios of 1, 2, and 2, on a 6x9 page.

CHAPTER XXVI

The Principle of Proportion

PROPORTION is always to be considered in connection with margins; with the dimensions of paper pages; and with the relative sizes of the type page and paper page.

Contrast and variety are necessary in printing, in order to lend interest to the design, but this touch of contrast, or

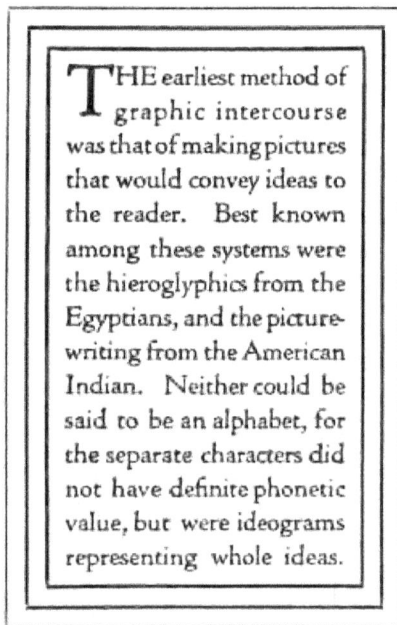

> THE earliest method of graphic intercourse was that of making pictures that would convey ideas to the reader. Best known among these systems were the hieroglyphics from the Egyptians, and the picture-writing from the American Indian. Neither could be said to be an alphabet, for the separate characters did not have definite phonetic value, but were ideograms representing whole ideas.

Fig. 180. Monotony in margins

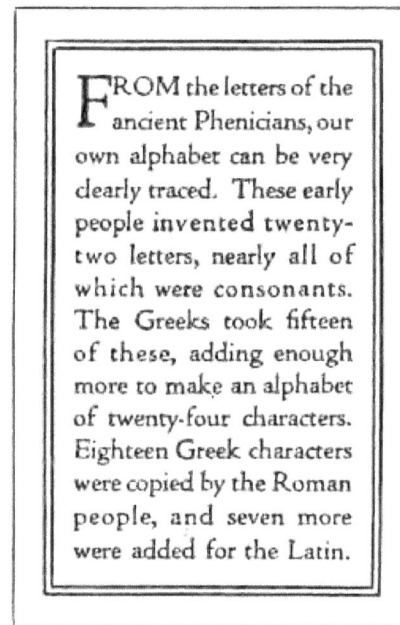

> FROM the letters of the ancient Phenicians, our own alphabet can be very clearly traced. These early people invented twenty-two letters, nearly all of which were consonants. The Greeks took fifteen of these, adding enough more to make an alphabet of twenty-four characters. Eighteen Greek characters were copied by the Roman people, and seven more were added for the Latin.

Fig. 181. Proportion in margins

irregularity, of elements of the form, should be applied in consideration of the principle of proportion, designated by one author as a "pleasing inequality of parts of an object."

216. **Proportion in margins.** Much of our printed work is bordered, and the margins inside and outside the border should be unequal, to be most pleasing. Equal margins are

monotonous and uninteresting, as the example in Fig. 180 shows. The proportion of 2 to 3 is generally accepted as most pleasing for such margins. This proportion of spacing is followed in the design in Fig. 181 on the preceding page.

For most work, it is customary to allow the wider space outside the border, since the border itself is really a part of the type design. However, this order of margins is not always followed.

217. Page sizes. It is a generally accepted rule that the most pleasingly shaped page is one the length of which is one and one-half times its width, or, in other words, a page with its dimensions in the proportion of 2 to 3. Some common page sizes are 4x6, 5x7½, 6x9, and 9x12 inches. Or, if the sheet is wide, it is often 6x4, 8x5, 9x6, or 10½x7 inches.*

Of course, it is not always possible or desirable to plan each job in these exact proportions, but it

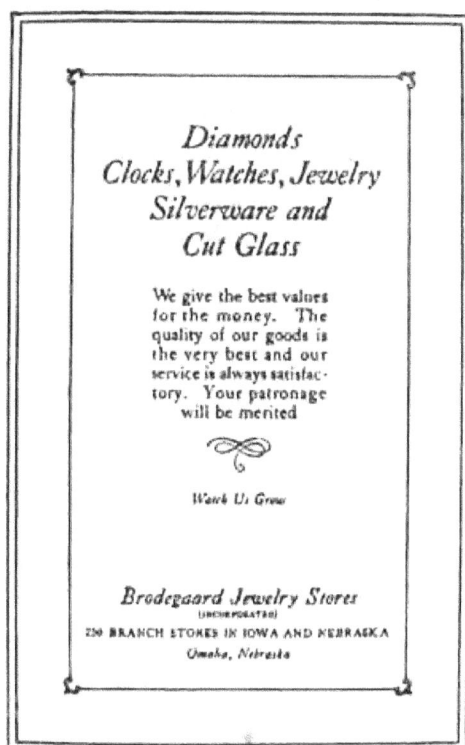

Fig. 182. In this design a "pleasing inequality" in the distribution of space adds much to the job

is a safe rule, that will always bring pleasing results, and a large proportion of printing is planned on this ratio.

218. Proportion of margin and text. In the plainer body composition, such as book work, it is generally considered that the most pleasing proportion of white space and text

* In ordinary printing, the first figure always indicates the width of the sheet, and the last figure its length. Thus, a 6x9 inch page is long, while a 9x6 inch page is wide.

is had when the area covered by the type form is equal to one-half the total area of the page, or when the type and the combined margins each occupy an equal area of space. When margins are too wide, the text loses in prominence and practicality. On the other hand, narrow margins give a crowded effect, and lessen the attractiveness and legibility.

E TAKE pleasure in announcing A LEGAL INSURANCE DEPARTMENT devoted exclusively to the needs of those engaged in the Legal Profession. Inquiries relative to insurance forms and contracts invited and information gladly given *gratis*. All lines of Insurance written with one day policy delivery service. We solicit your call and the pleasure of an interview.

A. KANN & SON
A Good Insurance Agency • Established 1903
2ND FLOOR NIXON BUILDING

GRANT 5614

Fig. 183. Design in which the smaller margin is outside the border. In this case the border and the edge of the sheet make a frame for the body

SUGGESTIONS

To find the proper allowance for margins, subtract the width of the body of the form from the width of the page; divide this by two, and then subtract the width of border from that. This leaves the total amount of white space on each side that is to be proportioned. Approximately two-fifths of it will be placed inside the border, and three-fifths outside.

PROBLEMS

1. What is the proper length of a page 6 inches wide? 3½ inches wide? 8 inches wide? 4 inches wide?
2. Make a lay-out properly arranging the margins for a form set 20 picas wide, to be printed on a 6x9 page, with a nonpareil border.
3. Make lay-out for a form 18 picas wide, with nonpareil border, on a 4x6 page.
4. Make lay-out for a form 21 picas wide, with pica border, on a 5½x8 page.
5. Make lay-out for a form 16 picas wide, with 1 point rule border, on a 3½x5½ page.

CHAPTER XXVII

The Principle of Shape Harmony

SHAPE HARMONY implies a harmony of shapes in all the elements that make up the printed design. There should be a harmony of shapes between the styles of type used in the form; between the various groups on a page; and between the design as a whole and the sheet or page on which the design is to be printed.

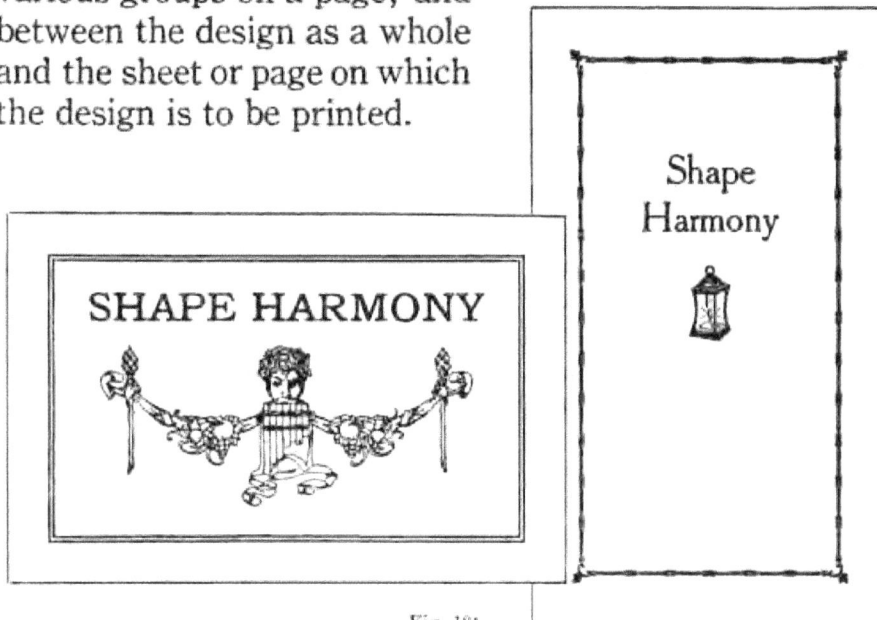

Fig. 184

219. **Type should fit page.** The general shape of the lettering used should be in harmony with the shape of the page. Condensed types may be used on narrow pages, and extended types on wide pages with pleasing effect. On the other hand, wide types and ornaments are not suitable for long pages, and the condensed types do not appear well on wide pages. Types of normal proportion have a wider use but they should be grouped to fit the shape of the page.

220. Shapes of lines or groups. The grouping of the type matter should be in harmony with the shape of the page. Short lines, and narrow groups of type, look best on long, narrow pages; wide groups should be arranged for wide pages. In Fig. 186 a type group is indicated, which is too wide and "stubby" for the page. A much more pleasing arrangement for the same copy is shown in Fig. 187.

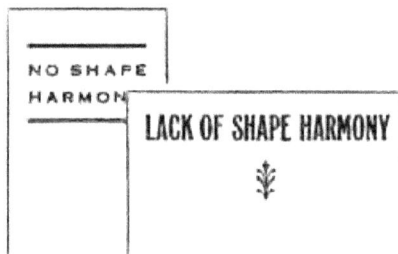 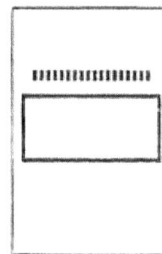 

Fig. 185 Fig. 186 Fig. 187

221. Harmony of types. When types of one series are used together, harmony in the letter forms is certain, but if it is desired to use more than one type face on one piece of printing, there must be something in common in their general shape characteristics. Condensed letters, for this reason, may not be used with extended letters, and types of oldstyle design are not suitable for use with the modern types. Also, letters of dainty, or ornamental, form do not harmonize with plain, bold letters of cruder design.

 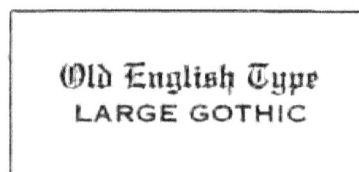

Fig. 188 Fig. 189

Sometimes it seems desirable to use a display line of Text type with "Gothic" lettering on a business card or a letterhead. If this is done, the Gothic letters must be small enough to avoid a clash in the strongly contrasted shapes of these two styles of type. Compare Figs. 188 and 189.

In the interest of shape harmony, it is well not to mix lines of lower-case letters and of capitals, in one job. The capitals are formal and dignified, and the squared, even effect of the lines do not harmonize with the broken, and uneven, lines of lower-case. Capitals are frequently used in formal work if the copy is brief, and lower-case is used in work of less conventional nature. A consideration of the nature and purpose of the job will govern whether capitals or lower-case letters shall be used. The stiffness or monotony of a form set in capitals may be lessened by setting certain subordinate lines or words in Italic, and a pleasing variation may be secured, if wisely done.

SUMMER
SCHOOL
GEORGIA SCHOOL
OF TECHNOLOGY

ANNOUNCEMENT
1914

Fig. 190. A splendid example of squared groups

222. **Harmony of type and border.** Borders should be chosen that have shapes in common with the lettering. Plain types must have plain borders, and more elaborate letters call for borders with units possessing shapes in common with them. Study the four figures on pages 176 and 177, and see why each border has been selected.

223. **Squared groups.** In display work, it is sometimes desirable to square the groups, by setting the lines to equal width. Neatly squared groups are quite attractive when they come naturally, but they should not be forced. Wide letter-spacing of parts of the group, bad divisions of words, or awkward breaks in the thought of the wording, should

not occur, in the attempt to make a squared effect. It is far more essential that the wording should be grouped in clear, logical order, and be easy to grasp and understand, than that it should assume some particular shape or arrangement.

Fig. 191

Fig. 192

224. Establishing harmony of shapes. When the page is to be a definite size, one should begin with the page size and plan all the details of the design in harmony with it. The general shape of the form must fit the shape of the page, and all the typographic units must be in harmony with it.

In the figures shown above, the same copy has been used for a wide page and a narrow page, and shape harmony in both cases has been established between the type faces, the grouping of the matter, ornaments, borders, and pages.

QUESTIONS

1. Explain what is meant by shape harmony.
2. What considerations govern the selection of a type face for a job?
3. How are the shapes of groups governed by shape harmony?
4. Discuss shape harmony in associated type faces.
5. How may Text and "Gothic" letters be used together?
6. Should cap lines and lower-case lines be mixed? Why?
7. How may variation be had in a form of all capitals?
8. What can you say of squared groups?
9. What considerations govern the choice of a border?
10. How would you proceed to established shape harmony in a job?

CHAPTER XXVIII

The Principle of Tone Harmony

TONE in printing is the density or strength of color made by the impression of the form. Light-faced types produce a light gray tone on the page, and bold types produce a dense black tone. Harmony of tone among the elements of the form is one of the essentials of good typography.

225. **To obtain tone harmony.** Tone harmony is had by the selection of borders, ornaments, or rules that will pro-

Fig. 193

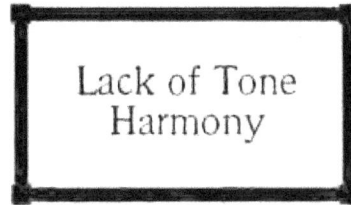

Fig. 194

duce the same weight of color, or tone, as that of the type used. If the type is of an even tone, then other materials used will be composed of strokes, or units, of the same tone.

If there is a contrast in the light and heavy elements of the lettering, the border may contain elements that match each of these tones, as in Fig. 197, in which the heavy lines of the border harmorize with the heavy elements of the letters, and the lighter lines with the light elements. When the body of a form consists of both display and body type, one element of the border may match the bolder display lines, and another the light gray tone of the body type.

If it is desired to use a certain ornament or border which is too bold for the type, it may be used by printing it in a second color, or a tint, which will thereby lighten its tone.

Fig. 195

Fig. 196

Fig. 197

Fig. 198

Fig. 199. A wide border may be used on a small form if the pattern is light enough to
harmonize in tone with the type, as in this design by Edw. Axel Sahlin

226. **Contrast in tones.** Sometimes a very pleasing effect may be had by a contrast of tones on the page. In Fig. 200 interest and "color" are added to the job by the contrast of the light gray and the heavy tones. This method of display requires some skill in designing, and, for the beginner, the even tones on the page are more likely to be successful.

Fig. 200. An example of contrast in tones

SUGGESTIONS

Make sure that you very thoroughly understand the five general principles of display, viz.: (1) fitness, (2) balance, (3) proportion, (4) shape harmony, and (5) tone harmony, and be ready to apply them in your work. They furnish the foundation for the development of a dependable sense of judgment and taste in executing good printing.

QUESTIONS

1. What is meant by tone harmony?
2. If type consists of contrasted light and heavy elements, what kind of a border is best?
3. How would you choose a border for a form consisting of display lines and body type?
4. How may a border or ornament heavier than the type be used consistently on a page?
5. Discuss the matter of contrast in tones.

CHAPTER XXIX

The Use of Decoration in Printing

LARGE proportion of all printed matter contains decoration of some kind. It may be only a border of simplest design or a small decorative spot at some appropriate place in the form, or the entire design may be a very elaborately decorative one, depending upon the nature of the job. When and how to use decoration, how to select it, and how extensively to use it, are problems that confront the young printer.

227. **Purpose of decoration.** We have earlier stated that the purpose of type is "to get itself read." The purpose of decoration is to make the type matter more attractive, to assist it in getting read, and to create the most favorable impression on the reader. Decoration must never exist for itself. It should be secondary to the purpose or mission of the printed matter it is to decorate. It would be a failure in any case if it did not support or strengthen the message, or if it should in any way overshadow the type or the text. A much-used quotation is particularly applicable to the use of decoration in printing: "Art is not a thing separate and apart; art is merely the best way of doing a thing."

228. **Must pass the test of fitness.** Before deciding upon the use of decoration, it is well to ask the following questions: "Does the work call for, or permit of, decoration?" "Will it enhance, or strengthen, the text matter?" "Will the decorative units considered be particularly fitting?"

Some classes of printing do not permit of any decoration but most jobs will take a moderate amount, if judiciously applied. A small per cent of printed work may be rather ornamental. Decoration depends upon the subject matter.

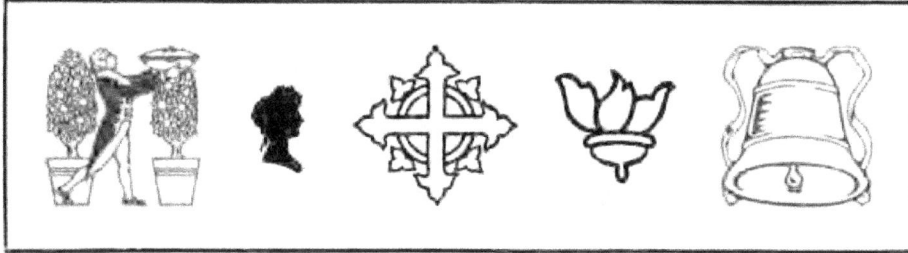

Fig. 201. A few representative ornaments kept in stock by the typefounders

The more formal printing does not admit of elaborate decoration. The title-page for a legal report might have a border of plain rules, but no ornaments should be used. A financial report may take a simple border, or an occasional small decorative spot, but restraint should be exercised in the use of ornament. On a musical program one may use ornaments suggestive of the text. If the program is light or informal, the design may be more or less decorative.

In religious printing, such decorative material may be used as will reflect the spirit of the message. The Maltese and Roman crosses, ornaments of a Gothic character, and mural decorations, are very appropriate for Church work. Missal initials—rather decorative in character, and of direct descent from the written and printed matter of the early Church—are always permissible in this class of work.

Each job should be carefully considered, and only the most appropriate decoration put in it. It is a safe practice, if there is any doubt as to whether a spot of decoration is desirable or not, to leave it out. One seldom spoils a job merely by having it too plain, but often jobs are ruined by being overdecorated, or by the intrusion of meaningless or irrelevant decoration, in an effort to make a finished design.

229. **Decoration must harmonize with type.** If decoration is used, it must harmonize with the type in shape and tone. It must also create the same general effect. If the formal, more dignified style of letter is used, the decoration must also have something of the characteristics of the type. If

Fig. 202. Some of the many type ornaments available to add interest to printing

Italic, or a type of the freer, more graceful style, is used, then the decoration should take on the same effect. Text lettering, with its ecclesiastical atmosphere, requires the kind of decoration that will be in harmony with it.

230. Ornaments should be conventionalized. Ornaments and decorative spots for the printed page should be conventionalized, or simplified, in accordance with recognized art principles, so that they will appear to lie flat on the surface of the paper. There should be little or no suggestion of perspective, or of the finer details of light and shade. In other words, they should be decorations, not illustrations.

In the figures shown on the following page, the use of an illustration in perspective, and a conventionalized ornament, are contrasted. It will be noted that the former does not harmonize with the flat surface of the paper or with the smooth, even impression of the type with which it is used. The latter, however, fits in admirably with both.

Practically all the ornamental material now offered by the leading typefounders is conventionalized, and will be found especially suitable for typographic design. A wealth of such material is now available, so that very appropriate ornaments may be found for almost every occasion.*

*For ecclesiastical printing, there are the crosses in various designs, and the many Gothic ornaments to be seen in connection with Text, or Gothic, type, in the specimen books. For musical programs, there are harps, lyres, pipes of Pan, etc. For printed matter representing plays or players there are masks, and other symbols of the stage activities. For educational or cultural subject matter, there are books, torches, hour glasses, lamps, etc. In fact, suitable pieces may be found for almost every subject.

Fig. 203

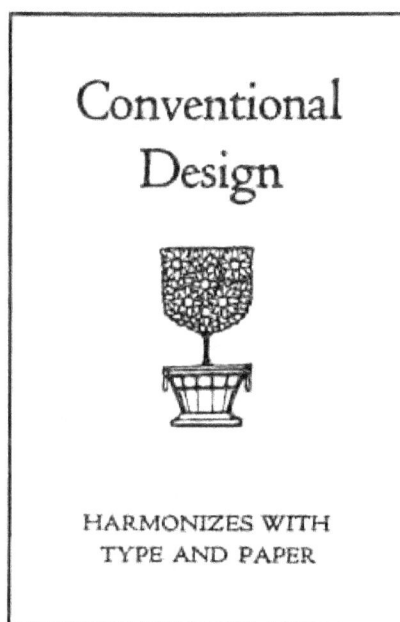

Fig. 204

231. **Hints on choosing an ornament.** Before selecting an ornament for a job, be sure that one is needed, and then pick it thoughtfully. Do not select an ornament because of the beauty of the ornament itself, but rather, that it may add beauty and effectiveness to the whole design. In the choice of an ornament, measure it by these standards:

(1) Is it in keeping with the subject matter?

(2) Is it a proper size?

(3) Will it harmonize in tone with the other units?

(4) Is its shape satisfactory?

(5) Will the job as a whole be definitely improved by it?

Unless each of these questions can be answered in the affirmative, it will be safer to leave out the ornament.

QUESTIONS

1. What is the purpose of decoration on the printed page?
2. What are some of the considerations of fitness in the use of decoration?
3. How may the elements of decoration harmonize with the type used?
4. Discuss pictorial illustrations and conventionalized ornaments.
5. What are some of the considerations in the choice of an ornament?

CHAPTER XXX

The Use of Initial Letters

INITIAL LETTERS are frequently used in printing, at the beginnings of new groups of text matter. In fact, this practice is older than the art of printing itself.* When carefully chosen, initials add very greatly to the appearance of the page, lending variety and interest, while their theoretical purpose is to call attention to where the reading matter begins. They must be selected and used in accordance with the general principles of good typography which have been mentioned in earlier chapters, namely, fitness (or appropriateness), proportion, shape harmony, and tone harmony.

232. **Typographical considerations.** Fitness implies a consistency between the initial and the text matter. A plain, undecorated letter should be used in conventional work of a formal nature; an ornate letter would be out of place. If decorative matter is made a part of the initial, it should be in keeping with the general character of the work, and it should be so designed as to appear to have been made for the particular style of lettering with which it is used.

Shape harmony dictates that the shape of the initial be suitable to the group in which it is used, and to the page on

---

* For some time after the invention of printing, the early craftsmen did not use printed initials. They attempted to make their books as nearly as possible like the manuscript books that preceded them, and they followed their lead in the matter of initials. They left spaces in the printed text, to be painted in by an artist. Many of these initials were richly finished, in burnished gold and color. A small index-letter, showing what the letter was to be, was generally written or printed in the space before the work was given over to the illuminator. Some wood block initials came to be used as book printing progressed, and finally metal blocks were made to print with the type matter. These are the forerunners of our modern initial letters.

which it is printed. A condensed letter would not be permissible on a wide page, and vice versa. Also, the style of the letter itself should harmonize with the type which it accompanies. The oldstyle types call for initials in oldstyle form, and modern-face types, for modern forms. A simple and sure method of caring for this matter is that of using a capital of a larger size of type in the same series, as an initial, such as a 24 point Caslon letter with text in 10 point Caslon. Type founders are helping to solve this problem of shape harmony by producing fonts of initials especially designed for use with certain classes of type faces.

There must be a suitable proportion between initial and text. The initial must be large enough to stand out pleasingly on the page, but not so large as to overshadow the type, or to monopolize space that should be given to reading matter. Consideration of the size and make-up of the page, and of the nature and purpose of the job, will help to solve this problem of proportion, or the size of the initial.

In smaller groups where decoration is not particularly desirable, letters of the depth of two or three lines of text will serve well as initials. If they are aligned with the text at both top and bottom, as the initials in the accompanying figures, they are known as two-line, or three-line, initials.

TWO-LINE initials are those which align both at the top of the first line of the text and at the base of the second line of it

Fig. 205. Two-line initial

IF THE bottom line of the initial letter can also be aligned with the bottom of the last line of the matter running alongside, a more pleasing effect will be had in the job

Fig. 206. Three-line initial

Tone harmony is especially necessary in the use of the initial. It is permissible for an initial to have a slightly heavier tone than that of the surrounding text, just as the leading lines on the title-page may be slightly heavier, and for the same reason, but if it is too bold, the page will then appear spotty, and legibility will be impaired. The initial should be light enough to appear as part of the paragraph, not as something set into it. One should always remember that an initial's only mission is to strengthen the appeal of the message, and it must not attract too much attention to itself. As one authority in typography states it, "It should not be allowed to overdo its legitimate work."

HERE is an initial which is too heavy for the type, thereby creating an effect of lack of harmony in the group
Fig. 207

HAVING substituted one of more a harmonious tone and shape, we secure a more pleasing effect than in Fig. 207
Fig. 208

233. Set first word in capitals. As the initial is the first letter of the first word in the group, uniformity in the word is preserved by setting the rest of the letters in capitals. This serves to unite the initial with the body type, and it also makes an even top margin with which to align the top of the initial, which is a very essential point. When a word of only two letters comes at the beginning of the group, it is customary to set the second, also, in capitals, as the one capital standing alone beside the initial is not pleasing. Sometimes two or three words may be set in capitals, for emphasis, or interest. The words "Initial Letters" at the beginning of this chapter, illustrate this practice.

Some printers occasionally use small capitals instead of capitals for the first word or words. When this is done, the initial will be carefully aligned with the small capitals.

In the use of Text types, this rule for capitalizing the first word is not followed, as Text-letter is not legible in all capitals. Only the lower-case letters are used.

234. Placing of initial letters. After an initial has been judiciously selected, the matter of placing it in the paragraph is to be considered. Letters must be properly and pleasingly aligned with the text matter, and the spacing between initial and text must be consistent with the size of the body type, and the general scheme of the page.

NEAT effects in the use of the initial are impossible unless the margins at the side and below the letter are of proper width

Wrong: no indention

NEAT effects in the use of the initial are impossible unless the margins at the side and below the letter are of proper width

Right: pleasing indention

NEAT effects in the use of an initial letter are impossible unless the margins around it are of the proper width

Wrong: too much indention

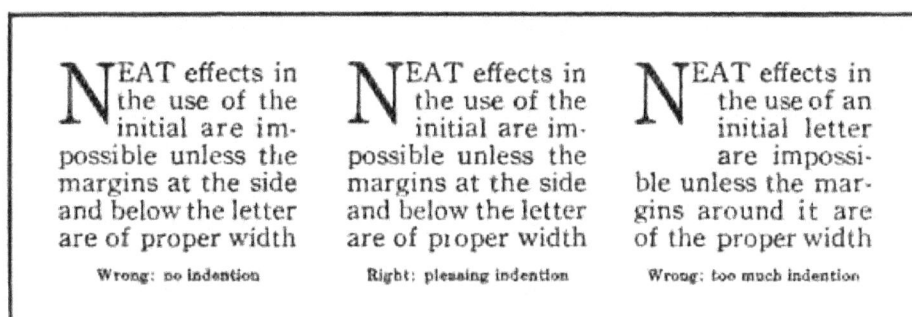

Fig. 209. Examples of right and wrong spacing around an initial letter

There should be enough space around the initial to set it away from the type lines with which it is not connected, yet not enough to make it seem a separate unit, or to leave an unsightly "hole" in the page. For most cases, if the lines alongside the initial are indented from a three-em space to an en quad, the effect will be quite satisfactory. However, when a particularly large initial is used with small type, an em indention is not too wide. In all cases, there should be an equal amount of space beside and below the initial.

235. **Letters that present special problems.** The letters A, L, T, V, W, and Y present special problems because of their irregular shapes. A and L are difficult to space pleasingly because of the wide shoulder at the side that makes the contact with the first line of type. Some printers solve this problem by

"BLESSED is the man that walketh not in the counsel of the ungodly, nor standeth in the way of sinners, nor sitteth in the seat of the scornful."

Fig. 210

mortising these letters to allow the first lines to approach the face of the initial. Even the letters B, C, D, O, and Q may sometimes be benefitted by a slight mortising at the upper corner, especially if they are comparatively large.

Also, it will be noted that with the letters T, V, W, and Y, the text matter may be set flush against the body of the initial. No indention is necessary because of the amount of white space that already exists at the sides of the letters.

LETTERS which are wider at the bottom than the top present a special problem in spacing. Mortising of letters at the top will permit the text to closely approach the initial

Proper spacing around this letter

LACK of uniformity in the spacing and clearness of of the group as a whole are the result of dealing with A and L in the same manner as with letters of other form

Wrong: the space is too wide

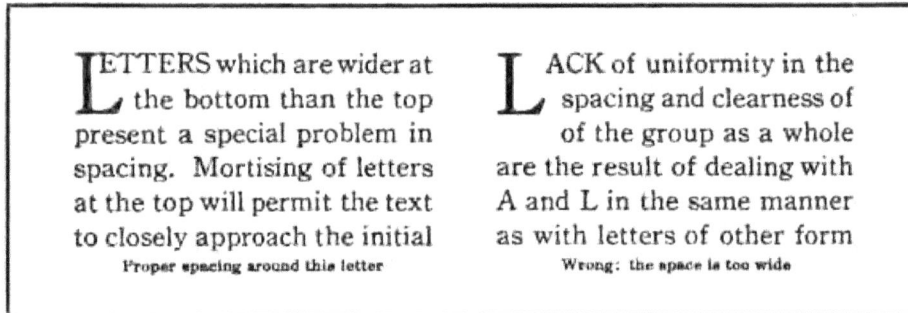

Fig. 211. Examples of proper and improper spacing around the letter L

236. Proper use of quotation marks. If quotation marks are to be used before an initial, they should be set in the same size of type as that of the paragraph, and not of the initial. Also, they should be set in the margin, so that the initial may align properly with the paragraph. In Fig. 210 the correct size and position of quotation marks is shown.

237. Informal treatments. In some classes of display printing, it may be desirable to let portions of such initial letters as T, V, W, and Y extend into the left margin. This eliminates from the body area the "hole," or white space resulting from the left shoulder of the letter, and makes an interesting effect, especially when page margins are ample. Fig. 212 shows another informal treatment with a letter of irregular shape.

YOUTH is the golden season of foolishness for which the wise would barter all their wisdom, the rich all their wealth, and call it a bargain, knowing the value of youth

Fig. 212

Occasionally, in the composition of forms containing modern-face types, an initial is formed by using a letter of a larger size in the same series, and aligning the base of this letter with the bottom of the first line of the paragraph, instead of an alignment at the top. While this style may be interesting in some particular kinds of printing, it would be safer for the student to avoid its use, as there is little to guide him in such practice, and the success of such a style depends in a large measure upon the skill of the typographer.

HEN an initial of this style is used, the first line of the text is aligned with the design, not the letter itself

Fig. 213

NITIALS of irregular shape are aligned with the text in such manner that the main body of the design will be in a line with the top of the first line of the text, and any projections will extend into the margin

Fig. 214

238. **Aligning irregular shapes.** Some decorative initials are of irregular shape, as the one shown above. When one of this nature is used, the top of the main body of the design should be aligned with the first line of the text.

A splendid assortment of initial letters will be found in the specimen books of the leading type founders, and a suitable style or kind may be selected for almost any need.

OMETIMES, however, it is necessary or desirable to make up an initial letter of a special character, for some particular purpose, and this may be done by using combinations of suitable rules, borders, and utilities, with individual types of the proper tone and style. When initials are thus made up, special care should be given to their design and construction.

Fig. 215

SUGGESTIONS

The student should begin with exercises in the use of the most common forms of initial letters. Then T, V, W, and Y, and also A and L, may be attempted. Representative decorative initials should be used with type groups. Careful attention should be given to fitness, tone, and shape, and to suitable spacing around the initial. Preserve proofs in your notebook.

A study of initials in type specimen books is also recommended.

QUESTIONS

1. What is the purpose of the initial letter in printing?
2. Tell what you can about the origin and development of the initial letter.
3. What are some of the typographic considerations in the use of initials?
4. What is the general practice with regard to the capitalization of words?
5. Tell what you can concerning the placing of initials in type matter.
6. What are some letters that present special problems in spacing?
7. If quotation marks are to appear with an initial, how should they be set?

CHAPTER XXXI

Paper

WE MAY safely state that the printer's product is made up of four things: technical skill, type, ink, and paper. It would be very difficult indeed for one to determine which of these four items is most important. In order to produce the best results in printing, it is quite necessary that one shall have a thorough knowledge of the different kinds of paper stock, and of the various properties and characteristics of each.

It would be difficult to understand paper without some knowledge of its manufacture. Space will not permit discussion of this phase of the subject here, but some of the best books on paper-making are listed in the bibliography, and a number of these should be carefully studied.

239. **Paper made from pulp.** Most of the paper used by printers is made of wood pulp, but writing papers are made principally of cotton and linen rags. Nearly all kinds of papers are now made in long webs, or continuous rolls, in modern paper machines. Wide screen belts convey a thin film of pulp up from the mixing vats and between large cylinders which squeeze out the moisture, and roll out the mixture to a smooth, uniform texture. If a hard finish is desired, the web of paper passes through heated calender rolls and becomes smoothed, or calendered. Enamel coated and other special papers go through further processes as the web travels through the machines. When the paper is finished, it is cut into sheets, sorted, and trimmed to size.

There are a great many kinds and grades of paper, but most of them come under the five general heads of news print, book papers, writing papers, covers, and cardboards.

240. News print is a cheaper grade of paper used for the printing of newspapers, handbills, and cheap circulars. It is made of wood pulp, usually of spruce, hemlock, or fir. It is supplied to the printer in flat sheets for the ordinary flatbed printing, or in large rolls for use in rotary presses.

241. Book papers comprise a large per cent of the paper stock used by the printer. They may be classified under the heads of machine finish book (commonly called M. F. book), sized and super calendered book (called S. & S. C.), antique, or egg shell, and the enamel coated papers.

M. F. book is the most common variety of white, soft, dull-finish paper. It is made in quite a number of sizes and weights of stock, and is used largely in books, magazines, and a large per cent of general job printing.

S. & S. C. book is made of essentially the same material as M. F., but it is harder and more glossy. Sizing is added to the stock in the process of manufacture, and it passes through an added number of calender rolls.

Antique finish, or egg shell book, is paper of soft, rough surface. It passes through the paper machine with little or no calendering, and so it retains its coarse, uneven finish. Egg shell is frequently used for programs and folders.

Coated paper is surfaced with a special clay which has been applied uniformly to the pulp base, and the paper is then calendered to a high degree of smoothness. It is made in both glossy and dull finish.* Coated paper is especially desirable when fine-screen halftones are to be used.

242. Writing papers are the papers made to be written upon with ink. They are bonds, ledgers, and flat writings.

---

* High-finish paper is hard on the eye because of the extent to which it reflects the light. To overcome this objectionable feature, many dull-coated book papers have been originated, and they are used rather extensively in the better class of printing. Dull-coated papers soil much more easily than the glossy, hard-finished papers, and this is to be considered in planning printed matter that must be handled a great deal.

Fig. 216. Stockroom of the Stone Printing & Manufacturing Co., Roanoke, Va.

Bond paper is the stock used for letterheads, and other stationery items. It is a strong, hard paper, and is made in bond, ripple, and linen finishes. Halftones, and fine lines of type, do not print satisfactorily on bond stock.

Ledgers are hard, durable writing papers of particularly smooth surface, for record forms, and loose-leaf work. Flat writings are cheaper papers of this class, composed largely of wood fibers, adaptable to pen and typewriter work.

243. **Hand-made papers.*** Some high-grade papers are still made by hand, particularly in Japan, and in southern Europe, and these are occasionally used in the printing of announcements, stationery, and distinctive booklets.

The hand-made papers are necessarily of rough, uneven surface, and for this reason, modern machine-made papers of soft or coarse finish are designated as antique papers.

244. **Deckled edges.** Some book papers, especially those of antique finish, have deckled edges. These are feathery, ragged edges, formed along the outer edges of the web as

*Paper was made almost entirely by hand processes until early in the eighteenth century. The raw materials were placed in tubs or vats in which they were mixed and beaten into a pulp by simple machinery, often driven by water power. The wet pulp was dipped from the tubs by hand, on flat molds made of fine wires stretched across wooden frames. As this milky substance settled on these frames, it became sheets of paper. The damp sheets were placed in a press which flattened them and squeezed most of the water out, and then they were hung on wires to dry and harden.

the paper is made. This finish appears either on one, or on two opposite, edges of the finished sheets of stock. Deckled edges give a pleasing touch to some kinds of printing.

245. **Covers** are extra heavy stock, usually made in colors, used for the covers of booklets, catalogs, etc. A very large variety of cover papers, in many colors, weights, and textures, will be found in the samples of all paper dealers.

246. **Cardboards** include many varieties of bristols, tag boards, coated blanks, and other similar heavy stock, for the printing of cards, tickets, posters, and the like.

247. **Sizes, weights, and quantities.** Most papers are sold in reams of 500 sheets, and the prices are quoted by the pound. If a ream of paper contains sheets 24x36 inches in size, and the ream weight is 70 pounds, it will be indicated as 24x36—70. The numbers that precede the dash always designate the size of the sheets, while the last number tells the weight of 500 sheets—or a ream—of the stock.

All writing papers are put up in sealed packages of one ream each. Cardboards are wrapped in packages of 100 sheets. Printers are charged a higher rate for odd amounts of paper which necessitate breaking standard packages.

FIGURING AND CUTTING STOCK

248. **Paper cutters.** There are two kinds of paper-cutting machines, one operated by means of a hand lever, and the other driven by power. In the latter, the knife is held in a stationary position until released by the operator, and after making the cut, the knife returns to its original position. Safety devices on the power machines protect the operator from the possibility of an unexpected stroke of the knife.

With both classes of cutters, the stock is placed on the cutting table, the back gauge is set to the desired measure, the paper is jogged up evenly against the gauge, a clamp just behind the knife is pressed upon the stock to hold it firmly in its position, and then the blade is sent through the stock. Usually, a sheet of strawboard or tag is placed on the bottom and the top of the lift of paper to be cut, to insure a sharp, clean cut, and to prevent soiling the stock or creasing it with the heavy pressure of the clamp.

Fig. 217. A power paper cutter

249. **Allowance made for final trim.** When stock is cut for a job, allowance is made for final trim as the successive cuts are made in the large sheets, so that the finished stock shall have smooth, clean edges on all sides. For example, if sheets of 25x38 inches are to be cut to 6x9 inches, the cuts across the width of the stock will be 19, 9½, and then 9 inches. The cuts across the length will be 12½, 6¼, and then 6 inches. By placing the best edge toward the back gauge each time, the finished stock will have smooth edges.

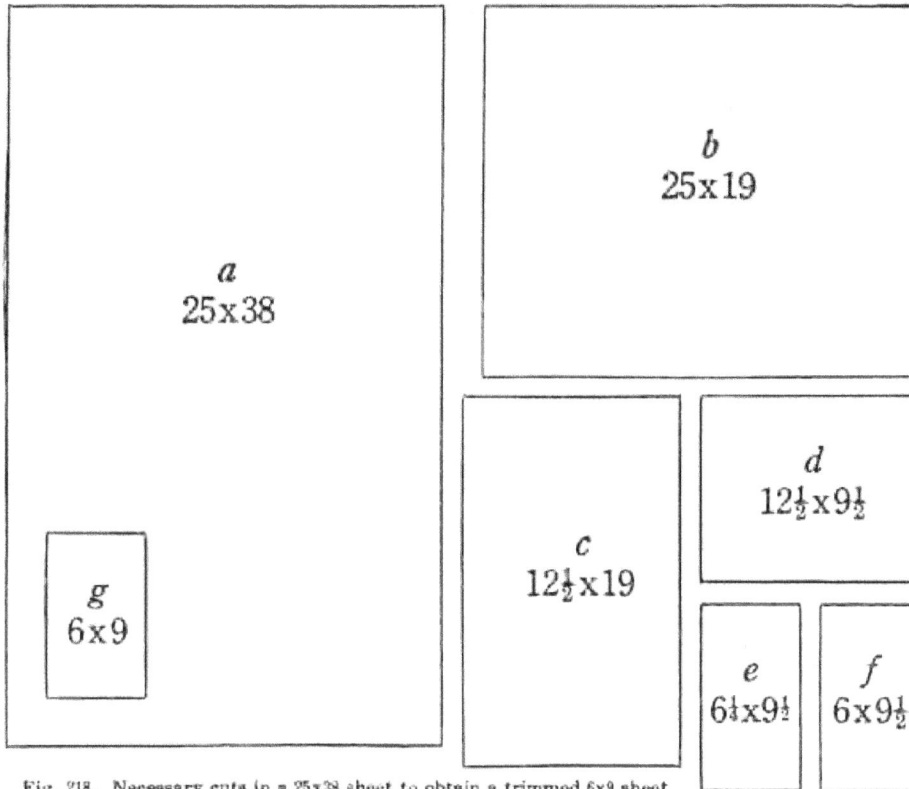

Fig. 218. Necessary cuts in a 25x38 sheet to obtain a trimmed 6x9 sheet

Methods of cutting stock differ slightly in various shops, and with the different types of machines. In the majority of cases, the first cut is made across the narrow way of the sheet, and then the succeeding cuts follow in such order that the wider cuts will come first. On the lever cutters, this method is a decided labor-saver. If this procedure is followed in cutting 25x38 paper stock down to 6x9 inches, the steps will come in the order indicated in Fig. 218.

250. **Spoilage allowance for printing.** In cutting paper for a job of printing, it is necessary to put in a few extra sheets for use of the pressroom, in setting the guides, making the job ready, regulating the ink, and also to allow for sheets that may become soiled, or misprinted, as the job is being run. A table of allowances for spoilage, based on a wide range of experiences, is in general use. See Fig. 220.

No. Copies:	50	100	200	300	400	500	600	800	1 M	1200	1500	2000	2500	3000	4000	5000	10M
2 to sheet	30	55	108	162	214	268	320	420	525	625	780	1040	1300	1560	2080	2580	5100
3 to sheet	20	37	72	108	144	179	214	280	350	414	520	693	867	1040	1387	1720	3400
4 to sheet	15	28	54	81	107	134	160	210	263	313	390	520	650	780	1040	1290	2550
6 to sheet	10	18	36	54	72	89	107	140	175	208	260	347	434	520	694	860	1700
8 to sheet	8	14	27	41	54	67	80	105	132	157	195	260	325	390	520	645	1275
9 to sheet	7	13	24	36	48	59	72	93	117	139	173	231	289	347	463	574	1134
10 to sheet	6	11	22	33	43	54	64	84	105	125	156	208	260	312	416	516	1020
12 to sheet	5	10	18	27	36	45	54	70	88	104	130	174	217	260	347	430	850
15 to sheet	4	8	15	22	29	36	43	56	70	84	104	139	174	208	278	344	680
16 to sheet	4	8	14	21	27	34	40	53	66	79	98	131	163	195	260	323	638
18 to sheet	4	7	12	18	24	30	36	47	59	69	87	117	145	174	232	287	567
20 to sheet	3	6	11	17	22	27	32	42	53	63	78	104	130	156	208	258	510
21 to sheet	3	6	11	16	21	26	31	40	50	60	75	96	124	149	199	246	486
24 to sheet	3	5	9	14	18	23	27	35	44	52	65	87	109	130	174	215	425
28 to sheet	3	5	8	12	16	19	23	30	38	45	56	75	94	112	149	184	367
32 to sheet	2	4	7	11	14	17	20	26	33	40	49	65	82	97	131	162	319

THE AMOUNT OF PAPER REQUIRED FOR A JOB

The stub lists various numbers of copies to be obtained from a full sheet of stock. The figures given indicate the number of full sheets required, including spoilage.

Fig. 219

251. Figuring stock for jobs. To find the proper amount of paper stock to cut for a job, first find out the dimensions of the sheets needed, and the size of the stock from which they are to be cut. Then find out how many of these pieces can be cut from one full sheet of stock. To do this, place the dimensions of the sheet to be printed under the dimensions of a full sheet of stock, and, by cancellation, find out how many cuts may be had each way of the full sheet. This will readily show how many pieces one may cut from each sheet of stock.

Then, find the total number of pieces needed for the job. This will be the number of completed copies desired,

STANDARD SPOILAGE ALLOWANCE		
Finished Copies Desired	Allowance for One Color	For Each Additional Color
100 to 250	10%	5%
251 to 500	6	4
501 to 1,000	5	2½
1,001 to 5,000	4½	2½
5,001 to 10,000	3½	2½
10,001 to 25,000	2½	2½
Over 25,000	2	2

When embossing, numbering, or any of the bindery operations are to be included, extra allowance must be made

Fig. 220

plus the allowance for spoilage. When the number of pieces per full sheet is divided into this total number of full sheets required for the printing, the quotient will be the number of full sheets of stock to be cut for the job. A study of the following problem will make this method clear.

PROBLEM: 2000 programs, 6x9 inches, to be cut from 25x38 M. F. book, at 12c per pound. How many sheets of stock will be required, and what will be the cost of the paper?

$$25 \times 38 \quad \text{(size of stock)}$$
$$6 \times 9 \quad \text{(size of piece)}$$
$$4 \times 4 = 16 \text{ (pieces per sheet)}$$

2000 (No. finished copies)
90 (spoilage allowance)

16 | 2090 | 131 (full sheets required)
16
49
48
10
16

140 (lbs.—double weight of ream)
.12 (price per lb.)
280
140
$16.80 (cost of 1000 sheets)
.131
1680
5040
1680
$2.20080 (cost of stock for the job)

Fig. 221. A practical problem in figuring stock, worked out in full detail

252. Finding cost of stock.* A common method of finding the cost of paper stock for the job is to find the cost of one thousand sheets of the stock, and then to consider the number of sheets required as so many thousandths of that cost. This is done by doubling the weight of a ream, then multiplying it by the cost per pound, and multiplying this amount by the number of full sheets required (using the decimal point to indicate thousandths.)† See figure above.

*The author is aware that there are other methods in use among printers, both for figuring the number of sheets required for the job, and the cost of them. Some of the methods are equally as good as the plans that we have recommended in the text.

† In cases in which only a portion of a ream of stock must be ordered especially for the job, this calculation would not be accurate unless the "broken ream" rate is used, for odd lots of paper are billed to the printer at a higher rate than stock in full reams.

$$\frac{\cancel{17} \times 22}{\cancel{5} \times \cancel{8\frac{1}{2}}} \quad \frac{\cancel{22\frac{1}{2}} \times \cancel{28\frac{1}{2}}}{\cancel{5} \times \cancel{3}} \quad \frac{\cancel{20} \times \cancel{26}}{\cancel{12} \times \cancel{18}}$$

$$4 \times 2 = 8 \qquad 4 \times 9 = 36 \qquad 2 \times 1 = 2$$

Fig. 222. The common method of cancellation used by the printer in figuring stock

SUGGESTIONS

In this chapter, it has been possible to give only a meager outline of the many kinds of paper and their uses. A study, in detail, of the actual papers themselves will be highly beneficial. In order to become acquainted with the texture of the various classes of paper, study the catalog and the case of samples of your paper dealer. Examine the texture of the samples, of the different classes of paper, and learn to distinguish kinds of paper as you encounter them. Also, collect sheets of different papers, trim them to size, and place them in your notebook, labeling as to kind, finish, and weight.

Do not attempt to cut paper until you have had personal instruction or supervision at the cutter. Then have your figures before you, and be sure that each cut is made strictly in accordance with them. Blunders at the paper cutter are usually costly ones.

GOOD BOOKS ON PAPER-MAKING

From Paper-Mill to Pressroom—Wheelwright. Geo. Banta Publishing Co.
Paper in the Making (Non-Technical). Dill & Collins Co.
The Manufacture of Paper—Sindall. D. Van Nostrand Co.
News Print—Haskell. International Paper Co.
How Paper Is Made—Wheelwright. United Typothetae of America.
Modern Manufacture of Writing Paper. The Eastern Manufacturing Co.
Commercial Engraving and Printing—Hackleman. Commercial Engraving Publishing Co.

QUESTIONS

1. What four items are mentioned as comprising the printers' product?
2. What are the principal materials from which paper is manufactured?
3. Name the five general classes of paper used in printing.
4. Name and describe four different kinds of book paper.
5. What are the principal kinds of writing papers?
6. What can you tell about hand-made papers?
7. What is meant by 24 x 36—80? 17 x 22—20? 20 x 25—100?
8. Describe the common method of cutting 6 x 9 sheets from 25 x 38 stock.
9. How would you proceed to find the proper amount of stock for a job?
10. What is the method recommended for finding the cost of stock?

CHAPTER XXXII

The Use of Color in Printing

THE use of color on the printed page involves many technical and scientific considerations that cannot be treated in a general textbook. Fine color printing is a very highly specialized art, which is becoming more and more limited to the special color-printing establishments. However, all printshops are called upon to do some two-color work, and therefore the printer should know how to use simple color schemes effectively.

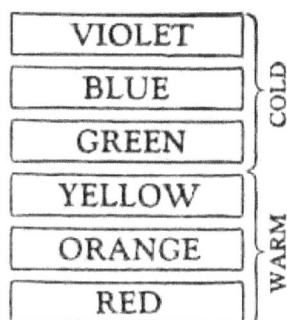

There are various theories of color which differ in many of the details, but whether they are built around a color wheel, sphere, or tree, some of their simpler facts are almost identical.

VIOLET	
BLUE	COLD
GREEN	
YELLOW	
ORANGE	WARM
RED	

Fig. 223. The colors of the spectrum in their regular order

Without attempting to fully explain any theory of color, this chapter will outline some of the simple facts which all printers should have regarding certain properties of colors, and their effects, warm and cold colors, and how to secure satisfactory harmonies. For other work in color, reliable books are listed in the bibliography.

253. **Primary and secondary colors.** Light is color. A ray of sunlight contains all the different colors. This is clearly seen in the rainbow, in which the sunlight is diffused, and the colors appear in separate bands across the sky. It is also demonstrated with the prism, which refracts the light and spreads out the colors, in the order shown above.

Three of these colors—red, yellow, and blue—will by proper combination produce all the others, and these are known as the *primary* colors. Orange is a combination of red and yellow; green, of yellow and blue; and violet, of blue and red. Orange, green, and violet are therefore classed as *secondary* colors. A chart of these colors appears below.

White and black are not considered as colors. White (or sunlight) is the blending of all the colors. Black, on the other hand, symbolic of darkness, is the absence of color.

254. **A simple color wheel.** If one expands the diagram of primary and secondary colors so that it will also include extra gradations of color between each of the six regular hues, a simple but practical "color wheel" may be made, with wedges of colors making up the circle.

Then, if each color is gradually darkened as the outer edge of the circle is approached,

Fig 224. Chart of primary and secondary colors

and tinted out as the wedge narrows toward the center, we have most of the elements required for simple color work.

A color wheel built on this plan is shown on page 215, and we shall refer to it frequently in this study.

255. **Colors have three dimensions,** and one is not likely to be confused in the specifications of colors if he understands this. The dimensions are hue, value, and chroma.

256. **Hue** refers to the particular position of the color around the color wheel; or, it is the respect in which blue, or green, or yellow, differ from one another. Hue may be considered, then, as the name of a color. The term red, or orange-red, names the definite hue of the color, but it does not tell whether the color is a light or dark one (which is

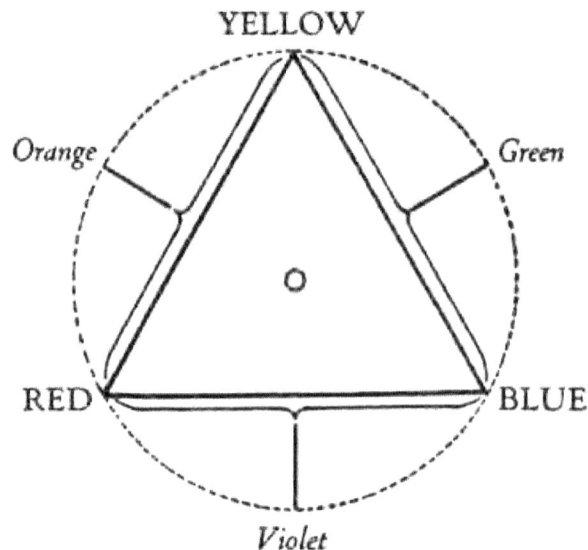

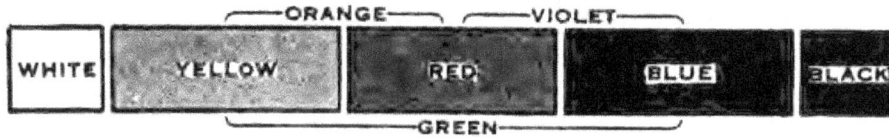

Fig. 225. Chart showing order of colors with respect to value

the value of the color), or whether the particular color is weak or strong (which is the chroma of the color).

257. **Value** is the light of a color, or the quality by which we distinguish a lighter color from a darker one. Value, in other words, specifies the distance of a color from the center, or the rim, of the color wheel. Different values of any one hue are designated as the tints, normal tones, and shades of that hue, depending upon the amount of light or shade in the color.

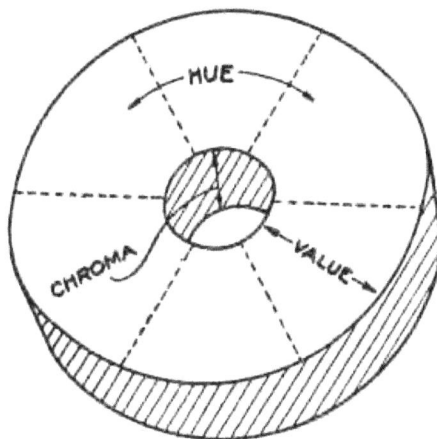

Fig. 226. Hue, value, and chroma in relation to the color wheel

The various hues of color differ from one another in value, or the amount of light each contains. Since value is light, white represents the maximum of value. Black is entirely lacking in value. The relative positions of the colors with respect to value is shown in Fig. 225, above.

258. **Chroma** is the strength or intensity of a color. One that has faded, or "grayed out," is said to have lost chroma. Chroma is not how light or how dark a red might be (for that is value), but how much "red" is in it. In simple two-color work, the printer is not as much concerned with the matter of chroma as with problems in hues and values, and only these two dimensions are shown on the color wheel.

Black, white, and the grays are classed as neutral tones, since none of the separate hues is apparent in any of them.

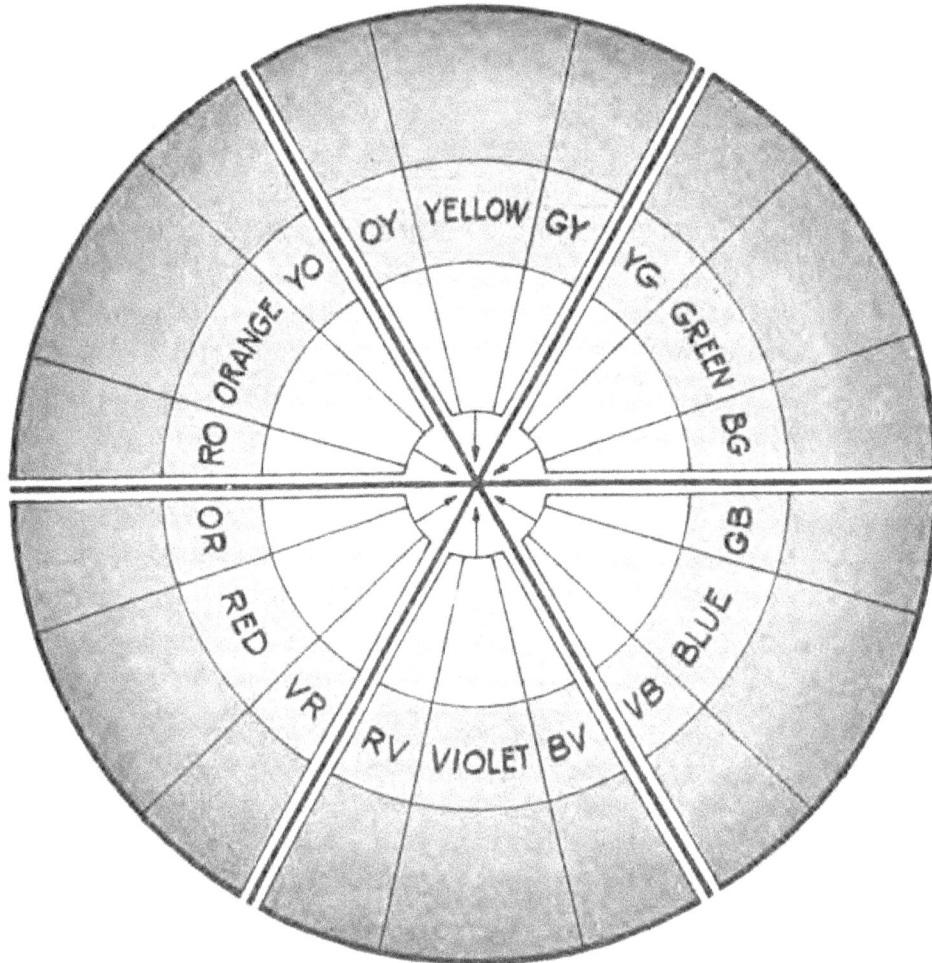

Fig. 227. A simple color wheel, from which color combinations
may be readily determined

259. **Warm and cold colors.** Each hue has its distinct
vibration, or length and intensity of color wave, as is evi-
denced by the fact that whenever the colors are refracted,
they invariably appear in the same order, with violet at one
side, and red at the other. This is also demonstrated in the
rays of the sun. In the heat of the day, they contain a more
even diffusion of all the hues, but as the rays get longer, in
the late afternoon, the weaker colors begin to fade out of
the rays, beginning with violet, blue, and green. As the sun

Fig. 228

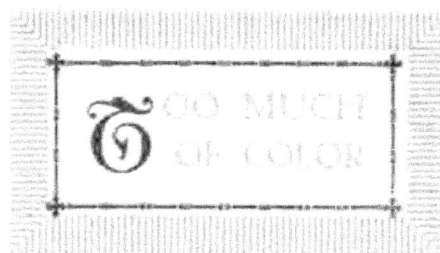

Fig. 229

is setting, the rays change from yellow to orange, and then at last the sun disappears in a deep, rich color. Thus, we find that violet is the weakest color, and red the strongest.

The stronger colors are more stimulating and exciting to the eye and nerves, and for this reason they are known as warm colors. The weaker colors are cold colors.

Red, orange, and yellow are the warm colors, and green, blue, and violet are the cold colors. Green may be changed to a warm color by adding a liberal amount of yellow.

Each color creates a different sensation in the vision and the mind of the reader.* Warm colors attract and enliven the interest, but when used too freely, they are also quite irritating and exciting. The cool colors, on the other hand, produce a sense of ease and comfort within the reader. It will be seen, therefore, that both are necessary in printing.

Warm colors should be used sparingly. A very small proportion of warm color is permissible on ordinary work, while the cold colors may be safely used in large areas. A comparison of the figures above will readily convince the student that a small proportion of warm color is best.

---

* Red is symbolic of intensity, passion, and excitement. It also represents patriotism and charity. In religious printing red symbolizes zeal and courage. It must be used very sparingly on the printed page.

Orange is symbolic of knowledge, civilization and enlightenment, just as is the torch or the lamp, in decoration. It is more satisfactory than red for use with black.

Yellow is expressive of elegance, richness, and light. It must be used sparingly.

Green is the color of coolness, and also of fruitfulness and abundance. It is a very restful color, and is easy on the eye.

Blue symbolizes loyalty, honor, peace, and permanence. It is also a restful color.

Violet is the color of royalty and dignity, as well as of somberness and depression.

260. **Complementary colors.** We have earlier stated that a ray of light contains all the colors. Complementary colors are those which, together, contain all the color elements of light. Red, for instance, is the equivalent of white light minus yellow and blue, the other primary colors. Green, which is made up of yellow and blue, is therefore the complement of red. In like manner, orange is the complement of blue, and violet is the complement of yellow. That the law of complementary colors is a natural one, is shown by the action of the eye in creating complementary colors.*

You will find by referring to the color wheel on page 215 that, in every case, the complementary colors will be found to be directly opposite each other on the chart. For instance, yellow and violet are complementary colors, and they are directly opposite. If green is added to the yellow, making green-yellow, then red, the complement of green, must be added to the violet, thus producing red-violet. In this way the colors are still kept opposite on the color wheel.

SECURING COLOR HARMONY

Harmony of colors in printing may be secured (a) by the use of complementary, or opposite, colors, (b) by the use of a shade and a tint of the same hue, (c) by printing in black and a suitable second color, or (d) by use of colored papers.

261. **Complementary color harmony.** If one will select two colors directly opposite on the chart, and use them in proper proportion, the cooler color predominating, a harmony of color is sure to be had. Two colors so chosen not

*HOW THE EYE PRODUCES COMPLEMENTARY COLORS. When the nerve cells within the retina of the eye become fatigued with one color, they seek relief by replacing that color with its complementary color. If we place a small piece of colored substance on a white surface and look at it intently for a number of seconds, and then quickly remove it, the eye will produce an image of the same size and shape, but of a directly opposite, or complementary, color. Also, after looking at the sun, one may then look away and see its image reproduced in a circle of dark blue, or violet. There are numerous ways in which this reaction of the eye may be noted. The complementary color produced within the eye is known as the negative after-image.

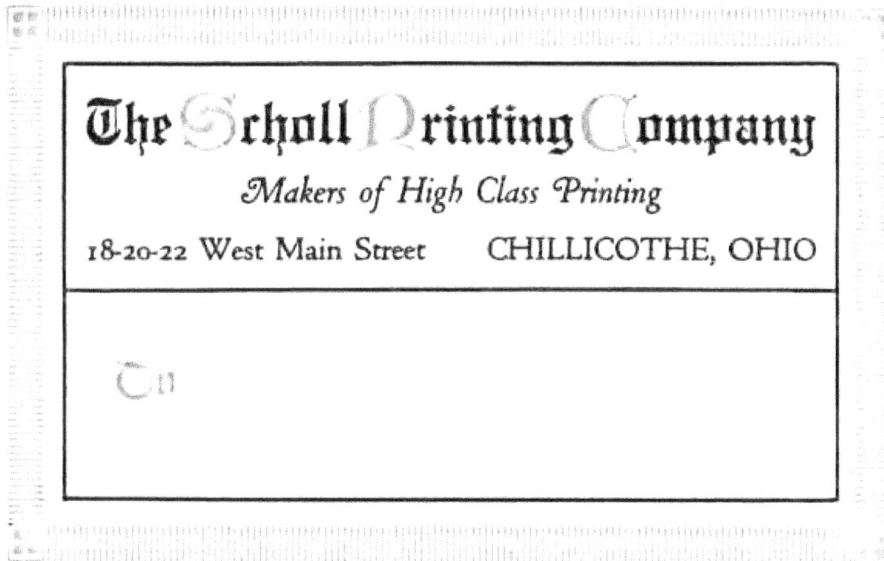

Fig. 230. More color is permissible on labels than on most other items

only produce a pleasing and harmonious effect, but they also serve to intensify each other, and to make each appear brighter and more attractive on the printed page.

262. **Harmony of tint and shade.** Beautiful effects, of a softer nature, may be had by printing a job in a tint and a shade of the same hue, as, for instance, the use of a tint of blue with a deep shade of blue. Such a combination may be printed on white paper, or on stock tinted in the same hue, or in the complementary, or opposite, hue.

263. **Use of black with colors.** By far the most common kind of two-color printing is that of using some color with black. All colors will work harmoniously with black, but if a cold color is used, it should be tinted, for the sake of creating the proper contrast, and of brightening up the page. The warmer colors must be used sparingly, as has been suggested above, and they should not be scattered too freely through the job, as this is confusing to the reader.

Hues of orange-red or red-orange are the most common colors to be printed on the page in combination with black.

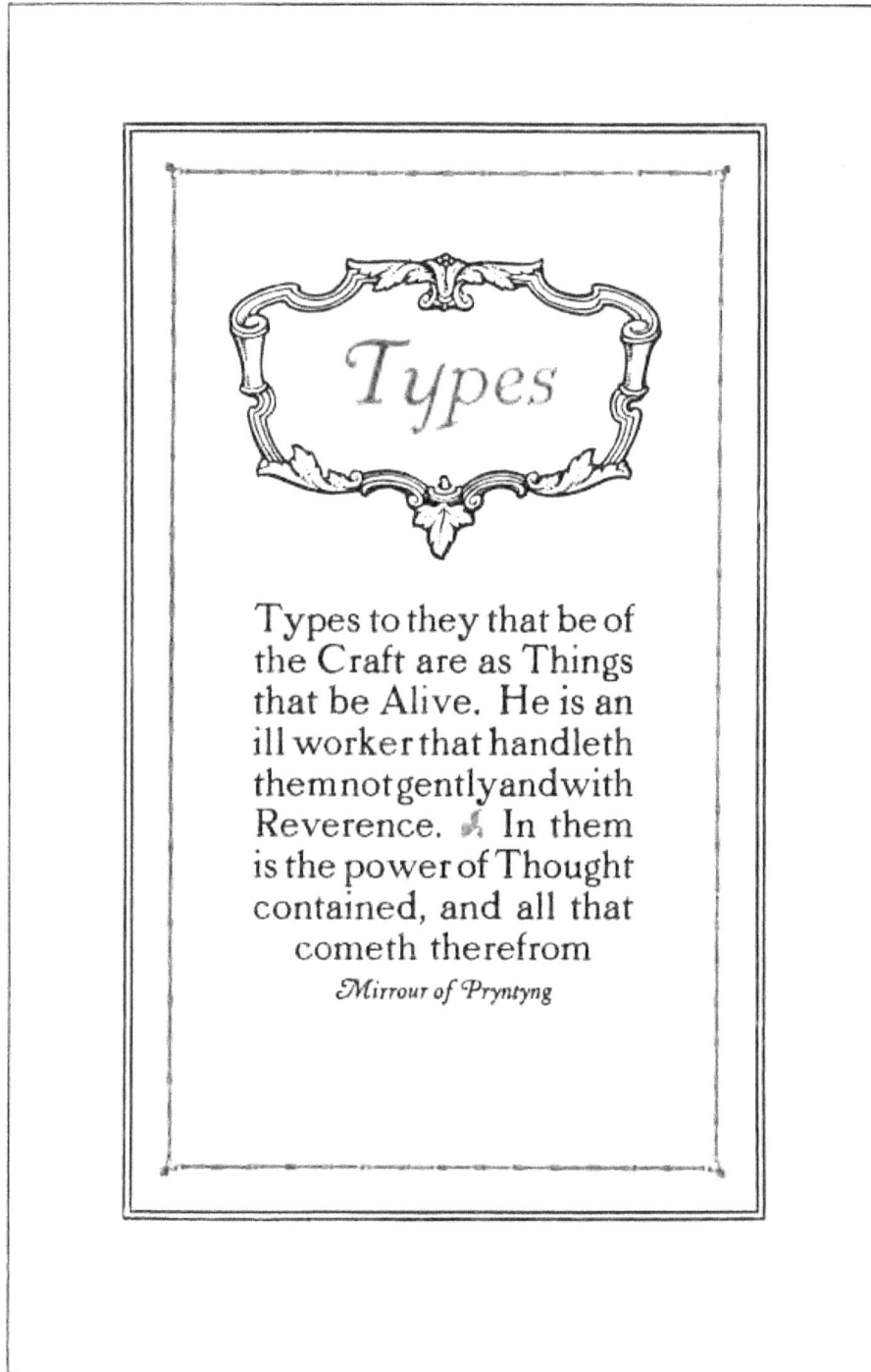

Types

Types to they that be of
the Craft are as Things
that be Alive. He is an
ill worker that handleth
them not gently and with
Reverence. ❧ In them
is the power of Thought
contained, and all that
cometh therefrom

Mirrour of Pryntyng

Fig. 231

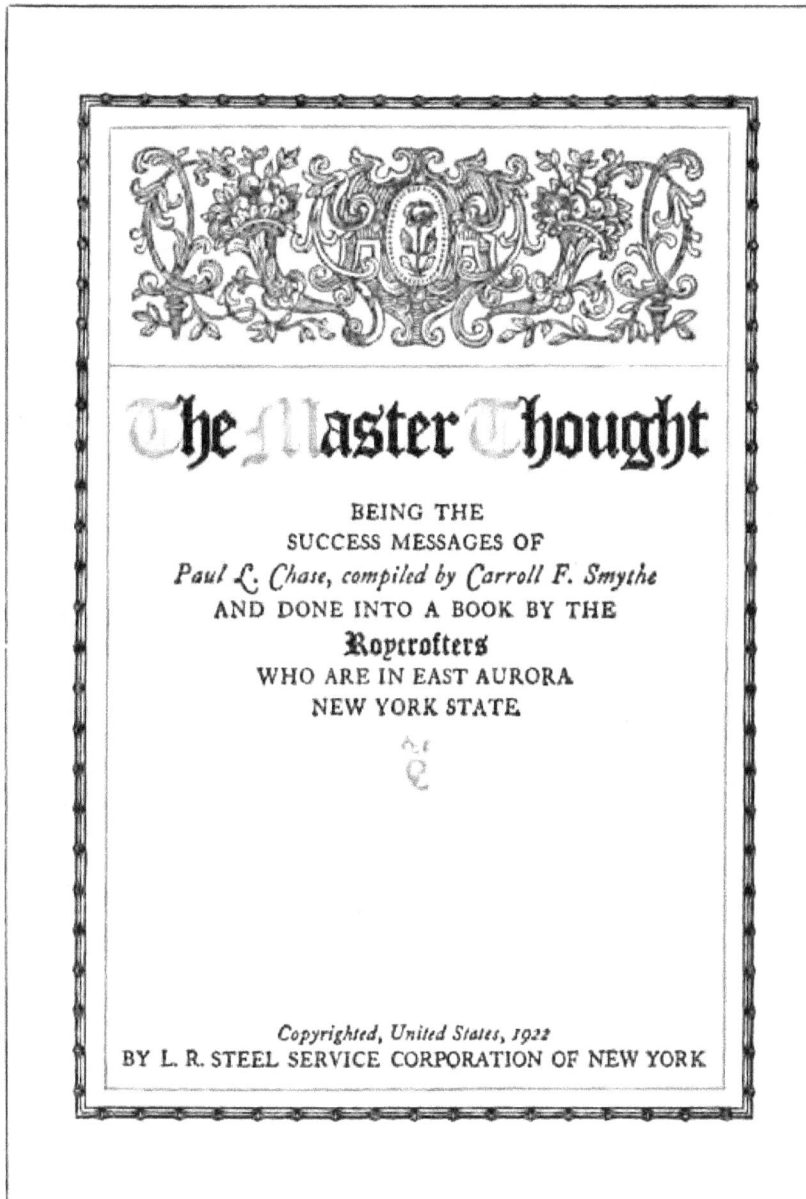

The Master Thought

BEING THE
SUCCESS MESSAGES OF
Paul L. Chase, compiled by Carroll F. Smythe
AND DONE INTO A BOOK BY THE
Roycrofters
WHO ARE IN EAST AURORA
NEW YORK STATE

Copyrighted, United States, 1922
BY L. R. STEEL SERVICE CORPORATION OF NEW YORK

Fig. 232. A pleasing distribution of color is secured in this cover design

264. Use of colored papers. Color combinations may be worked out by using a colored paper, and printing it with one or more colors of ink. If one color is used, it should be either the same hue of the stock (but a darker shade), or ink of the complementary color. If two colors are used, one may be the same hue as the stock, and the other of the complementary color, or they may consist of a shade and a tint of either of these colors. The nature of the job, and and the color of the paper, will govern the choice of colors.

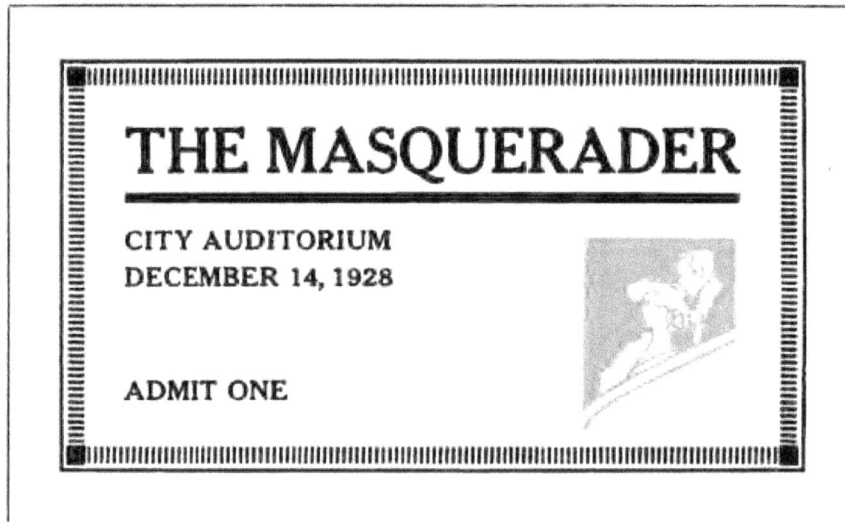

Fig. 233. An ornament of heavier tone than the type may be used if printed in a lighter color, as in this ticket

GOOD BOOKS ON COLOR IN PRINTING

Design and Color in Printing—Trezise.   The Inland Printer Co.
Color and Its Application to Printing—Andrews.   The Inland Printer Co.
Advertising: Its Principles and Practice.   Ronald Press Co.
The Grammar of Color.   Strathmore Paper Co.
A Color Notation—Munsell.   Munsell Color Co.
Modern Type Display—Frazier.   The Inland Printer Co.

QUESTIONS

1. Name the primary and secondary colors, and tell how the latter are made.
2. What are the three dimensions of a color? Define each term.
3. What are meant by warm and cold colors? Name those in each class.
4. What can you tell about the effects created by the individual colors?
5. In what proportion should warm and cold colors be used? Why?
6. How does the human eye produce complementary colors?
7. How are complementary colors located with respect to each other, on the chart?
8. Discuss the method of securing color harmony with complementary colors.
9. What considerations govern the use of a color with black ink?
10. How may color harmony be secured in the use of colored papers?

CHAPTER XXXIII

The Composition of Tickets

TICKET jobs furnish the student with excellent material for practice in the fundamentals of display composition. Tickets are small, easy to set, and will admit of individual ideas of treatment, as they are less formal than most jobs.

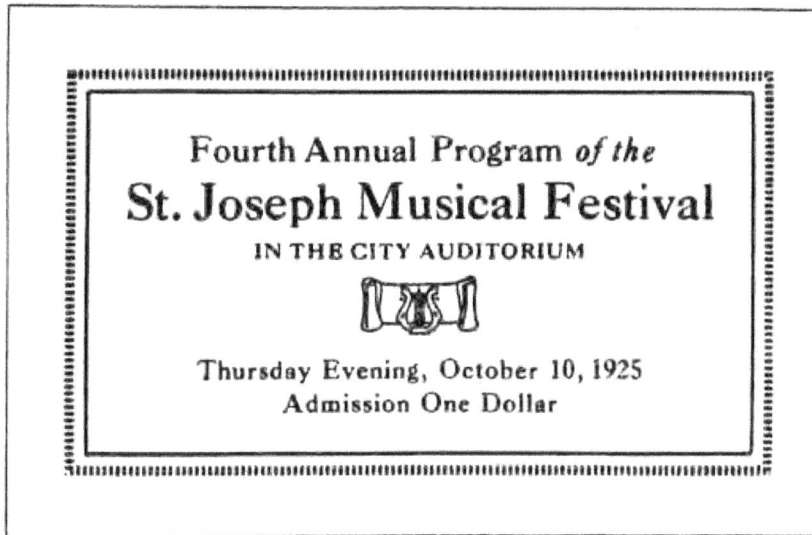

Fig. 234. A ticket form in which suitable decoration is used

265. **Sizes.** The size of a ticket will usually range from $2 \times 3\frac{1}{2}$ to $2\frac{1}{2} \times 4$ inches, depending upon the amount of copy, and the nature of the display. However, there are no fixed or standard sizes or shapes, and the exact dimensions are frequently left to the judgment of the compositor. A good proportion should be had between the width and length.

The stock for ticket jobs is ordinarily cut from white or colored cardboard. Odd scrap, or strip, stock is sometimes utilized, and occasionally standard die-cut cards are used.

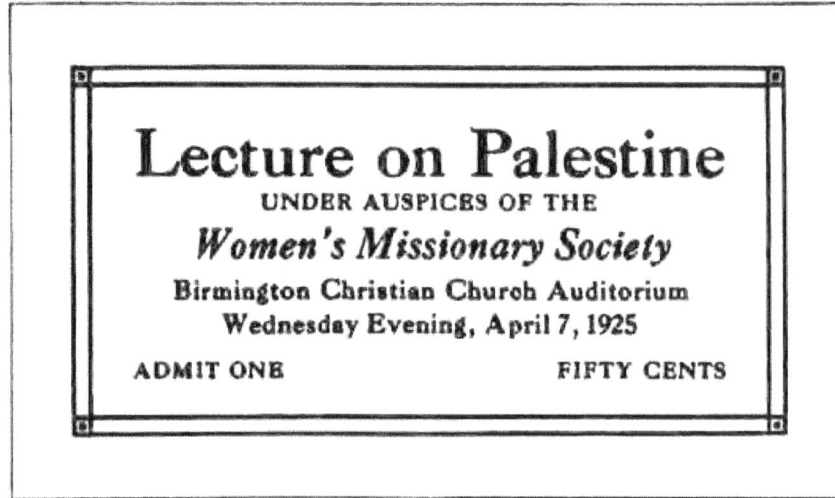

Lecture on Palestine
UNDER AUSPICES OF THE
Women's Missionary Society
Birmington Christian Church Auditorium
Wednesday Evening, April 7, 1925

ADMIT ONE   FIFTY CENTS

Fig. 235

266. Styles in tickets. There is no fixed form or style for the typography of tickets, and each individual job should be planned with the thought of fitness for its specific purpose. In addition to the admission feature, there is also an element of advertising in tickets, and therefore the copy should be pleasingly and appropriately designed, and the principles of good display should be applied.

The copy should be broken up into logical units, and the different items should be displayed in accordance with their relative importance. The amount of decoration used will depend upon the nature of the copy, in each case.

Representative ticket designs are shown herewith, and a study of these will be helpful to the student.

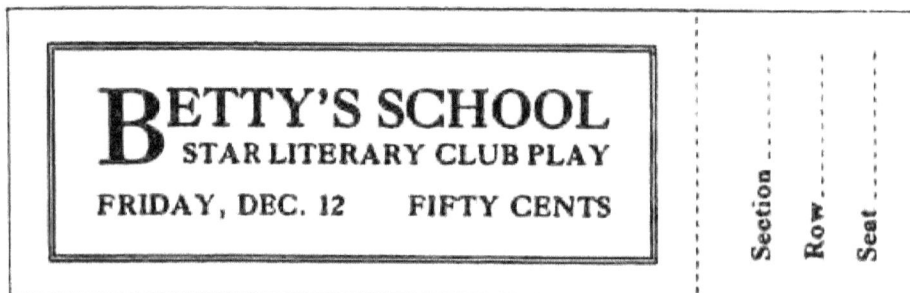

BETTY'S SCHOOL
STAR LITERARY CLUB PLAY
FRIDAY, DEC. 12   FIFTY CENTS

Section ....
Row ....
Seat ....

Fig. 236. A ticket with reserved seat stub

CHAPTER XXXIV

The Composition of Business Stationery

BUSINESS or professional stationery is most effective when all the different items that are to be used together are designed in the same general style. For example, when Caslon Oldstyle is chosen for a firm's letterhead, it is well to set the envelope, business card, invoice heading, and all other similar forms, in the same series of type, and to follow the same general method of arrangement and display. With this idea in mind, we shall deal briefly with some of the common practices in the composition of the principal items of business stationery—letterheads, envelopes, and cards.

LETTERHEADS

267. **Typography of letterheads.** Probably the most important item of business stationery is the letterhead. It is in a special sense the representative of the user, and much depends upon the impression it makes on the reader. As a rule, the simplest letterhead is the best.* It should be neat, dignified, and orderly. It should not be overbold, nor set in too large type, and should not be too highly colored. Ordinarily, it should be set in one series of type, and the fewest possible sizes should be used. The style of the letterhead, and the extent and character of the decoration used, will depend upon the nature of the business it is to represent.

---

* "My idea of a good letterhead is that it should very clearly and simply, and in good taste, show the firm name, the goods carried, or the business, and the address and telephone number. A cut in some cases helps out the general appearance, if it emphasizes the business. Good paper, and clean, sharp impression from a proper- ly designed heading are requisites for a good letterhead. I believe in a uniform style for all the business forms of a house. My advice is to make the heading as simple as possible and to carry the needed information in the most legible way." — Hal Marchbanks, of The Marchbanks Press, New York City.

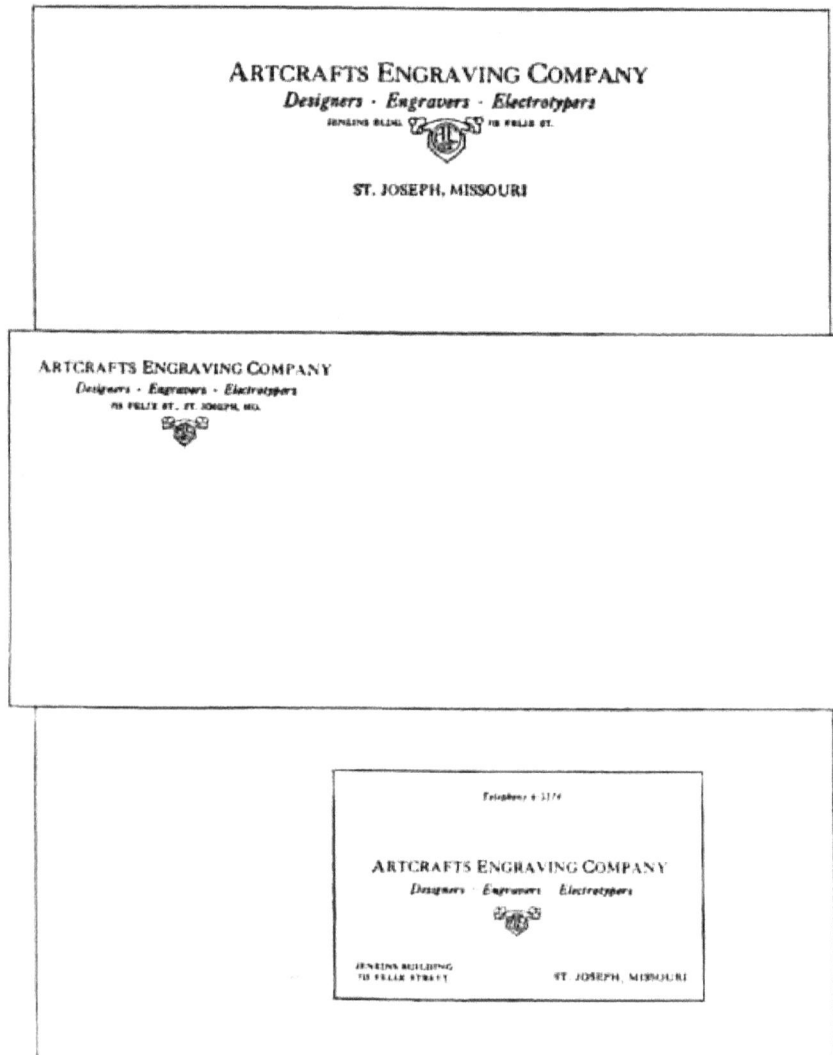

Fig. 237

In the arrangement of the matter, the name of the firm or person should be given first place, the line of business, second, and the address, third. If the letterhead carries additional copy, the form should be carefully grouped and balanced in such a way that suitable prominence will be given to these three principal items of the copy.

Fig. 28. A commercial letterhead, well displayed and neatly balanced

268. Sizes of letterheads. The standard size of letter-heads is $8\frac{1}{2}$ x 11 inches. These are cut without waste from 17 x 22 paper, and they are folded three times to fit into the No. $6\frac{3}{4}$ envelope, or folded twice for use with the No. 9 or No. 10 envelope. For short letters, some firms use sheets of standard width, but less than standard length. Usually these are $8\frac{1}{2}$ x $5\frac{1}{2}$ (called half-sheet letterheads), or $8\frac{1}{2}$ x $7\frac{1}{4}$ (commonly designated as memorandum heads).

A smaller letter sheet, size $7\frac{1}{4}$ x $10\frac{1}{2}$, is widely used by professional people, and it is also steadily gaining favor for general correspondence. The sheet is folded twice length-wise to fit the No. $7\frac{1}{2}$, or two-fold, envelope.

A few representative letterheads are reproduced on the following pages, and in these different typographic treat-ments have been followed, to suit the nature of the copy.

HARRIS GRAIN COMPANY
600 NORTH WASHBURN AVENUE
Detroit, Michigan

Fig. 239. An attractive form for two-fold stationery

GEORGE W. EASTIN
ATTORNEY-AT-LAW
217 DONNELL COURT
St. Joseph, Missouri

Fig. 240. Professional letterheads usually follow the plain, conventional style

228

CROSSROADS MERCANTILE CO.

Dealers in General Merchandise

FARMING IMPLEMENTS · HARDWARE · GROCERIES · AUTO ACCESSORIES

CLOTHING · HATS · BOOTS · SHOES

REDFIELD, MO.

Fig. 241

CROSSROADS MERCANTILE COMPANY

DEALERS IN GENERAL MERCHANDISE

REDFIELD, MO.

Farming Implements
Hardware
Clothing, Hats

Auto Accessories
Groceries
Boots & Shoes

Fig. 242. Two arrangements of the same letterhead copy by Axel Edw. Sahlin, of the Roycrofters

TRUST BROTHERS PRINTING COMPANY

Producers of Quality Printing

SEVENTY ROBERTS STREET

PITTSBURGH, PA.

Fig. 243. A very neat and dignified arrangement of a printers' letterhead

E. P. ARCHIBALD

Advertising Writer & Designer of Printing

516 ATLANTIC AVENUE

BOSTON

Fig. 244. Simplicity and good taste are emphasized in this design by Mr. Archibald

ENVELOPES

269. Envelope sizes. The envelope most used in business correspondence is the No. 6¾ (sometimes listed as 6½), but there is an increasing demand for the No. 9 envelope, as it will take a letter sheet when it is folded twice lengthwise, thus leaving the printed heading uncreased. The No. 10 envelope is rather large for the standard letterhead, and is seldom used unless enclosures are to accompany the letters. The No. 6 envelope may be enclosed in any of the others, and it is used principally for return correspondence. The sizes of common commercial envelopes are given in Fig. 245, herewith.

> *Standard Sizes of*
> *Business Envelopes*
>
> No. 6   3⅜ x 6 inches
> No. 6¾   3⅝ x 6½ inches
> No. 7½   3⅞ x 7½ inches
> No. 9   3⅞ x 8⅞ inches
> No. 10   4⅛ x 9½ inches

Fig. 245

270. Envelopes should match letterheads. Inasmuch as the regular envelopes are usually designed for use with letterheads, the style of composition should suitably match the typography of the letterheads, as has been suggested at the head of the chapter. For most purposes, the form should be small and neat, and the general style should be such as will reflect the nature of the business represented.

271. Position of the wording. Most envelopes are printed in the upper left corner. Occasionally, display matter is spread over the entire left side, or even more, of the surface, although there seems to be little justification for this practice. The matter should always be well designed, and be consistently grouped together, and it should never interfere with the clearness of the mailing address.

On personal and professional stationery, the name and address is often printed on the flap instead of the corner of the face. This practice is steadily growing in favor.

**THE MARTIN-FERRIS
TRANSFER COMPANY**

Specialists in All Kinds Heavy Moving

WILLIAMSPORT · PENNSYLVANIA

Fig. 246

PATTERSON BROTHERS
Fine Tailoring
826 MAIN, MARION, OHIO

Fig. 247

BENJAMIN WILLIAMS
Real Estate and Insurance
Mortgage Loans
HEBRON, NEBRASKA

Fig. 248

The U. T. A. School of Printing
T. G. McGrew, *Superintendent*
1500 East Michigan Street
Indianapolis, Indiana

Fig. 249

232

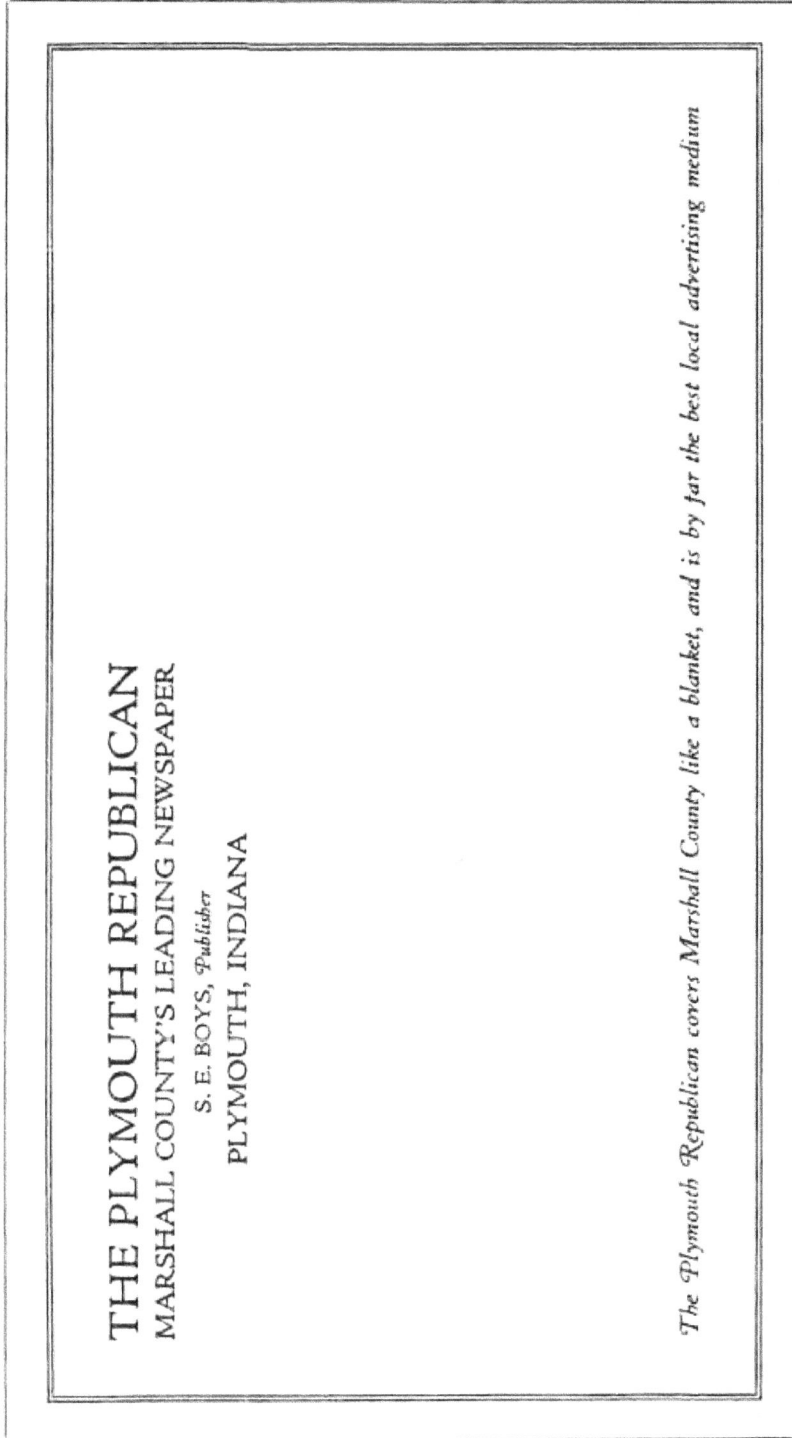

THE PLYMOUTH REPUBLICAN
MARSHALL COUNTY'S LEADING NEWSPAPER

S. E. BOYS, *Publisher*

PLYMOUTH, INDIANA

The Plymouth Republican covers Marshall County like a blanket, and is by far the best local advertising medium

Fig. 250. A form covering the full face of the envelope

Sometimes the entire face of the envelope is considered as a unit in the designing of the form, as in the case of the job reproduced on the opposite page. While this design is appropriate, and quite attractive, for most work the simple corner design, or address on the flap, is most suitable.

BUSINESS CARDS

272. Sizes of cards. Business cards, like tickets, vary in size. Most of them range from about $2x3\frac{1}{2}$ to $2\frac{1}{2}x4$ inches. Professional cards, and also the more formal business cards bearing only the name, business, and address, are usually small, but those with fuller copy, or that are arranged in a less formal style, are of somewhat larger size.

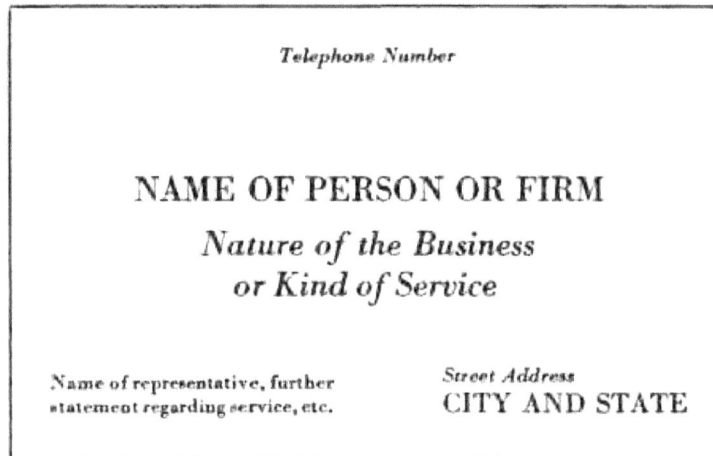

Telephone Number

NAME OF PERSON OR FIRM

Nature of the Business
or Kind of Service

Name of representative, further
statement regarding service, etc.

Street Address
CITY AND STATE

Fig. 251. Lay-out for the usual form of business card

As a rule, special die-cut cards are used for this work. These are cut from 22x28 bristol, and are packed 500 in a box. The sizes of die-cut cards are designated by number, 117, 88, 70, 63, 55, 48, or 36, the number in each case indicating the quantity of cards that may be cut from one full sheet of stock. Sizes 117 and 88 are quite frequently used for professional cards, but most business cards are printed on the sizes 70, 63, or 55, which are somewhat larger.

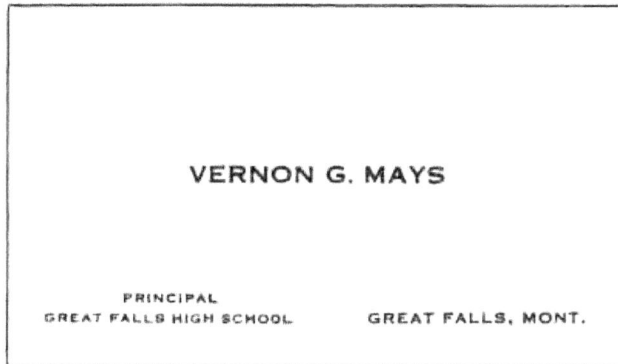

Fig. 252. A typical professional card

Fig. 253

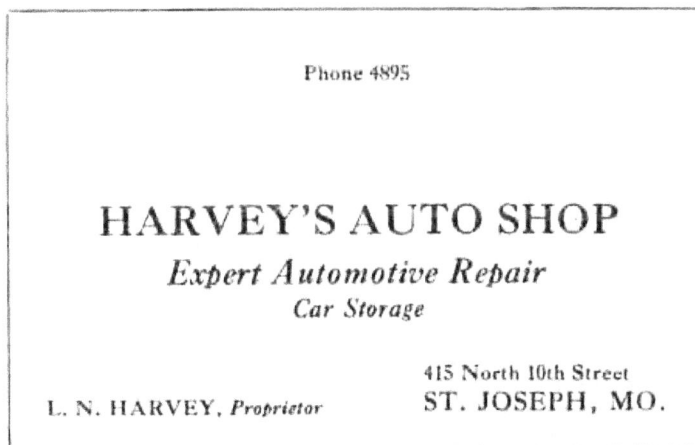

Fig. 254

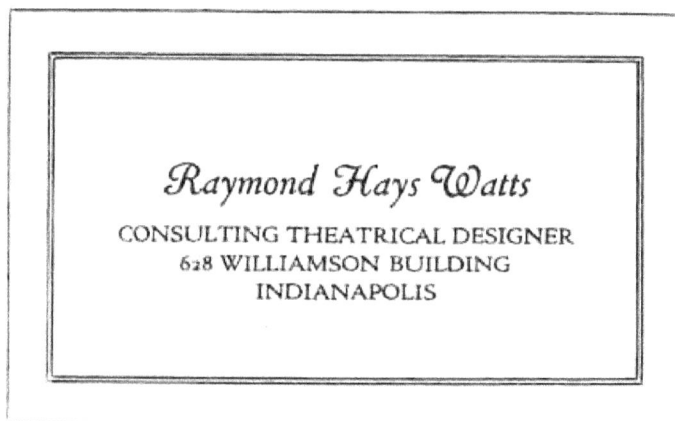

Fig. 255

Fig. 256

Fig. 257

273. **Typography of cards.** Professional cards, and the formal business cards, should be set in capitals, in the small sizes of a plain, dignified letter. Copperplate Gothic, and other similar lining Gothics, or the various card Romans, are ordinarily used for professional cards. Good business card faces include any of the Caslons, Bodoni, Litho Roman, and a number of other good display types. As usual, only one series of type, with its accompanying Italic, should be used on a business card, for the most pleasing effect.

A margin of 12 to 18 points should be allowed on the smaller sizes of professional cards, and at least 18 points should be allowed on the larger ones. Thus, if the card is three inches wide, the type might be set 16 picas wide. On a four-inch card the usual type measure will be 21 picas.

Borders are seldom used on the ordinary business card, but they are permissible in informal treatments, as some of the examples on the preceding page will show.

The copy should be laid out in such a manner that the items answering the questions (1) "Who?" (2) "What?" and (3) "Where?" should be given suitable prominence in the display. The matter should be carefully grouped, spaced, and balanced, so that it shall be in logical order, easy to read, and that it shall not appear crowded. The principles of simplicity, balance, proportion, shape and tone harmony, and fitness, are safe and reliable guides in designing cards.

Examples of formal and informal treatments of business cards have been reproduced on the two preceding pages.

RELIABLE BOOKS ON DISPLAY COMPOSITION

Design and Color in Printing—Trezise.   The Inland Printer Co.
Modern Type Display—Frazier.   The Inland Printer Co.
Nifty Ideas for Thrifty Printers—Frazier.   The Inland Printer Co.
The Art and Practice of Typography—Gress.   Oswald Publishing Co.
Parsons Handbook of Letter Headings—Johnson.   Parsons Paper Co.

A study of the typographic sections of *The Inland Printer*, including the monthly review of specimens, will be extremely helpful to all students.

CHAPTER XXXV

The Composition of Advertisements

ADVERTISING copy must be skillfully written, logically arranged, and appealingly displayed, in order to bring the desired results. As this latter element is definitely in the realm of the printer, some of the main considerations in the typography of advertisements will be treated here.

274. **The purpose of an advertisement** is to attract the attention of the reader to its message, to convince him of the need or the desirability of obtaining the merchandise or service offered, and to induce him to take action in the matter. The ad must therefore be (1) attractive or inviting to the eye, (2) easy to read, and (3) it must exert a favorable influence on the reader, in order to accomplish this.

275. **Ads should be well designed.** Assuming that the copy has been properly written and logically organized, the treatment of its typography has much to do with its effectiveness. The general arrangement must be such as will attract favorable attention. It should most suitably—and simply—express the thought that is embodied in the copy. It should in every possible way support and emphasize the message it bears; therefore it must be orderly and legible, and its appearance should be agreeable to the senses of the reader. Careful thought should be given to the display and arrangement of every ad, before setting it, and a definite, clear-cut plan should be worked out, and then followed.

276. **Legibility especially important.** Ads should be set in good, clear, legible type faces. Of equal importance is simplicity in design, and a judicious grouping and arrangement of the different masses in the form, that the eye of the reader may take in the wording, and the mind absorb

Speed and hill climbing

The present Pierce-Arrows travel from point to point 15% faster than before. Their hill-climbing ability —pulling out of holes or through sand—is 25% greater because of the Dual Valve Engines in them.

Governed in an indicated speed, their greater power permits them to maintain that pace, to also make more trips and serve a wider range each working day

Pierce
Arrow

THE PIERCE ARROW MOTOR CAR COMPANY BUFFALO, N. Y.

CHASSIS PRICES
1 ton $1700
2 ton 2900
3 ton 4300
All Prices F.O.B. Buffalo

Fig. 259. Fitness: the bold type and border, and the general style, are suitable to this subject

---

CAHOKIA

A SUPER POWER PLANT BE-HIND YOUR INVESTMENT

Safety

Whoever has a stake on community growth has an investment as strong as granite. Further, whoever has an investment in something all the people need all the time has not feet over that bugaboo—safety for savings. Cahokia offers that soundness of investment. And it pays six per cent dividends! Maximum return is here linked up with maximum safety.

Demand for electricity in St. Louis doubles every five years.

CAHOKIA IS A SUPER SECURITY

Call Securities Department

UNION ELECTRIC
LIGHT & POWER COMPANY

Fig. 258. Fitness: the orderliness and quiet dignity of this design is especially appropriate

the sense of the message, without a conscious effort. The thought in the subject matter should "flow" smoothly and easily through the medium of the type design.

Other elements which affect legibility, such as length of lines, leading, and spacing, are particularly applicable to the setting of ads. It should also be remembered that the lower-case letters are much more easily read than lines of capitals, and therefore large groups of capitals should be avoided. It will be well to review the chapter on Legibility before beginning the composition of advertisements.

277. Follow the principles of display. Ads should closely follow the recognized principles of display. A regard for balance and proportion are evident in all good advertisements. Harmony of tone and shape are to be considered in the choosing and assembling of typographic materials. Fitness suggests that the type chosen, as well as the style of display, shall be in keeping with the subject matter, and shall create the proper atmosphere for the particular appeal that is to be made. Whether the display shall be dainty and artistic, formal and dignified, or bold and rugged, will depend upon the nature and purpose of the ad.

Simplicity and order must be considered in the arrangement of the matter.* The most important items should be given due prominence over the other copy. One should not try to display the entire ad. In fact, an effort to display

*"The practice of making good advertising typography is not a matter of playing with pretty types and prettier theories, with all the time in the world at one's disposal. This is what it is in fact: a striving to make an equilateral triangle out of three things that will never quite come together; namely, superlative quality, lightning speed, and bargain prices. There is no quarrel with these conditions, for they are inherent in business and advertising, and must be met.

"We must remember that good advertising typography is largely a matter of being simple; of good workmanship with few tools; of setting type naturally without attempting to force it into arbitrary shapes and patterns; of not trying to display everything and decorate everything; in a word, of knowing what NOT to do. Take the principle of good margins and spacing, add to it that of using as few type faces as possible, in as few sizes as possible, and you have all the theory you require. You will have a recipe for the kind of typography that pays, and one that will be safe and sufficient until the crack of doom." —From a speech of Everett Courrier, a noted typographer of New York City.

Fine English Suitings

AT GREATLY REDUCED PRICES

MADE by our own experienced and skillful workmen into stylish and modish suits for careful dressers. The materials are imported direct from the best English Mills. in patterns exclusively controlled by us. During the ensuing eight weeks we shall offer these at a very great reduction to Angelica citizens. Perfect fit guaranteed in every case

One Price $22.50

RUFUS FABIAN TAILORING COMPANY
ANGELICA, NEW YORK

Fig. 260. An ad in which tone harmony, ample margins, and a fitting type face combine to make a strong, effective ad

a number of lines in a small ad usually results in confusion, an unattractive display, and a decided loss in legibility and forcefulness. Remember that "all display is no display."

278. **Borders** are necessary on most ads. The border defines the limits of the ad, and holds the attention of the reader within the space. It also preserves the unity of the ad by holding together the different groups of which it is composed, and it increases the interest and legibility.

As in all other items of printing, the border should be harmonious with the type, and should appear as a fitting frame for the body. It should not be overbold, or draw attention to itself because of any marked irregularities, or eccentricities of design, but should appear as a unit with the body matter. Usually, the plainest borders are the best.

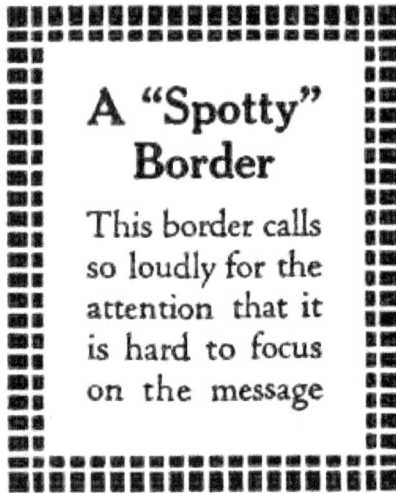

A "Spotty" Border

This border calls so loudly for the attention that it is hard to focus on the message

Fig. 261

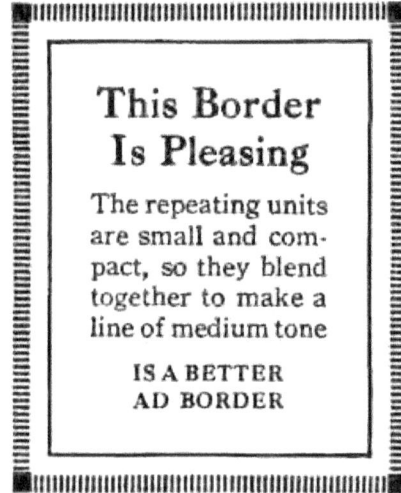

This Border Is Pleasing

The repeating units are small and compact, so they blend together to make a line of medium tone

IS A BETTER
AD BORDER

Fig. 262

Borders that consist of separate repeating units should not be used if they will appear "spotty," and so confuse the reader, or draw his attention away from the message. The border in Fig. 261, above, consists of units which are quite disturbing to the reader, but in Fig. 262 the border is made up of finer units which blend together, and therefore make no displeasing effect. The inner panel of rule in the latter also helps to unite the units into an even band of color.

279. **The value of white space.** Ample margins of white space around the body of an ad are quite necessary for the best results. They set the message apart from any other printed matter on the page, and also make a sharp contrast with the group of type matter, so that the wording is emphasized, and made easy to read. A crowded ad, with little or no white space, is unattractive to the eye, and has little chance of being read. Note particularly the liberal use of white space in the advertisements reproduced in Figs. 260 and 263, and see how it adds interest to both of them.

280. **Harmony among neighboring ads.** A very pleasing effect is secured when all the ads in a publication are set in one good type series, with its Italic. A good compositor

Bank of France Travelers' Checks

A NEW type of travelers' check has been devised to relieve the tourist in France of the burden of fluctuating exchange rates, and the inconvenience occasioned when attempts are made to change money in all parts of France. These checks are issued by the Compagnie Francaise du Tourisme of Paris, [the new French government tourists' bureau] through The National City Bank of New York. Among their chief advantages are:

Easy Convertibility

Checks are cashed by all branches of the Bank of France, and can be used at shops, hotels, etc., AT THEIR FULL FACE VALUE, practically everywhere in France or the French colonies.

Convenient Denominations

Checks are issued in books of ten, in denominations of 100, 500 and 1000 francs.

Refund on Unused Checks

Unused checks will be exchanged when brought back home, for dollars at the current buying rate of exchange for bankers' checks on Paris.

Terms of Sales

Checks can be purchased in the United States at the current selling rate of exchange for bankers' checks on Paris; they are sold for the equivalent in dollars of their franc value, plus a commission of one-half of one per cent and a nominal fee of twenty-five cents per book of ten checks to cover the stamp duty of the French government.

The fact that these checks are guaranteed by the Bank of France and issued in a negotiable form familiar to the French people, explains their popularity in France

SOLD BY

The National City Bank of New York

55 WALL STREET

Fig. 263. Bold headlines and strong contrasts are not always necessary to make a strong ad. In this one, tone harmony, intelligent grouping of the matter, and ample margins, make a forceful ad.

243

Antiques and Old Glass

Hooked Rugs, Indian Pottery,
Pine Chests, and many
other articles of Glass
and Furniture

Shop open afternoons

CHARLES E. COMINS

One East Main Street   WARREN, MASS.

ARTHUR J. SUSSEL

Arts   Antiques

S. E. CORNER 18TH AND SPRUCE STREETS
Branch 928-30 Pine Street
PHILADELPHIA   PENNSYLVANIA

Marblehead Antique Exchange

is open for the summer with
a large collection of Early
American pine and maple
furniture, china, mirrors,
hooked rugs, etc.

Front and State Streets, Marblehead, Mass.

ANTIQUES

Reasonably priced for quick sale

LEILA J. FARR

Stratton Road   EAST JAFFREY
NEW HAMPSHIRE

Telephone 124-3

For Wedding Gifts
OLD SILVER

GOOD taste increasingly recoils from
the use of the modern machine-
stamped commercial silver which is so
out of harmony with mellow furniture
and choice old glass.

So I urge: for gifts of lasting worth
and appreciation, give old silver. It is
not necessary to spend a great deal for
such gifts — a single serving spoon; a
pair of them; a small set of tea or coffee
spoons; a tiny pitcher, may be inexpen-
sively purchased at my shop.

GEBELEIN

79 Chestnut Street :: BOSTON, MASS.

A name that stands for the finest in silver.

The
Webster Place Antique Shop
At FRANKLIN, New Hampshire

COLLECTORS especially interested
in maple and pine furniture or
hooked rugs will do well to visit our
shop. They will have difficulty in
finding elsewhere so large a stock and
so varied an assortment.

And there is much besides of other
American antiques: furniture of all
kinds in different woods; whale oil
lamps and bellows; glass; pink lustre
and other china; pewter; iron; brass
and tin.

*In your travels this summer
visit the shop.*

The WEBSTER PLACE ANTIQUE SHOP
On the Daniel Webster Highway at
FRANKLIN, NEW HAMPSHIRE
CLYDE C. BROWN, Proprietor

Fig. 264. Reproduction of a page of advertisements from the magazine, Antiques, whose
advertisements are all set exclusively in the Caslon Oldstyle series

Invite Us to Your Next
——"BLOW-OUT"——
By Calling 8272
GEIGER-WHITE
TIRE SERVICE

WAS IT INSURED?

That's the first thought that comes to mind when one sees, or hears of, or reads about a fire. Should your property be endangered what would it mean to you financially?

See us about sufficient coverage to protect you against any possible financial loss from fire or other eventuality. Do it TODAY.

LESTER PAYNE

Representing Philadelphia Fire and Marine Insurance Company

AUTO SUPPLY CO.
Agents for Gabriel Snubbers
Automobile Accessories
1003 Frederick Ave.   Phone 3814)

24-Hour Kodak Finishing Service
MAJESTIC STUDIO
E. J. PRAWITZ
6-1104W   712 Edmond

TOOTLE
THEATER
HIGH CLASS MUSICAL COMEDIES
——AND——
FEATURE PHOTOPLAYS
Continuous Show from 1 p. m.
11 p. m.
Change of Bill Sunday and
Thursday

Don't envy a good complexion just try a facial at

Spring & Haxton's Beauty Shop

Marcel   Shampoo

Manicure   Scalp Treatment

Call -313 for appointment

Remember
Your Family and Friends
with a
PHOTOGRAPH
WITZEL'S STUDIO

Poland's Cash Grocery

Quality - Service - Price

Chase's Candies and Richelieu Groceries

"A Store With a Conscience."

Fig. 266. An inharmonious combination of ads which lessens the force of any one of them

may thus secure very creditable results with a simple outlay of type faces, and may produce ads that are forceful and effective. The quiet dignity produced by this harmony among ads increases the appeal of each of them.

The superiority of a common style of advertising display is particularly seen on the pages of small publications, such as school newspapers, in which many ads are grouped together. When these are set in several styles of type, with different borders, as in Fig. 265, there is confusion, and all the ads lose in effectiveness. Fig. 266, on the other hand, is harmonious and pleasing, and the ads are more effective.

Fig. 266.   A section of very simple, but most effective ads, in a pleasing harmony of style

281. Sizes of newspaper ads. The standard width for newspaper columns is 13 picas. Six point column rules are placed between the columns. Thus, the space occupied by a double-column ad is 26½ picas, and that of a three-column ad is 40 picas, etc. In some newspaper plants, special border pieces are made up, so that a two-column border may be fully 26½ picas wide, or a four-column border may be 53½ picas wide, but more often the border will be built out to even pica widths (26 picas, and 53 picas, respectively), and then a nonpareil slug will be placed alongside the ad, between the border and the column rule.

The depth of an ad is measured in inches. A one-inch single-column ad is 13 picas wide and 6 picas deep. A ten-inch double-column ad is 26½ picas wide and 60 picas deep.

The measure of the depth of an ad refers to the exact amount of space taken up by the ad, and not to the length of the border. Usually, the ads are separated from matter above and below by cut-off rules, and a slug is then placed at the top and the bottom of the ad, between the border and the cut-off rules. The

TWELVE PICAS OVER ALL

A Two-Inch Ad

The depth of an ad includes the total amount of space from cut-off to cut-off, and therefore allowance should be made for these outside margins when the skeleton is being built up for the ad

Fig. 267. Proper size for a two-inch ad

measure of the ad is from rule to rule, thus including the spacing outside the border. Accordingly, a ten-inch ad will be set in a border 59 picas long instead of 60 picas, to allow for these outside margins. This is shown in Fig. 267, above.

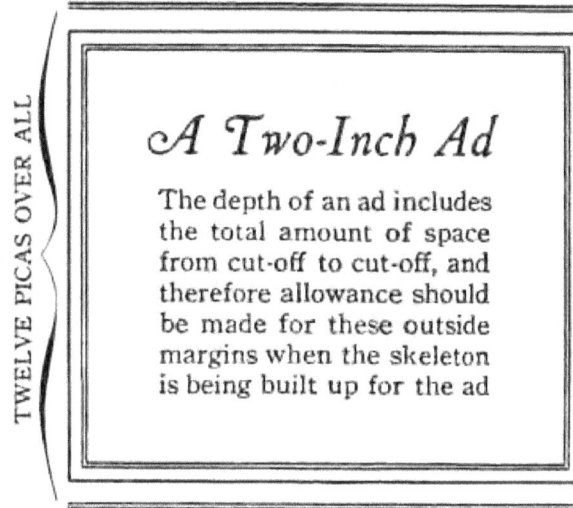

SUGGESTIONS

In the setting of ads, it is customary to build the border to the proper dimensions, in skeleton form, first, and then to insert the body matter as it is set. Be sure to allow for head and foot slugs in the total length.

A study of the ads appearing in various publications, and particularly in the leading printing trade journals, will be very helpful to the student.

SOME GOOD BOOKS ON ADVERTISING

The Typography of Advertisements—Trezise. The Inland Printer Co.
Advertising—Its Principles and Practice. Ronald Press Co.
Making Type Work—Sherbow. Published by the author
Effective Type-use for Advertising—Sherbow. Published by the author
The Psychology of Advertising—Scott. Small-Maynard Co.
Modern Type Display—Frazier. The Inland Printer Co.

CHAPTER XXXVI

The Composition of Programs

PROGRAMS do not follow any fixed standards of size or style, but they are designed to properly represent the occasions for which they are printed. They therefore offer the student good opportunity for the exercise of judgment and originality in planning their typography.

282. **Single-sheet programs.** The simplest and cheapest plan for a program is that of assembling the matter into a single-page form, and printing it on one side of a sheet. In such a case the title or occasion, time, and place form the heading, while the details of the program itself constitute the body of the form. The size of the sheet will depend on the amount of copy, and the nature of the design, but the proportions, to be most pleasing, should closely follow the recognized ratio of width and length that governs all good printing. Common sizes range from 4x6 to 6x9 inches. A typical single-sheet program is illustrated on the next page.

283. **The four-page program,** or program folder, is one that consists of a title-page, or initial page, at the front, on which is displayed the information as to event, time, place, etc., and the program proper on one or more of the following pages. Ordinarily, if only two pages are printed, the title-page will appear on the first page, and the program on the third; or if three pages are used, the program copy will spread across the second and third pages. The fourth page may also be used if necessary. When the folder contains both a menu and a program, it is customary to locate the menu on the second page and the program on the third.

A consistent style of typography should run through all the pages of a program. For most work, a single series of

PIANO RECITAL

by

Mme. JEANNE DOUMERGUE

Aeolian Hall, March 10, 1923

✖

PROGRAMME

I

NOVELETTE, No. 2, D Major . . . *Schumann*
FINALE, *Fantaisie*, op. 17 . . . *Schumann*

II

PRELUDE, F Major . . . . . . *Chopin*
POLONAISE, A Major . . . . . *Chopin*
MAZURKA, A Minor . . . . . *Chopin*
SCHERZO, C Sharp Minor . . . *Chopin*

III

LA CARILLON DE CYTHERE . . *Couperin*
LA CATHEDRALE ENGLOUTIE . . *Débussy*

IV

TOCCATA, G Major . . . . . . *Bach*
SONATA, No. XIII . . . . . *Scarlatti*
UNDINE . . . . *Ravel*
EL ALBAICIN . . . . *Albeniz*

V

MAGIC FIRE, *Die Walküre* . . *Wagner*
FINALE, *Tristan und Isolde* . . *Wagner*

THE PIANO IS AN ALBRECHT

Fig. 268. An attractive single-sheet program in Caslon Old Face. Periods
separated by em quads are here used as leaders

MENU

SOUP

CONSOMME ROYAL
SALTED CRACKERS

FISH

MOUNTAIN BROOK TROUT

OLIVES   LETTUCE   CELERY

BAKED BLUE FISH
GREEN CORN

BAKED SPANISH MACKEREL
BRUSSELS SPROUTS

ENTREES

ROAST SPRING LAMB
BAKED POTATOES

ROAST CANVAS-BACK DUCK

CRANBERRY SAUCE   CRAB APPLE JELLY

DESSERT

PINEAPPLE ICE CREAM
LADY FINGERS

COFFEE   TEA   CIGARS

Fig. 269. A typical arrangement for a menu page, showing the usual
grouping of the items in the bill-of-fare

type should be used, or at least, faces should be associated
that are harmonious in all respects. When a program and
menu appear together, the same general treatment should
be given both pages. Also, the typography of the title-page
should harmonize with that of the body pages.

Program of General Teachers' Meetings
ST. JOSEPH PUBLIC SCHOOLS

1924

September 6	Organization Meeting

September 27
    Address—"The Challenge"   Supt. C. A. Greene
                           Public Schools, St. Joseph, Mo.

October 25
    Address—"History of the Peace Treaty of
        Versailles"   .   .   Dr. R. J. Kerner
                        University of Missouri, Columbia

November 22
    Address   .   .   Pres. Uel W. Lamkin
                 State Teacher's College, Maryville, Mo.

December 13
    Address — "The Function of Literature in
        Education"   .   .   Dean I. N. Evrard
                 Missouri Valley College, Marshall, Mo.

1925

January 10
    Address — "Educational Policies and Out-
        look"   .   .   Supt. Charles A. Lee
                 State Supt. Schools, Jefferson City, Mo.

February 7
    Address—"The Romance of Teaching"
        .   .   .   .   Dr. John F. Caskey
             Pastor Francis Street M. E. Church, St. Joseph, Mo.

March 7
    Address—"Our Task"   Pres. H. C. Wayman
                 William Jewell College, Liberty, Mo.

April 4
    Address   .   .   Mr. Louis T. Golding
                 Editor, News-Press, St. Joseph, Mo.

Fig. 270. Program in Cloister Oldstyle, with suitable ornament and border

Synopsis of Acts

ACT I. Castle and grounds of Count Arnheim. Thaddeus rescues Arline from a wild deer. He refuses to drink to the Emperor, but is rescued by Gypsies, who steal Arline.

ACT II. (Twelve years later).
Scene 1. A side street in Presburg. Arline asleep. Florestein robbed.
Scene 2. Another side street in the City of Presburg. Daylight.
Scene 3. Fair scene in the Public Platz, in Presburg.

ACT III. Interior of Count's Apartments in Hall of Justice. Arline is recognized as his long lost child.

ACT IV. Salon in the Castle. Ball in Arline's honor. Queen is frustated.

All ends happily

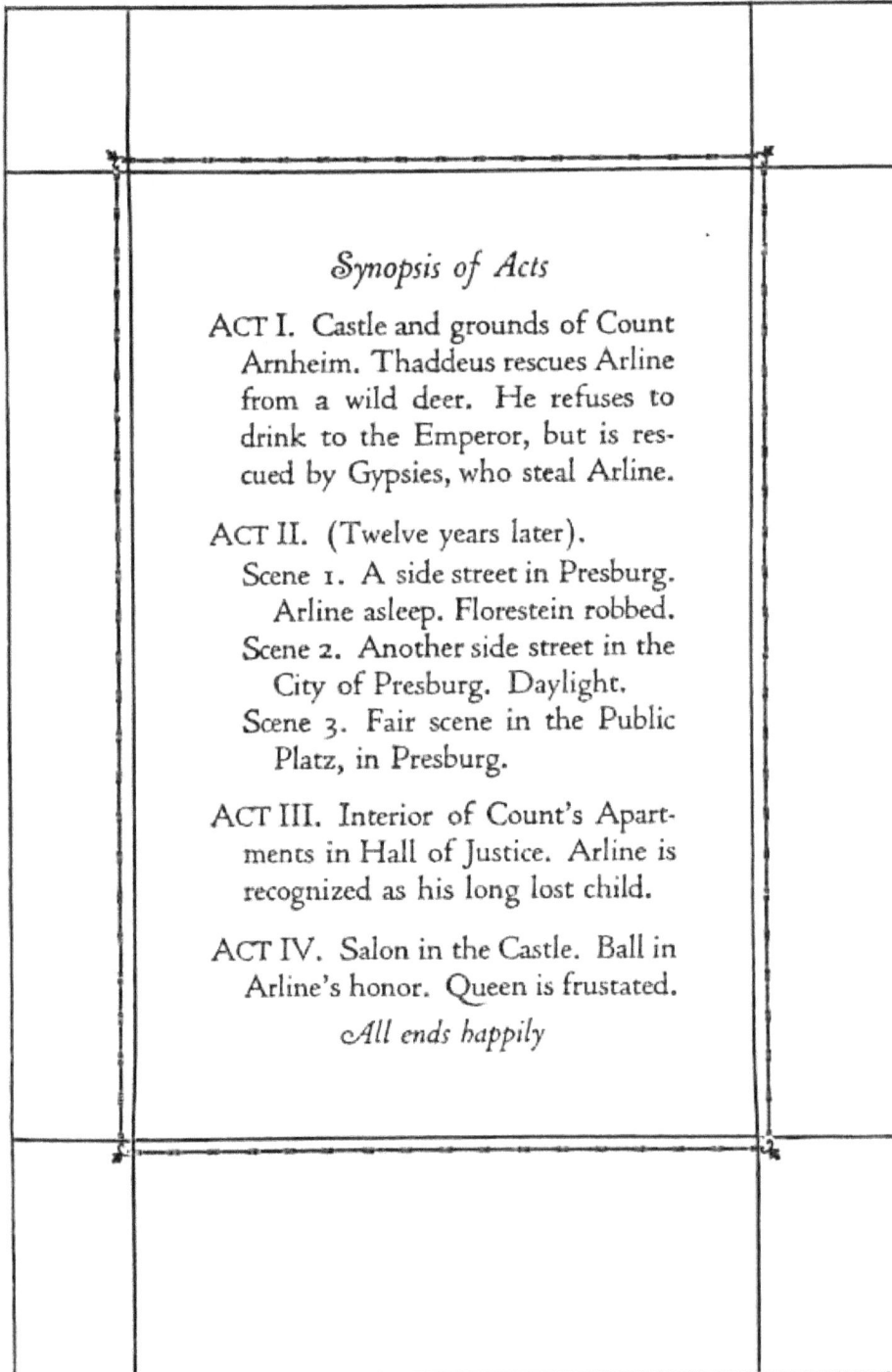

Fig. 271. Page of an informal program, with balanced page margins

MUSICALE

NEUVILLE ACADEMY

SATURDAY EVENING
OCTOBER THE TWENTY-THIRD
MCMXXVI

HUNTINGTON PARK

NEW YORK

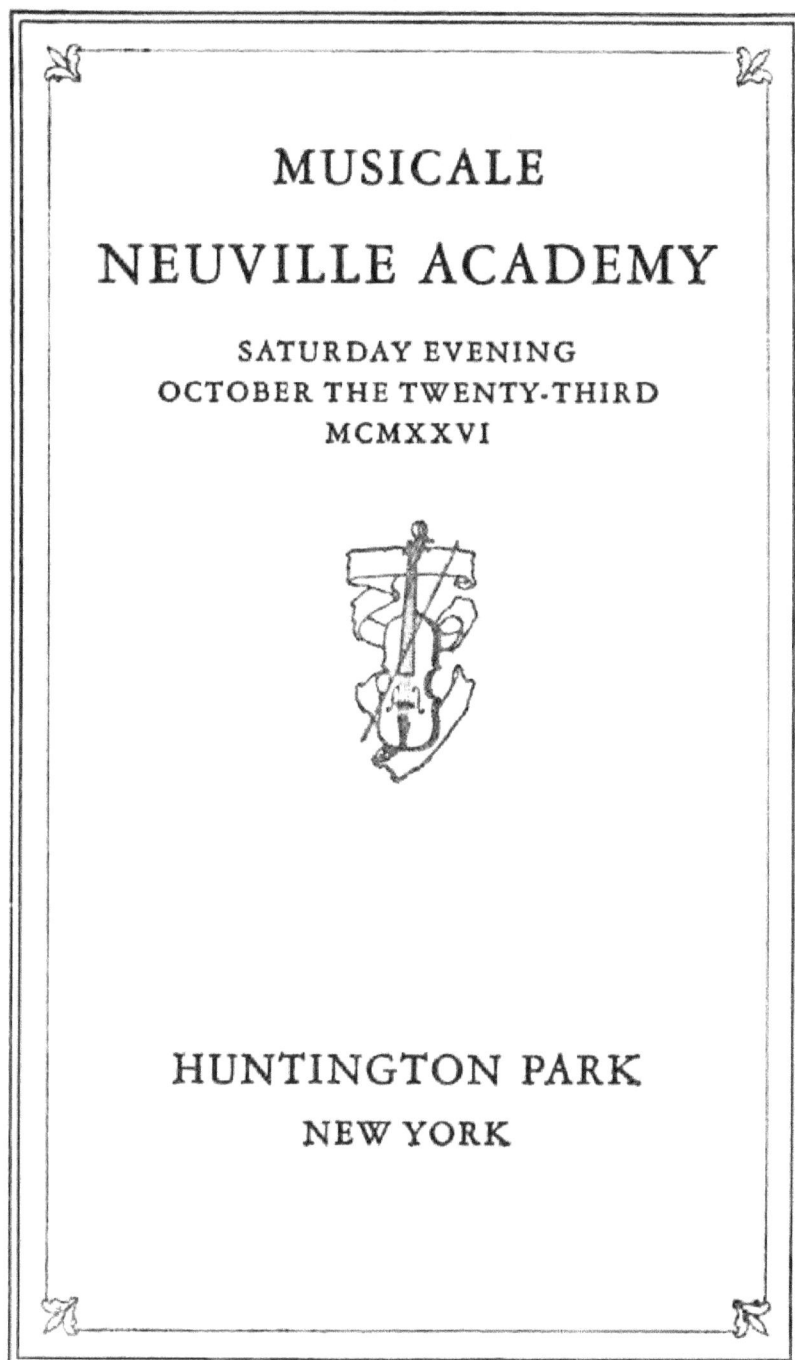

Fig. 272. Initial page of a four-page folder, with appropriate treatment

PROGRAMME

MISS EMILY BOARDMAN	Violin
MR. WILLIAM PORTER CHANDLER	Baritone
MRS. WHITNEY PARKMAN	Piano

1. Berceuse, Op. 41   Chopin
   MRS. PARKMAN

2. Le Rêve du Prisonnier   Rubinstein
   MR. CHANDLER

3. a. Concerto, G Minor   Bach
   b. Barcarolle, Op. 62   Saint-Saëns
   MISS BOARDMAN

4. La Vierge à la Crèche   Perilhon
   MR. CHANDLER

5. a. Waltz, F Sharp, Op. 52   Schubert
   b. Nocturne, Op. 12   Chopin
   MRS. PARKMAN

6. Minuet, Op. 22   Gluck
   MISS BOARDMAN

Miss Natalie Ridgeway accompanying

Fig. 273. Program page designed in harmony with the initial page

284. Ornamentation of programs. A reasonable amount of decoration may be introduced into most program forms. Well-chosen ornaments, such as harps or lyres on musical programs, candles or torches on educational programs, or crosses or mural ornaments on religious programs, often add to the attractiveness and charm of the job. Whether a form shall be severely plain and formal; enlivened by a slight touch of ornamentation; or shall appear as a rather decorative design, must depend upon the character of the program or event for which it is to be printed.

285. Choice of types. Naturally, the choice of type for a program will be based on the consideration of fitness. A light, dainty letter—such as Garamond, Drew, Sterling, or Della Robbia—may be used with propriety when representing an event of a light, airy nature; more sober and formal letters—such as the Caslons, Bodoni, Bookman, Venetian, or Scotch Roman—will be suitable for programs in which dignity, culture, or education are to be emphasized.

Programs for church services, or other religious occasions, are frequently printed in some form of Text-letter, or in a combination of Text with some harmonious oldstyle Roman or Italic. If Text type alone seems too heavy, such a combination as Caslon Text or Cloister Black with Caslon Oldstyle or its Italic, is a good, appropriate substitute.

Some programs are set entirely in upper- and lower-case Roman, others in Roman and Italic, and sometimes small capitals are also used. Various combinations are seen in the programs that are reproduced in this chapter.

286. Use of leaders. In programs set in rather narrow measure, as in Fig. 273, in which there is comparatively little white space, the leaders are often omitted. However, most programs carry leaders, either in the form of regular hyphen leaders, or lines of periods separated by quads, and in accurate alignment vertically throughout the form.

CHAPTER XXXVII

Cover-Pages and Title-Pages

IF THE fundamental principles of display have been mastered, the student should have very little difficulty with the composition of cover-pages and title-pages, as there are very few additional rules to be given for this class of work.

The cover-page is the outside page on the front cover of a book, catalog, or pamphlet. It usually contains the title and author of the work, if a book, or a very brief statement labeling the contents, if a catalog or a similar publication. The cover-page copy is, in fact, the label of the book, brief and clear, readily seen and instantly read. The title-page, on the other hand, is the introductory page of the body of the book, which contains the title, author, publisher, and any other necessary information about the book or author. Nearly all books have both a cover-page and title-page, but some small booklets combine the elements of both into one form, to conserve space, so that one initial page preceding the body pages serves in the double capacity.

COVER-PAGES

287. **Cover-page designs** are perhaps the least restricted of any kind of commercial printing. There are practically no rules to govern the details. Judgment and good taste must guide the printer in working out each problem.

The cover, in its style, should reflect something of the spirit of the book, and should invite the prospective reader to become acquainted with its contents. It should have a subtle power of attraction that will help get the book read.

The design, or treatment of the copy, should always be appropriate to the subject matter. A book treating a very

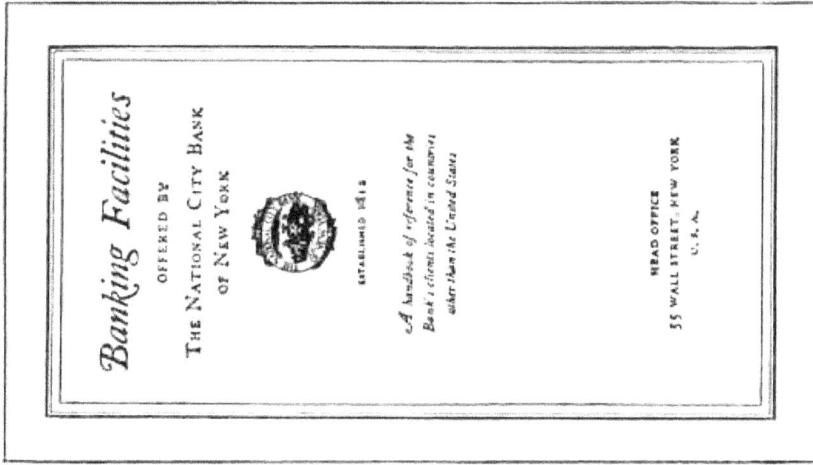

Fig. 275. A neat title-page in Caslon Oldstyle Italic.
Both designs are by David J. Gildea

Fig. 274. A title-page in Caslon. Interest is added
by use of Italics, and the pictorial spot

formal, classical, or dignified subject should have a simple, sober, formal treatment of its cover. Elaborate ornament or design would be out of place on such a book. A pamphlet on recreation, or travel, or a book containing matter in a comparatively light vein, may receive a freer and more elaborate treatment of its cover-page material.

Some designs cover the entire front page, while others confine the complete design to a small portion of the page. When the design is particularly small in comparison with the page, the out-of-center balance is often pleasing.

288. **Cover stock to be considered.** The material used for the cover of the book will affect the character of the cover design. Colored covers require bolder types than do white or lightly tinted ones. Whether the stock is rough or smooth also affects the problem, as the type used must harmonize with the paper. Types with fine lines, or quite small or light-faced letters, will not appear well on rough stock, and will also be subjected to undue wear.

TITLE-PAGES

289. **The colophon.** Early manuscript books contained no title-pages. Making books was a very laborious process, paper was expensive, and no space was given to "extras." The first printers added a small paragraph after the body of the book, telling the circumstances of the printing. This was called the colophon.* Later, the colophon was sometimes arranged in verse, and even displayed in open form. As book printing became further developed, the items that were ordinarily listed in the colophon were brought to the front of the book and displayed on the first page, thereby forming what is known as the title-page of the book.

* The colophon of an edition of *Xenophon*, published in 1511, when translated from its Latin text, reads as follows: "Here endeth the book. In the year of our Lord 1511 and on the second day of September. Printed at the expense of the worthy Bartholomew Trot." Many of these colophons bore the name of the printer, and other details, and some even contained compliments to the printer, or quotations from the Scriptures.

290. **Typography of title-pages.** Title-pages are somewhat more formal than the cover-pages, and they follow a recognized order for the arrangement of the matter. The details of design may vary greatly, in accordance with the nature of the book, and its general typographic style.

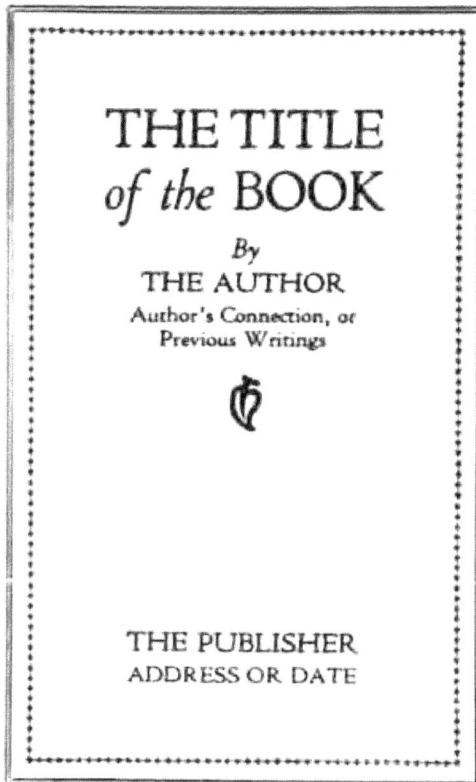

THE TITLE
of the BOOK

By
THE AUTHOR
Author's Connection, or
Previous Writings

THE PUBLISHER
ADDRESS OR DATE

Fig. 276

The customary arrangement of the matter on the title-page is shown in the accompanying figure.

Naturally, the name or title of the book should be given leading prominence at the head of the page. The name of the author is usually the next item in importance, and it will be displayed accordingly. The name of the publisher is placed at the bottom of the page, with the date of publication, or address, or both. If additional items are to appear on the page, they will be subordinated to these main features, in the interest of clearness.

There should be a harmony of type style and of general treatment between the title-page and the other pages of the book. Harmony of tone and shape should be carefully considered in the planning of the title-page.

A few representative title-page designs are reproduced on the following pages. They show a variety of treatments, each appropriate to its subject, and a careful study of these designs will aid the student in his planning of title-pages.

TWELFTH

ANNUAL REPORT

OF THE BOARD OF DIRECTORS OF
THE SEDALIA PUBLIC LIBRARY
FOR THE FISCAL YEAR
ENDING APRIL 30

1926

SEDALIA, MISSOURI

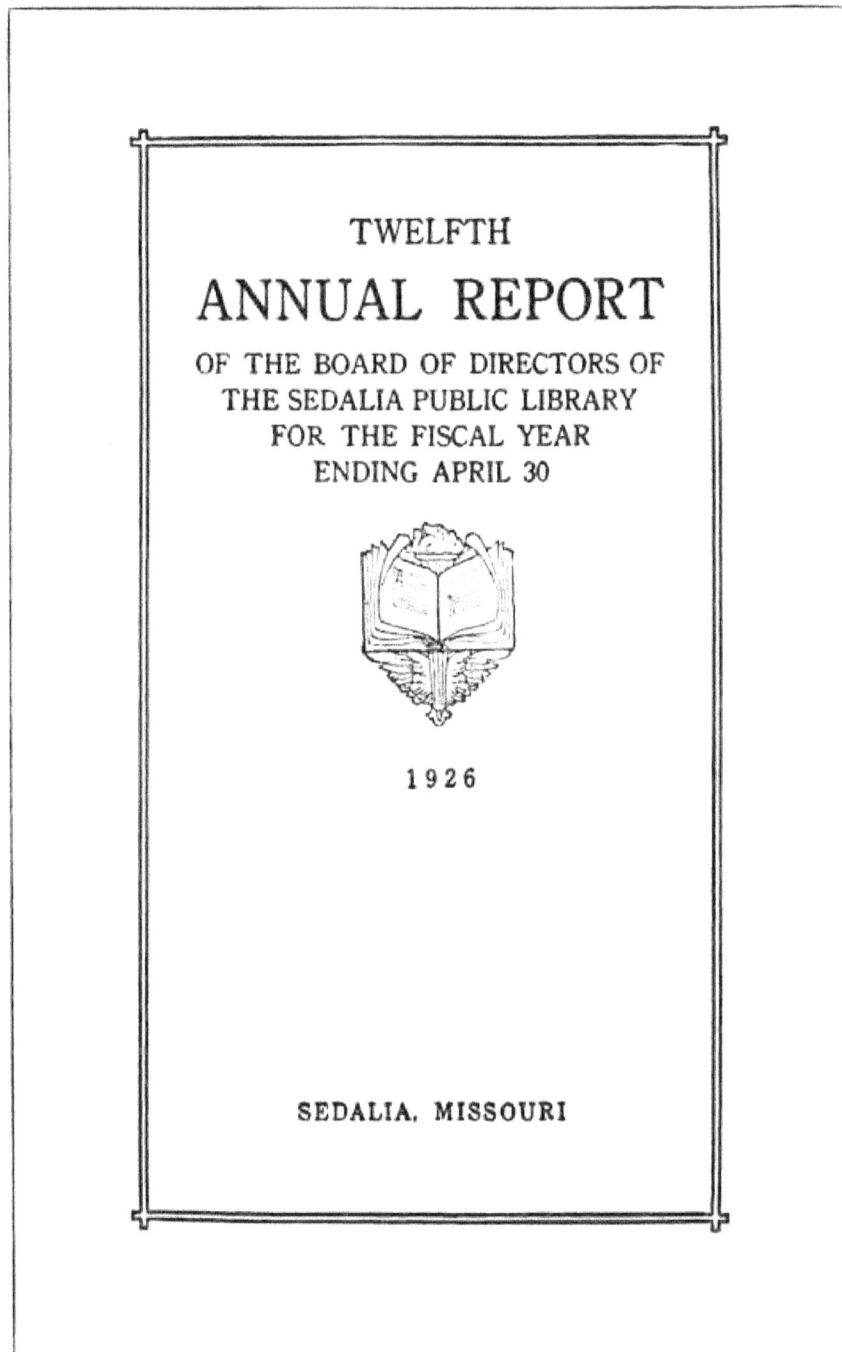

Fig. 277. A very interesting title-page design, set entirely in Century Oldstyle capitals.
Ornament was printed in second color. Design by D. B. James

Deckle d'Aigle

A NEW FOUR DECKLE EDGED BOOK
PAPER *and* OVERLAPPING COVER

*A Brochure Showing
Various Styles of Printed Engravings
and Type Work Offering
Irresistible Evidence*

AMERICAN WRITING PAPER COMPANY
HOLYOKE, MASSACHUSETTS

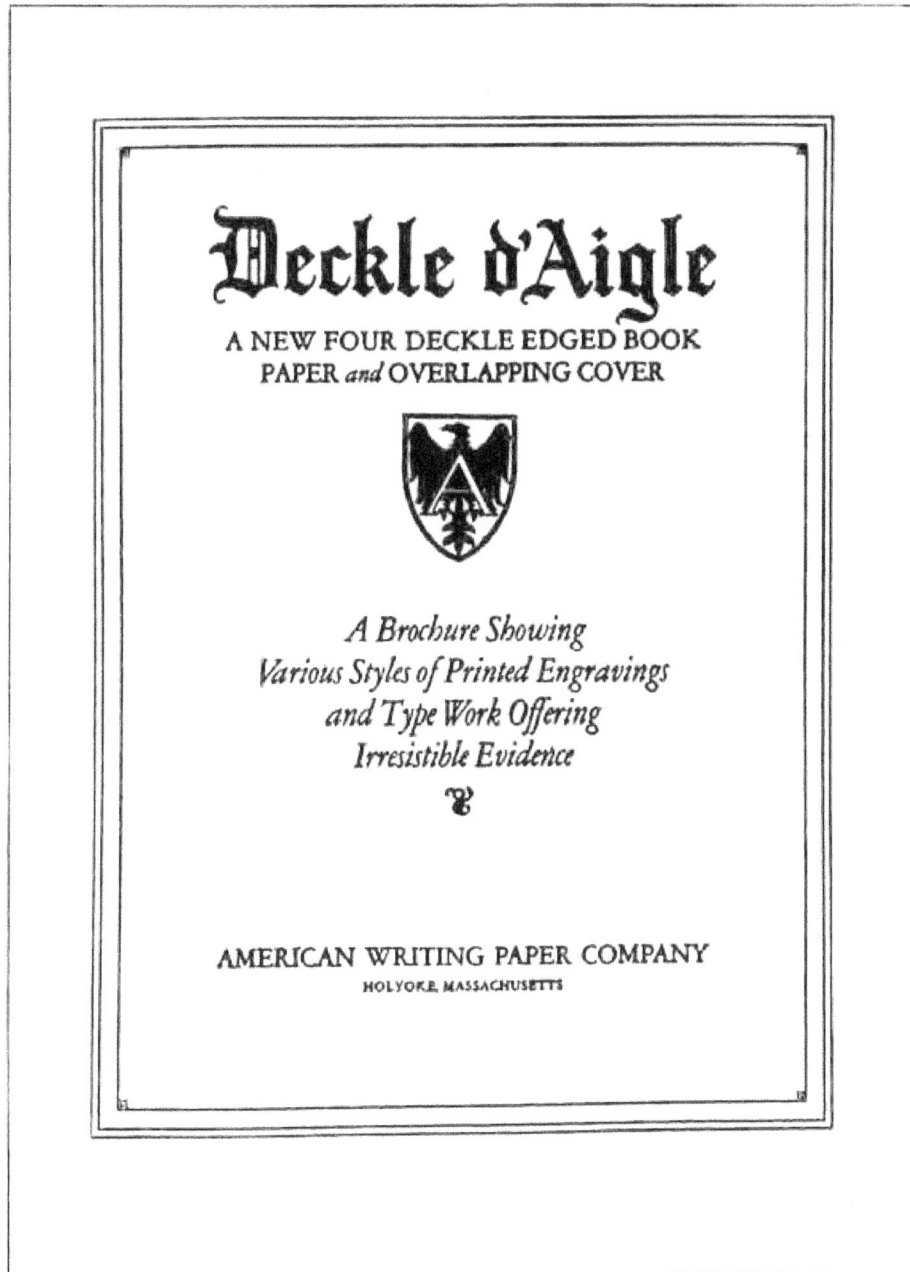

Fig. 278. A title-page design especially suitable for printing on antique paper. Note the
use of text-letter in the heading, for emphasis and added interest

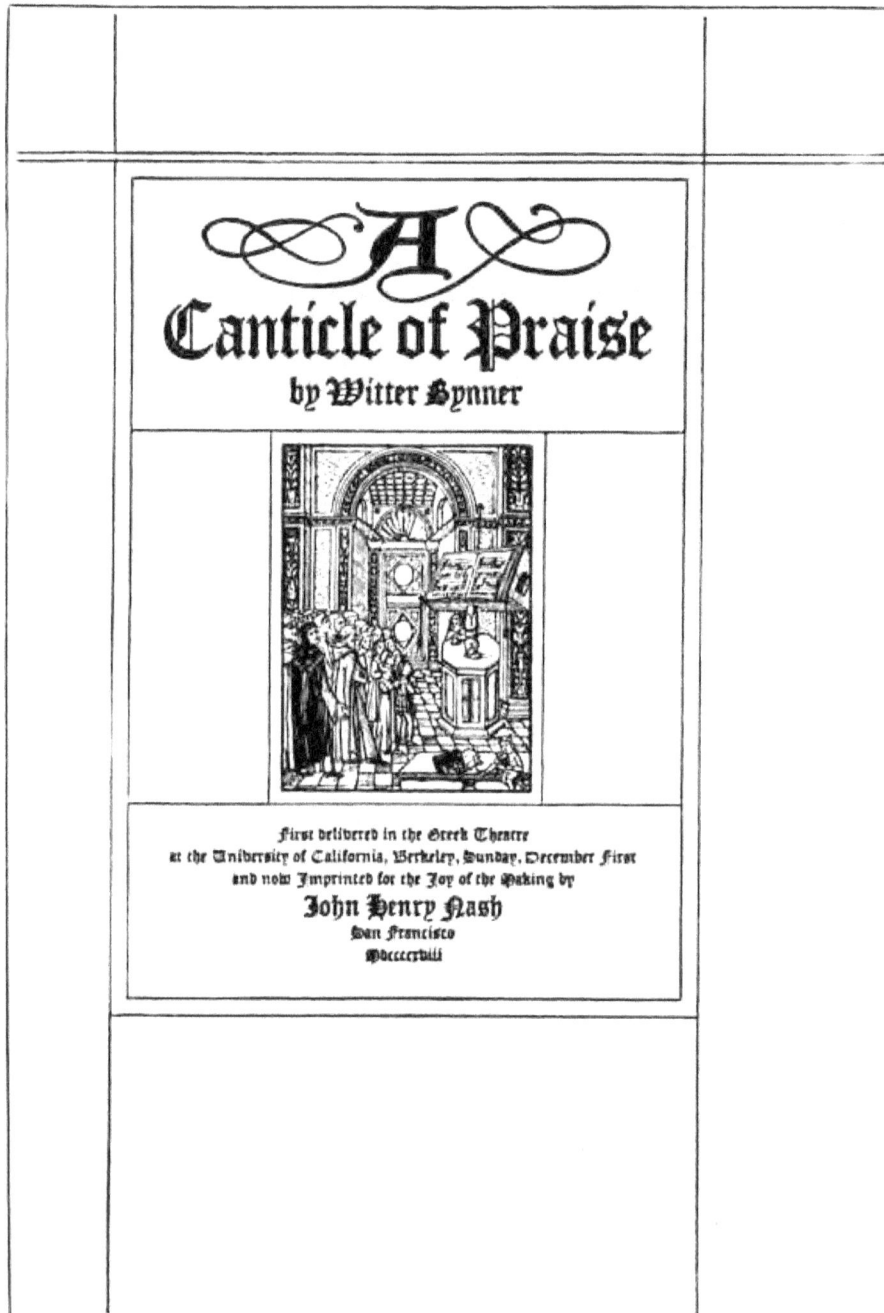

Fig. 279. Title-page in the style of the early ecclesiastical books. In the original
the rules were printed in orange-red

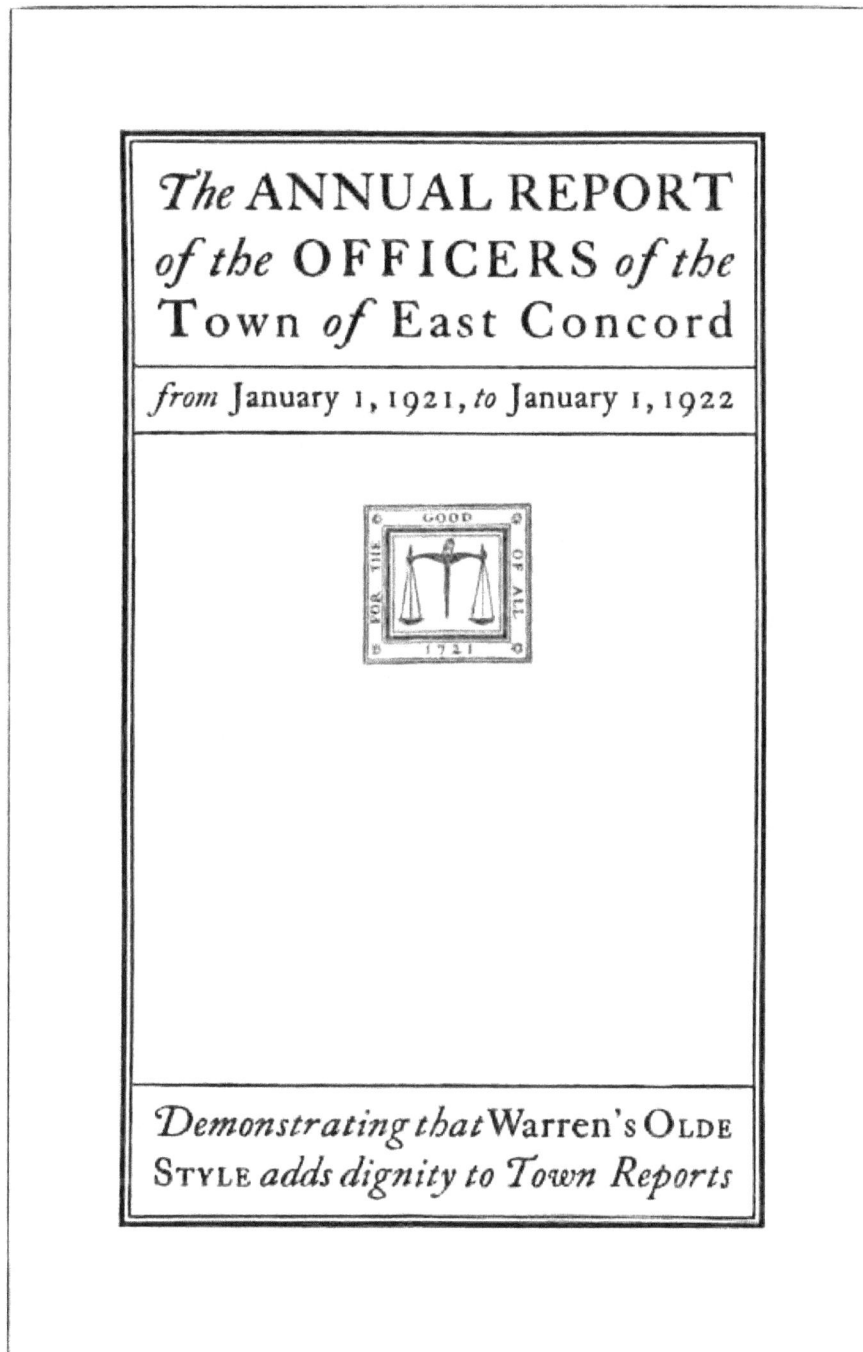

The ANNUAL REPORT
of the OFFICERS *of the*
Town *of* East Concord

from January 1, 1921, *to* January 1, 1922

Demonstrating that Warren's OLDE
STYLE *adds dignity to* Town Reports

Fig. 280. Panels and squared groups in a title-page design. Where the copy gracefully fits into
such a scheme, it is pleasing, but the arrangement must not appear forced or strained

CHAPTER XXXVIII

The Composition of Books

MUCH of the typographical instruction that has been given in preceding chapters applies with equal weight to the composition of books, catalogs, and pamphlets. It will not be repeated here, but some of the special considerations in book composition will be briefly treated in this chapter.

291. Order of the contents. In the regular bookwork, there is a recognized order for the various divisions of a book. The ordinary book will contain at least a title-page, copyright page, the table of contents, the text, or body of the book, and the index, in the order named. In addition, a half-title, dedication, preface, introduction, or list of illustrations may be included before the text matter, and a glossary, or appendix, or both, may follow it. The proper order for contents appears in Fig. 281.

Proper Order for the Contents of a Book

Front fly-leaf, blank
Half-Title
Title-Page, backed
 by Copyright Page
Dedication
Preface
Table of Contents
List of Illustrations
Introduction
Text, or Body of the
 Book
Appendix
Glossary
Index

Fig. 281

All of these features except the copyright notice should be printed, or started, on a right-hand page. Chapter headings that come within the text will take either right-hand or left-hand pages, as they chance to fall, in the make-up.

The half-title is the first printed page of the book, containing only the name, or title. If the title is short, it will appear in a single line, but if it contains a number of words, they may be grouped, to satisfy shape harmony. The type used should harmonize with the style of the title-page. It should be balanced on the page, and therefore the group will be located slightly above the center of the page. The half-title is always followed by a blank page.

The notice of copyright is placed at the balance of the page immediately following the title-page, and it is set in small type. The imprint of the printer, or a statement that the book was printed in the United States, usually appears in small type at the bottom of this page.

If a dedication is included, it occupies the first right-hand page following the title-page. The copy should be set in the same series as the text, but the style will depend on the nature of the copy, and the idea of the author.

The preface, as well as the introduction, varies in length, sometimes covering only a portion of a page, and sometimes covering several pages. It is usually set in the same style as the text. If very short, it may be in a size larger than the text, but if it is rather lengthy, it is sometimes set in a size of type smaller than that used in the text.

The contents, the list of illustrations, and the index are usually set in type a size smaller than that of the text.

292. **Page numbers** of a book are designated as folios. Roman numerals (xviii or XVIII) are used to number the pages of the divisions preceding the text, and the Arabic numerals (18) are used for the text and following divisions. The numbering of the preliminary pages begins with the half-title, and the numbering of the body of the book begins with the first page of the regular text matter.

Usually the folios appear at the outer ends of the lines containing the running-heads, but in some books they are centered just below the last line of the page. On pages containing chapter headings, running-heads are not used, and folios are omitted, or brought to the foot of the page.

293. **Running-heads** are used in practically all books, and on many of the smaller booklets, and they add interest and variation to the otherwise plain body style of the pages. Ordinarily, they consist of lines of type of the same face as

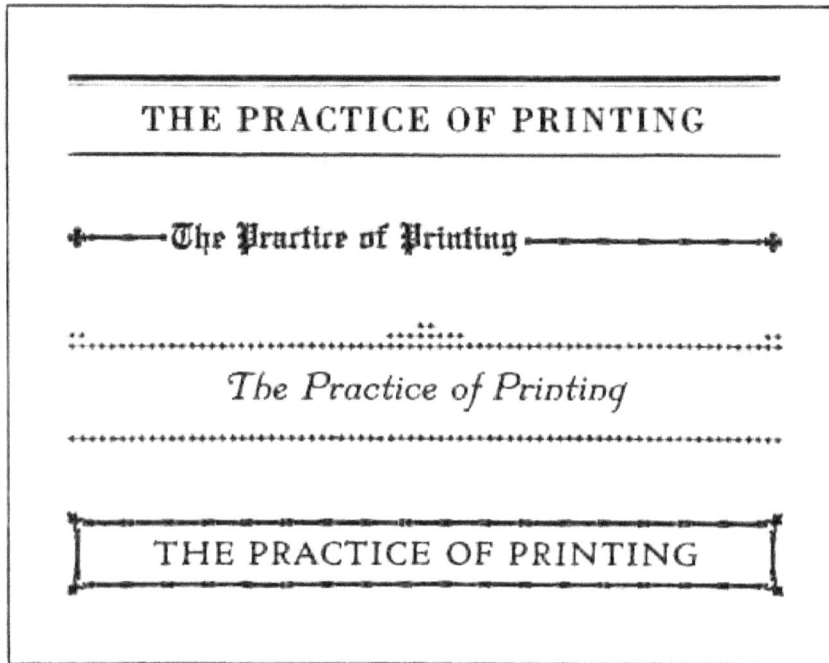

Fig. 282. A few decorative running-heads

that of the text, with or without an underlining rule of the proper tone. In booklets of an informal nature, a touch of decoration may be given the page by means of a pleasingly designed running-head. Some examples are shown above.

If the running-head is used, it must be in a style fitting the nature of the work, and there must be a harmony between title-page, running-head, and body matter. In some books, a line of capitals of the same face as the text, but a size or so smaller, is used. A line of Italic the same size as the body type, or a size larger, is also appropriate. Lower-case Roman letters are very seldom for running-heads, but if used, they should be somewhat larger than the text.

For booklet work in which informal effects are desired, the decorative running-head is appropriate. A wide variety of designs may be worked out, but one must always give due consideration to appropriateness, and tone harmony.

Some of the more formal styles of running-heads are used at the heads of the pages throughout this chapter.

294. **Sizes of books.** The terms quarto, octavo, etc., as applied to the sizes of books, are now rather confusing, and indefinite. Book sizes were originally determined by the number of folds given the full sheets, or "signatures," of which the book was made up. The size of the sheets was about 18x24 inches. Thus, a sheet folded once made four pages about 12x18 inches in size, and was called a folio. A sheet folded twice made eight pages about 9x12. This was called a quarto (4to). An octavo (8vo) was a sheet folded three times, making sixteen pages 6x9 inches.

In modern book terms, this textbook would be known as a duodecimo (12mo), a designation originally given to books made up of signatures containing twelve leaves, or twenty-four pages, each. The term, as now applied, refers to the size of the page rather than to the manner of printing. A few of the standard sizes of books are as follows:

Folio............12 x19 inches	Medium 12mo.... 5¼x7⅞ inches
Quarto..........9½x12 inches	Medium 16mo......4½x6¼ inches
Medium Octavo..6 x 9½ inches	Super Royal 32mo..3¼x5½ inches

295. **Proportions of margins and text.** It is generally considered that the most pleasing proportion of white space and type matter on a book page is had when the area that is covered by the type form is equal to one-half of the total area of the page, or in other words, when the type and the margins each occupy an equal amount of space. This rule cannot be rigidly adhered to in all cases, however.

When the margins are too wide, the text will lose somewhat in prominence, and practicality; such an arrangement

58. Simple type-assembling exercises. Do not attempt to set any finished work at first. Begin with single words, placing them in the stick in the correct manner, reading them in the stick, and then replacing the type into the correct boxes. By this method, you will become accustomed to the proper procedure of typesetting, and will then be ready for actual work.

```
111  111  111
1111  Illinois St.
OO  ooo  OOO
Oh,  look,  7000
222 555 666 999
25   62   59   96
iii  111  jjj
```

Among other exercises, set up the characters appearing in Fig. 44, one line at a time, and replace them after you have carefully examined and compared the letters. Follow this by setting up your name, address, and other items that may be of interest, but do not fill in more than a line at a time, and do not attempt to obtain a print from these first few exercises.

JUSTIFICATION AND SPACING

59. Justification of lines. Justification is the practice of spacing out lines of type so that each line will be firm in the stick, and all lines will be set to exactly the same width. Each line must be spaced in such a way that it will be snug and firm, but not too tight. There must be no "play" in the line, yet it should not be difficult to remove any individual letter from the line as it stands in the stick.

If a line is too loose, types may drop out of the form, either when the type is taken from the stick or the galley, or even after the form is locked for the press. Also, the letters may lean slightly toward one end of the line, so that the types will not strike the sheet squarely, causing only one side of the faces to print, after the form has been placed on the press. This is known as the type being "off its feet."

If a line is too tight, it may spring the composing stick, throwing other lines out of true justification. If it reaches the stone without readjustment, it will seriously interfere with the locking up of the form. Also, when types are forced into the stick, they are apt to become bent or broken in the process.

The art of accurate justification is one of the most necessary accomplishments of a compositor. The beginner should especially strive to learn and practice it in the most thorough manner. The proper measure of success in all one's future work in typography depends on the ability to justify lines of type accurately, and no one should slight this important phase of the work.

60. Justifying work in uneven lines. Let your first work in composition consist of exercises in using uniform spaces between each of the words in the lines, placing the justification at the ends of the lines. This method is indicated in Fig. 45, above, in which type-high spacing has been used.

Use 3-em spaces between words, and an em quad between sentences. Space out all the lines with quads and spaces, always putting all the largest pieces to the outside, and the thinner spaces next to the type, as has been done in this illustration. Be sure that each of the lines is justified *perfectly* before you leave it, regardless of the amount of effort, or time, that seems necessary to accomplish it.

As a project in this simpler style of composition, set up the exercise given in Fig. 46. Set it line for line as it now appears, placing all the extra spacing at the ends of the lines. If you use 8 point type, set your stick 18 picas wide; if 10 point, set it to 20 picas; if 12 point, set it to 23 picas.

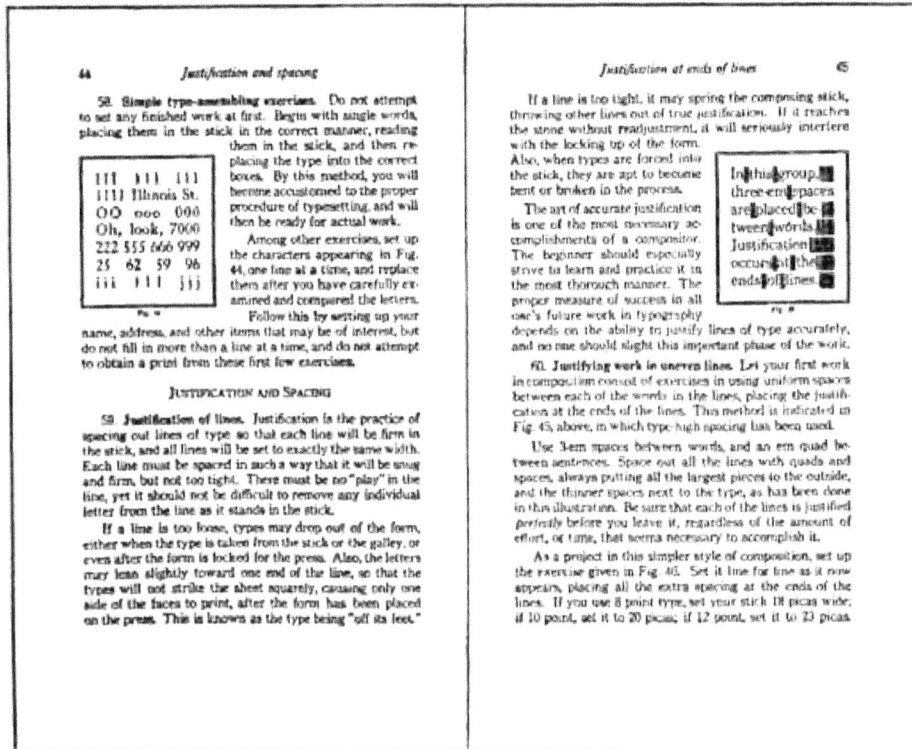

Fig. 283. Pages in which the areas of text and margins are in equal proportion, and the margins are balanced each way in the proportion of 2 to 3

also gives a sense of waste. On the other hand, if scanty margins are allowed, it will give a crowded effect, and the text will appear rather scattered, or disconnected. Properly spaced pages are more pleasing, and also more legible.

296. **Balanced page margins.** In cases in which it is necessary to have rather narrow margins, the form should be placed almost in the center of the page, but inclined a little toward the inner margin and the top of the page. If wider margins may be planned, there should be a more noticeable variation in them. No hard-and-fast rule can be given for margins that will fit all cases, but a pleasing effect is secured when the inside and the head page margins are noticeably narrower than the outside and the foot margins. The proportion of two to three each way is frequently followed in planning page margins, as illustrated above.

297. **Details that mar the page.** A number of details in the general make-up of the page must be properly arranged in order to make a pleasing and effective page. Some of the common defects that are to be avoided are illustrated on the opposite page. Each of these is numbered, and the numbers coincide with the following numbered paragraphs.

1. The last line of a paragraph should not be carried over, alone, to the top of a new page, as it breaks up the even contour of the page form, and disturbs the unity of the paragraph. This line either should be retained on the preceding page (by shrinking the spacing), or another line should be carried over with it to the top of the page.

2. The first line of a paragraph should not stand alone at the bottom of the page. The next line should be retained with it, or the entire paragraph should be carried over.

3. A word should not be divided at the close of a page, as it is unsightly, and confusing to the reader.

4. The last word of a paragraph should not be divided onto a new line, where it can be avoided by respacing.

5. When the last line of a paragraph comes within less than an em of the full measure, it should be spaced out to full width to avoid the ragged effect thus made.

6. When illustrations are inserted into the text, there should be uniform margins between the cut and the type, on the three sides. As a rule, about a pica is allowed, but this depends upon the nature of the illustration, and the general style of the page. To insure equal margins, and a consistent grouping of the matter, it is a common practice to have at least two full lines of the paragraph just above the cut, and at least two full lines immediately below it.

7. Not only should divided words not appear at the ends of a number of contiguous lines, but various punctuation marks should not appear too frequently along the margin, as they break up the neat, even contour of the type group.

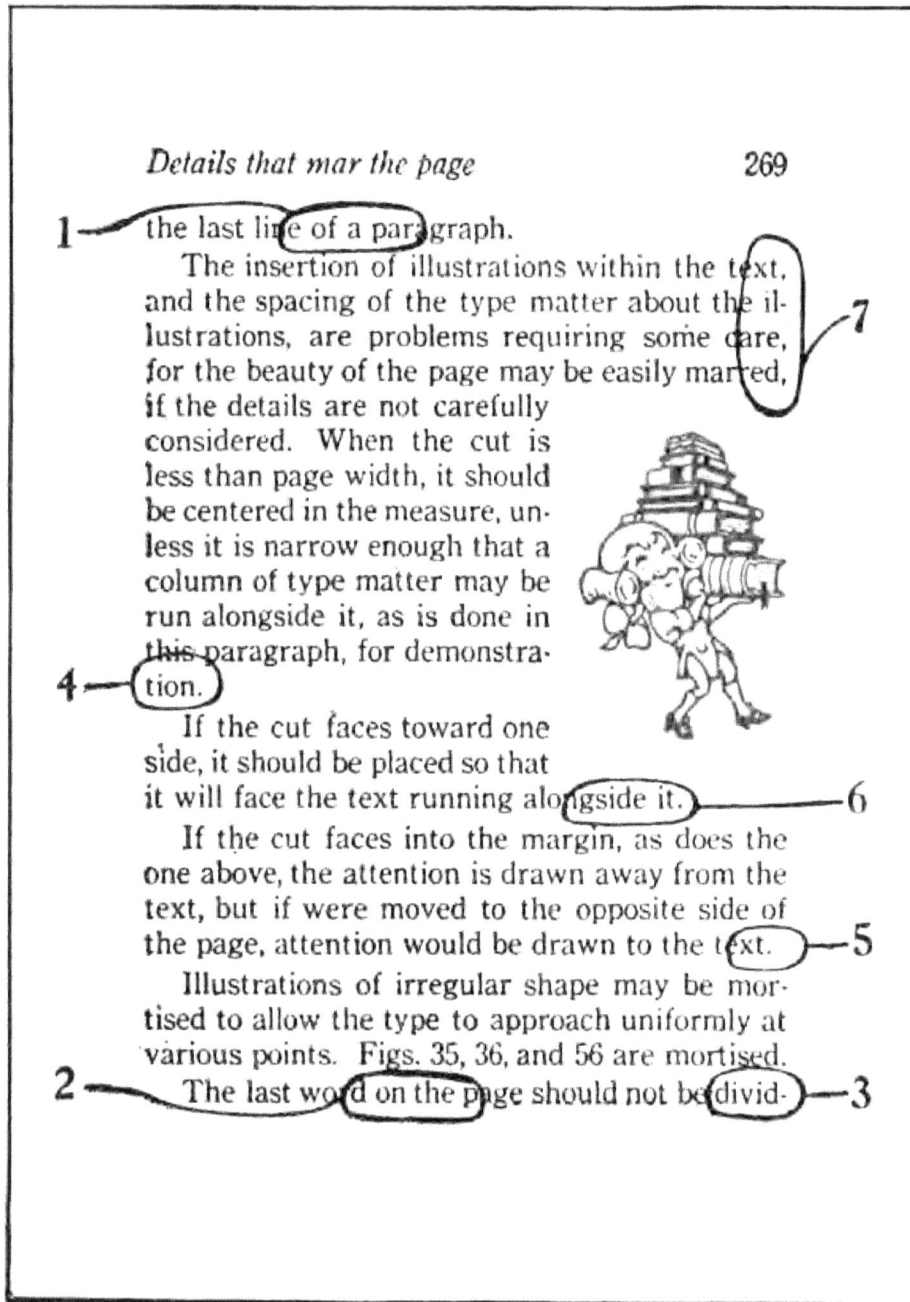

Details that mar the page 269

1 — the last line of a paragraph.

The insertion of illustrations within the text, and the spacing of the type matter about the illustrations, are problems requiring some care, 7 for the beauty of the page may be easily marred, if the details are not carefully considered. When the cut is less than page width, it should be centered in the measure, unless it is narrow enough that a column of type matter may be run alongside it, as is done in this paragraph, for demonstra-
4 — tion.

If the cut faces toward one side, it should be placed so that it will face the text running alongside it. — 6

If the cut faces into the margin, as does the one above, the attention is drawn away from the text, but if were moved to the opposite side of the page, attention would be drawn to the text. — 5

Illustrations of irregular shape may be mortised to allow the type to approach uniformly at various points. Figs. 35, 36, and 56 are mortised.
2 — The last word on the page should not be divid- — 3

Fig. 284

298. Placing of illustrations. When illustrations appear on the pages, they should be placed where they will secure a proper balance in the double-page spread. Usually, one illustration on a double page will be located slightly above the center, and next to an inner margin; two illustrations will appear opposite each other, each next to an outer margin; a third one will be located below the first two, and against an inner margin. A study of the locations of the illustrations in this text, or in any good book, will give the student an idea of the common practice in this matter.

Whenever possible, it is advisable to set the cut into the body of the composition, and to run a column of the text alongside it. If the cut is too wide for this, it should then be centered in the measure, and placed at the balance of the page. If the illustration is of square finish, and the same width as the text, it may be placed at the head of the page, but irregular shapes at the head or foot of the page interfere with the regular contour of the page form, and thereby create an unfinished and displeasing appearance.

Illustrations which face toward either side of the page should be placed so that they will face the matter running alongside. If they should face the margins, attention would be drawn from the text, destroying the unity of the page.

299. **Choice of paper.** In the selection of paper stock for a book or catalog, the character of the type and cuts to be used, should be considered. Type faces with hair-lines do not print to best advantage either on enameled stock, or on extremely rough paper. The extent of handling to which the book will be subjected is also to be considered. If fine half-tones are to be used, smooth coated paper is necessary, but if type only, or type and line engravings, are to be used, a dull, soft-finish stock is more suitable in most cases, as it is much easier on the eye. White is preferable for books and catalogs, unless some particular tint of stock gives an added significance and interest to an individual job.

300. **Calculating the space to be covered.** For purposes of estimating the probable amount of space that might be covered by a given amount of copy, a standard table giving

the average number of words per square inch is used. This table appears in Fig. 285. While it cannot be accepted as an accurate guide, it assists the printer in making general estimates. The figures are for matter set solid, and leaded.

Square Inches	6 pt. Solid	6 pt. Leaded	8 pt. Solid	8 pt. Leaded	10 pt. Solid	10 pt. Leaded	12 pt. Solid	12 pt. Leaded
1	47	34	32	23	21	16	14	11
2	94	68	64	46	42	32	28	22
4	188	136	128	92	84	64	56	44
8	376	272	256	184	168	128	112	88
12	564	408	384	276	252	192	168	132
16	752	544	512	368	336	256	224	176
20	940	680	640	460	420	320	280	220
24	1128	816	768	552	504	384	336	264
32	1504	1088	1024	736	672	512	448	352

Fig. 285. Table of words per square inch

301. **Informal booklets.** There are no set standards for the typography of catalogs and informal booklets. Much is left to the technical skill and good taste of the printer, and each must be made an individual problem. If the principles of good typography are consistently followed in the planning of the details, results are usually successful.

For the guidance of the student, a few representative styles in informal booklets are reproduced on the following pages. Title-pages and text pages are shown in each case.

SUGGESTIONS

For further instruction in book composition, the most detailed, and most authoritative, work is THE PRACTICE OF TYPOGRAPHY SERIES, four very excellent volumes by the late Theodore L. DeVinne, published by the Oswald Publishing Company. The titles are *Plain Printing Types, Correct Composition, Modern Methods in Book Composition,* and *Title-Pages.* While these all deal with body and book composition, the last two are especially rich in details of book construction that will be valuable in this connection.

HIGH SPOTS

Best Selling Arguments Covering Our Products

SOME time previous to the meeting of the Sales Force of the Miller Saw-Trimmer Company held in Pittsburgh, January 30 and 31, 1918, each of our representatives was requested to submit a letter covering the five best selling points of both the Miller Saw-Trimmer and The Miller Automatic Platen Press Feeder. The replies covered a wide range of thought and brought out some splendid suggestions which, we believe, offer new angles of approach to all the members of our selling force.

AT THE convention, copies of a number of the best of these letters were submitted to the salesmen in attendance with the request that each man vote for the best letter in each group. As a result of this vote, Letter No. 1 on the Miller Feeder, written by Mr. John Farnsworth, and Letter No. 10, on the Miller Saw-Trimmer, written

Fig. 287. Initial text page in harmony with title

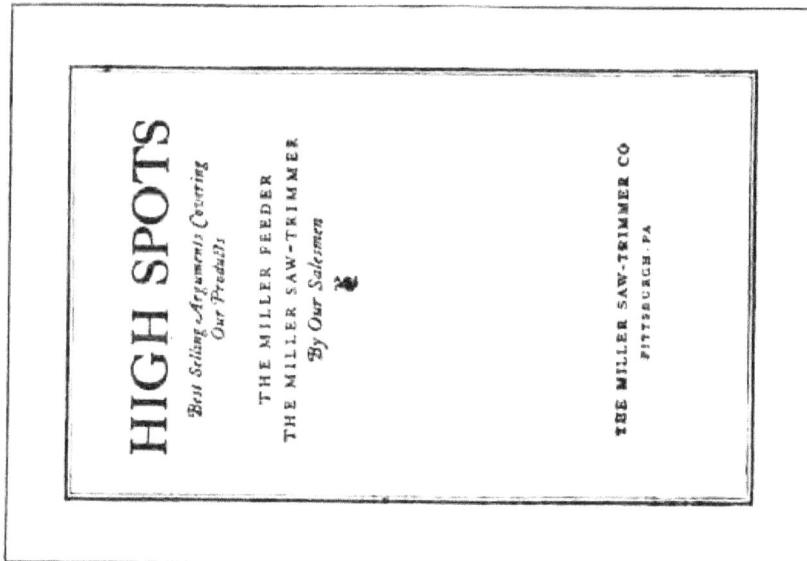

HIGH SPOTS

Best Selling Arguments Covering Our Products

THE MILLER FEEDER
THE MILLER SAW-TRIMMER

By Our Salesmen

THE MILLER SAW-TRIMMER CO

PITTSBURGH, PA

Fig. 286. Title-page of an attractive booklet

Fig. 289. The shaded portions indicate second color

Fig. 288. Title-page a notable printer's house organ

274

THE HISTORY OF LETTERS

A Short Sketch of the Successive Stages
in the Making of an Alphabet.

T WOULD be a mistake to even suppose that a system of graphic intercourse was man's possession at the beginning of the world. It is probable man has lived longer without such a system than he has with it. We have many evidences that the race was old when the art of writing was first acquired. Great nations were developed, flourished, and passed away; monarchs ruled in splendor; cities were built, and a high degree of culture existed during this ancient time. Long before the world had any means of recording literary writings, long poems were composed and recited through successive generations. The Greek poet, Homer, produced his renowned history of Troy in this early age, and thus great work

[3]

Fig. 291. Cloister ornaments and initials match the type

The HISTORY of LETTERS

Second Edition

A STORY OF ALPHABETS
by RALPH W. POLK

Fig. 290. Booklet in the Cloister Oldstyle series

The Subject of.

CHRISTMAS

By LEIGH HUNT

So many things have been said
of late years about CHRISTMAS
that it is supposed by some there
is no saying more. Oh, they of

Fig. 253. Initial page of text, in pleasing harmony

THE

Subject of

Christmas

BY

LEIGH HUNT

OAKLAND:

The Kennedy Company

MCMXII

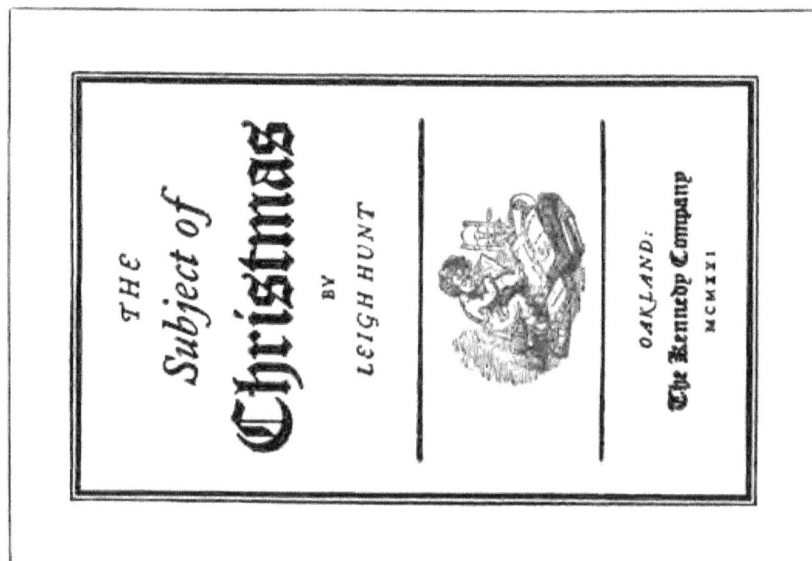

Fig. 252. Booklet set in the style of early typography

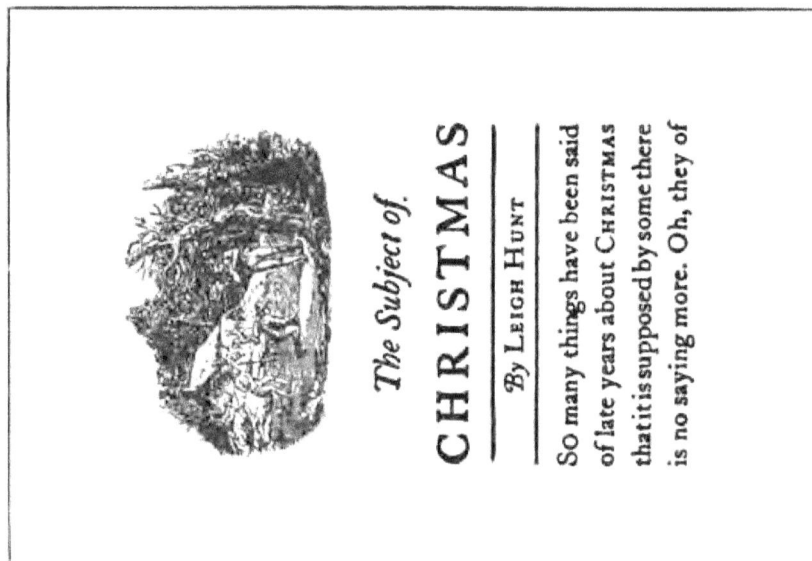

CHAPTER XXXIX

Printing Plates

PRINTING PLATES for the ordinary letter-press printing may be grouped into two general classes—those for the reproduction of original copy, and those for the duplication of cuts or type forms already made up. In the former are included halftones and zinc etchings, while the latter class comprises electrotypes, nickeltypes, and stereotypes.

Fig. 294. Halftone from a photograph

Fig. 295. Etching from line drawing

REPRODUCTIVE PRINTING PLATES

302. **Halftones** are plates made by a photo-mechanical process on sheet copper.* The tones of the copy are broken up into a pattern of fine dots, corresponding in strength to the light and shadow of the copy, and these dots are made to stand out in relief on the plate, as printing surfaces.

The copy to be reproduced is placed on a frame in front of the camera (Fig. 296), focused for size, and a negative is

*The word "cut" is a term which refers to a halftone, an etching, or, in fact, to almost any illustration to be used on the printed page except the type founders ornaments. This term continues in quite common use, although a number of the leading photo-engravers recommend that their product be called "plates" or "engravings."

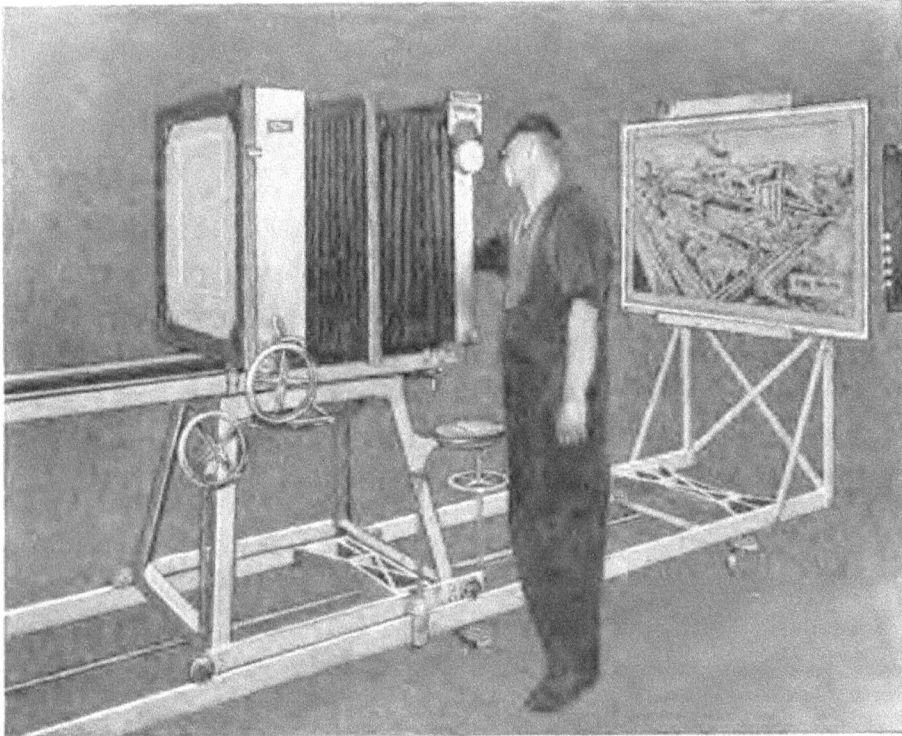

Fig. 296. Photoengraver securing a negative of the copy for a halftone. View in plant of the Artcrafts Engraving Co., St. Joseph, Mo., in which the plates for this book were made

made under strong artificial light. A halftone screen of the proper density is placed between the copy and the plate, and the image is transferred through the diminutive squares of the screen. This is followed by other necessary chemical processes, and then the negative is printed on a polished and sensitized plate of copper, which in turn, is etched by chemicals, until the dots stand out sufficiently in relief.

When the plate is etched, it is sent to the finishing-room to be trimmed, routed, and beveled. Square halftones are sawed out and beveled along the edges, in preparation for mounting. Outline halftones, which have some shoulder, are carefully outlined with a tool as a guide to the router who removes all the unnecessary background. The finisher smooths the edges, and does any other necessary tooling.

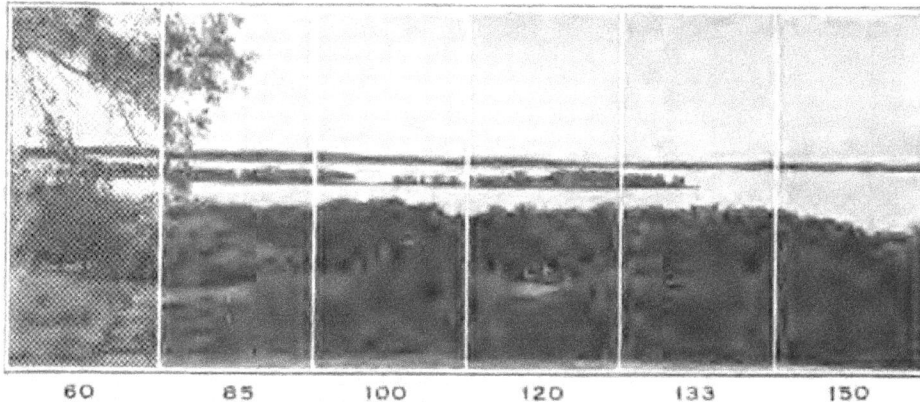

Fig. 297. Specimens of most of the common halftone screens

Halftones are mounted on a base of well-seasoned wood, are squared and trimmed to size, and then they are run through a type-high planer to insure the proper height.

Copy for halftones usually consists of photographs or wash drawings, although almost any manner of copy might be reproduced by this process, if desired.

303. **Halftone screens.** Halftone screens are designated as fine or coarse, depending upon the texture of the screen used in the making. The finest halftones in practical use are those on which the 150-line screen (i.e., 150 lines to the inch) has been used. These are for printing on the very finest grade of enameled papers. For the average run of work on good book papers, 120 to 133-line cuts are used, as they are fine enough to show all the detail that is ordinarily necessary, yet not so fine as to cause difficulty in printing. Coarse halftones must be used in newspapers, or on other rough papers. The common screens are shown above.

On the opposite page (in Fig. 299) is shown a portion of the printing surface of a halftone, greatly enlarged, so that the manner of securing the different tone values is clearly seen.* Fig. 300 shows how it would print on paper. Place the book a few feet away, and see the effect of these dots.

* The illustrations on the opposite page are reproduced here through the courtesy of   The Commercial Engraving Publishing Company, Indianapolis, Ind.

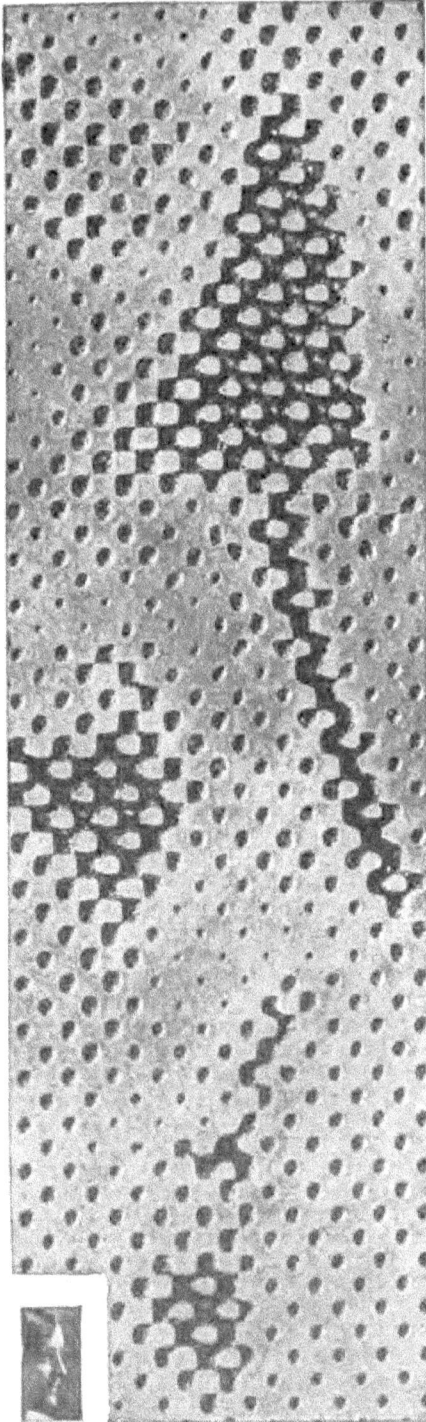

Fig. 298   Fig. 299   Fig. 300

Fig. 301. A line drawing in which portions have been left for shading

304. **Zinc etchings** are plates for the reproduction of line drawings, or other copy consisting of lines, dots, or masses of black, which are in sharp contrast with the background. Photographs, wash drawings, or subjects containing fine gradations of light and shade cannot be reproduced by this method. Pen drawings are usually used as copy for zinc etchings, and when shaded effects are desired, these are produced by closely assembled lines, dots, or stippled work.

When shading is desired in an etching, it is often made by a mechanical process, known as Ben Day work, by which the necessary tones or patterns may be put on the drawing, the negative, or the zinc plate, before the job is etched.*

* The Ben Day machine consists of a board with a rigidly hinged frame. The former holds the drawing or plate upon which the shading is to be done, and the removable frame holds a celluloid film, upon which the particular pattern of shading appears in relief on the under side. Ink is applied to the film with a roller, and the frame containing the film is turned face down on the drawing. The top side is then rubbed firmly with a stylus, thus transferring the ink to the copy. Usually a frisket or mask of tissue paper is placed over such portions of the drawing as do not require shading,

Fig. 302. This etching has been shaded mechanically by the Ben Day process

Zinc etchings are made in a manner somewhat similar to halftones, but the copy is not photographed through a screen, and the resulting print is therefore an exact reproduction of the lines and masses as they appear in the copy.

305. **Copy** for a halftone or zinc etching should be clear and sharp, and in strong contrast with its background. As a rule, it is impossible to obtain a satisfactory plate from copy on colored paper; white only should be used.

There is no fixed rule for the relative sizes of the copy and the finished plate. Usually, the copy will be somewhat larger than the plate, but this is not necessary. A design can be enlarged or reduced to almost any desired size, but

or, if a portion of a metal plate is to take the shading, a wash of a transparent solution such as gamboge is applied, and this serves the same purpose as a mask. The freshly inked pattern is then powdered with rosin, and the gamboge is removed, leaving the shading on the desired parts of the plate. The frame holding the film may be accurately shifted to new positions above the copy, so that it is possible to re-ink the film and transfer the design as many times as desired, and thus thickened lines may be formed, stippled dots made to run together, and many patterns made.

it is better to reduce than to enlarge, because in enlarging any slight defects which may exist in the copy are very strongly intensified, while in reducing, they are even less noticeable. On the other hand, when the reduction is too great, some of the finer details of the copy may be lost.

It should always be kept in mind that whether the copy is reproduced in the same size, or is enlarged or reduced, the proportion of the width to the height will always remain *exactly* the same. It is impossible to make a square plate from an oblong copy, or vice versa. A simple method for finding out the exact size of a plate to be made from larger copy is to multiply the short dimension of the copy by the long dimension of the plate to be made, and then to divide that sum by the long dimension of the copy.

PLATES FOR DUPLICATION

306. **Electrotypes.** The most common process for the duplication of type forms or plates is that of electrotyping, by which metal plates are made in exact duplication of the original patterns. The principal steps are as follows:

The form or plate is surrounded by type-high bearers on the four sides, and locked in a strong chase. It is then dusted with graphite to prevent sticking, and an impression is taken in a wax plate, under heavy pressure. This wax mold is properly shaved, and built up, and is treated with black-lead, to make it a conductor of electricity. Then it is placed in a tank containing an acid solution, and a copper shell is deposited on the mold by the electroplating process. This thin copper shell, when stripped from the wax, is in the exact form of the face of the original pattern. The shell is backed with lead, planed and tooled, and is then mounted on wood or metal base, or is shaved to the proper thickness (11 points) for use on sectional steel base.

Electrotype plates (commonly called electros) are very often used for the printing of books and catalogs, or other long runs. This textbook, for example, is printed from page plates obtained from the original type pages. For long runs in job printing, a number of electros are often made from one form and locked together for the press, thereby saving considerable presswork, as well as wear on the type.

307. **Nickeltypes** are plates made by this same method except that nickel instead of copper is deposited on the face of the mold. After a thin shell of nickel has been built up, the mold is transferred to the copper solution, and the remainder of the shell is made by depositing copper on the back of the nickel. Nickeltypes are more expensive than copper electrotypes, but they are much harder, and are not susceptible to the chemical action of colored inks.

308. **Stereotypes** are duplicates of type forms or plates, in solid type metal, either type-high or of the proper height for mounting on patent base. Matrices of papier-mache are made of the form to be duplicated, and these are placed in casting boxes, into which molten metal is poured. Stereotypes are used almost exclusively in newspaper work, for the duplication of ads, illustrations, etc., and also for the full-page plates used in rotary newspaper presses.

PATENT BASES FOR PLATES

309. **Sectional bases for unmounted plates.** For some purposes, particularly in the printing of books, unmounted plates are used. These are attached to patent bases which make them type-high, and hold them in the proper position. The most used system of plate bases consists of sectional blocks and register hooks, which may be assembled in page units of the required size and shape. The blocks are made up in fonts, or assortments, containing pieces of various sizes, all in multiples of pica dimensions, so selected that it is possible to quickly make up a base for any size of plate.

Adjustable register hooks (which are commonly 6x6, or 8x8, picas in size) are usually inserted on one side and at the foot of the plate, with solid catches at the two opposite sides, but sometimes the adjustable hooks are placed on all sides, in order that the plate may be moved into perfect register by the adjustments of the hooks, without interfering with the lock-up in the chase. The hooks are operated with a steel key, or a steel ratchet, and, as they are tightened up, they grip the beveled edges of the plate, and hold it securely in place.

Fig. 303

The assembly of blocks gives a smooth, unbroken base for the plate, which insures a solid, even impression. Underlays may be put on the back of the plate, and the plate may be returned to its exact position, without disturbing the register. Margins between pages of plates thus mounted are built up with metal furniture, the same as with pages of type matter.

Fig. 304. An adjustable register hook

BOOKS FOR FURTHER STUDY OF PLATES

The most outstanding book on the subject of printing plates and the various processes of reproduction is Hackleman's *Commercial Printing and Engraving*, published by the Commercial Engraving Publishing Company, Indianapolis. A copy of this book should be on the reference shelf of the school printshop. Other good books on plates are as follows:

Vol. 29— Reproductive Processes. U. T. A. Technical Library
Vol. 15— Electrotyping and Stereotyping. U. T. A. Technical Library
Halftone and Photo-Mechanical Processes—Horgan. Inland Printer Co.
A Handbook of Photoengraving—Amstutz. Inland Printer Co.

CHAPTER XL

Linoleum Block Printing

BLOCK printing is one of the earliest forms of graphic reproduction, and it is still extensively practiced in the form of linoleum block work, especially in public schools. Linoleum block printing requires a very simple equipment, and the stock is inexpensive, and is very easy to cut.

Non-inlaid and unglazed linoleum should be used, and it must be mounted on wood, and made type-high. It is usually more practical to buy the blocks ready-made, as they are far more satisfactory, and cost no more than the necessary materials for the mounting of the regular linoleum.

310. Putting the design on the block. The design may be drawn or painted directly on the linoleum, or it may be transferred to the plate from a tracing on transparent paper. In either case, it must be remembered that the plate should be carved in reverse, and that the letters or design must therefore appear in the opposite order to the copy.

If the tracing method is followed, the original copy is traced on a sheet of transparent paper, which is placed in reverse upon the block, with a carbon between, and the image is traced on the block. The sheet should be secured to the block with thumb tacks or strips of gummed paper, to prevent slipping. Sometimes the tracing is made with a very soft pencil, and then the tracing is placed on the block, face down, and a transfer is made by rubbing the back of the paper. The transfer must be clear and distinct.

311. Engraving the block. Using the smallest gouge, or veining tool, outline the design, keeping as close to the line as possible without cutting into the face of the design. Hold the tool at an angle of about 45 degrees, and carve slowly, with a careful, steady stroke. This will give a beveled edge to the work, increasing its strength and durability. When the outline is completed, take a larger tool and remove the remaining areas to be cut away, so that all the non-printing portions will be cut down to the burlap. With a little practice, this may be easily done. Cut away from the lines of the printing face rather than toward them, at all times.

Before printing, pull a proof of the work. Smooth any ragged or uneven lines, and correct any other defects.

312. **Printing the block.** Lock the block near the center of the chase, and place it in the press. Prepare a tympan of hard paper, and cover it with a strong manila draw-sheet. Make sure that the grippers are out of range. Then print the block on a sheet of book paper, and note the nature of the impression. If it should be too heavy, reduce the tympan. If the impression is light, packing may be added, but if it is uneven, the block should be made ready by building up the low parts from the back. If a sheet of paper, smaller than the face, is attached to the center of the back of the block, some of the pressure will be removed from the edges of the plate, improving the appearance of the work, and eliminating much of the wear on the printing surface.

313. **Designs in color.** When a design is to be reproduced in more than one color, it is necessary to have a tracing for each color, and to transfer each one accurately to a separate block. The block containing the outline of the design will be used as a key, and the others must be registered with it, both in the transferring, and in the printing.

SUGGESTIONS

Linoleum blocks, in standard sizes, or cut to order, and the special tools for this work, may be secured from The Linoleum Block Printing Supply Company, Jersey City, N. J. The following books are available:

Linoleum Block Printing—Chas. W. Smith. Published by the author.

Linoleum Block Printing—Phillips and Williams. The Linoleum Block Printing Supply Company.

APPENDIX

Printing Equipment for High Schools

THE author is frequently requested to furnish a list of necessary items of equipment for a high school printshop. Naturally, the individuality of each problem is so marked that it is impossible to give a definite reply in detail without careful consideration of the local problem, in each case. The objective of the printing course (is it to be prevocational, vocational, or cultural?), the housing facilities, and the amount of money available for the purchase, have much to do with determining the equipment.

High school shops usually are arranged to accomodate classes of from twelve to twenty students. It is inadvisable to provide for less than twelve persons, from an economic standpoint, and it is common experience that the printing instructor cannot efficiently handle groups exceeding eighteen to twenty persons. Therefore, equipment providing for maximum classes of twenty would seem to be most practical for the high school shop.

In order to carry on the work in the proper manner, and to teach the various processes correctly, there are certain minimum requirements that must be included in any equipment, however small. These are: a press, a proof press, a paper cutter, a lay-out of type, with suitable cases and cabinets, leads, slugs, and other spacing material, composing sticks and galleys, an imposing stone, wood furniture and other lock-up materials, ink, and paper. None of these items may be omitted.

Naturally, the simpler the outfit, the simpler must be the results that may be expected from it. In proportion as the course is to be enriched in scope and content, the equipment must be larger and more complete.

The author would recommend the following list as a *minimum* initial equipment for the small high school shop not attempting vocational, or advanced, work. The type in this list includes one body Roman face in several sizes, with its accompanying Italic and bold-face. In the minimum equipment, type in one series is preferable, as it will be more serviceable than a number of small fonts of miscellaneous styles, but, of course, one must not expect to do all classes of work acceptably with a single series.

In all cases where the budget will permit it, a larger and more complete equipment should be purchased, but where a conservative beginning is necessary, this might be considered as a nucleus, around which a more extensive school printing plant may be gradually built up.

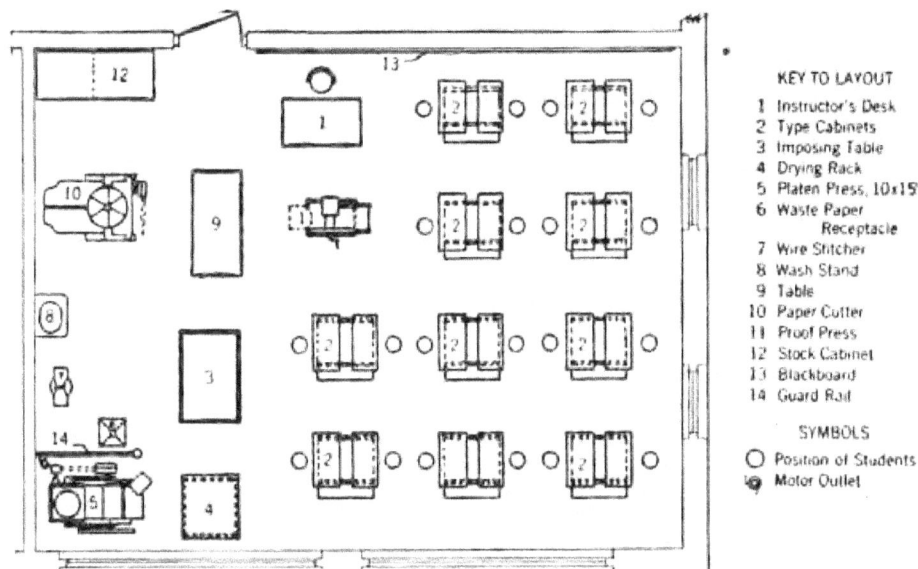

KEY TO LAYOUT

1 Instructor's Desk
2 Type Cabinets
3 Imposing Table
4 Drying Rack
5 Platen Press, 10x15
6 Waste Paper
     Receptacle
7 Wire Stitcher
8 Wash Stand
9 Table
10 Paper Cutter
11 Proof Press
12 Stock Cabinet
13 Blackboard
14 Guard Rail

SYMBOLS

◯ Position of Students
⚡ Motor Outlet

A suggested shop lay-out for the minimum equipment listed below

A Minimum Equipment for the Small High School Shop

Machinery:

One 10x15 Platen Press, with electric motor
One Proof Press
One 30-inch Lever Paper Cutter
One Wire Stitcher

Type:

40 lbs.	8 pt. Century Schoolbook
400 lbs.	10 pt. Century Schoolbook
20 lbs.	12 pt. Century Schoolbook
One font	18 pt. Century Schoolbook
One font	24 pt. Century Schoolbook
One font	8 pt. Century Schoolbook Italic
One font	10 pt. Century Schoolbook Italic
One font	12 pt. Century Schoolbook Italic
Two fonts	8 pt. Century Schoolbook Bold
Two fonts	10 pt. Century Schoolbook Bold
Two fonts	12 pt. Century Schoolbook Bold
One font	18 pt. Century Schoolbook Bold
One font	24 pt. Century Schoolbook Bold
5 lbs.	8 pt. Spaces and Quads
100 lbs.	10 pt. Spaces and Quads
5 lbs.	12 pt. Spaces and Quads
Two fonts	18 pt. Spaces and Quads
Two fonts	24 pt. Spaces and Quads

Cases, Cabinets, etc.:

10 Type Cabinets, each with full-size blank
    case, two pairs brackets, and lead rack
40 California Job Cases, with pulls
 2 Quarter-Size Rule Cases
 1 Cabinet Style Imposing Table, complete
    with reglet and wood furniture fonts

Miscellaneous Items:

100 lbs. 2 pt. Labor Saving Leads, 4 to 25
100 lbs. 6 pt. Labor Saving Slugs, 4 to 25
  5 lbs. 2 pt. Labor Saving Brass Rule 1022
  5 lbs. 2 pt. Labor Saving Brass Rule 2082
  1 font Miters for 2 pt. Rule No. 2082
24 Pressed Steel Galleys, size 6x10
 4 All Brass Job Galleys, size 9x14
20 Composing Sticks, size 6x2
 1 Composing Stick, size 8x2
 1 Pint Safety Benzine Can
 1 Benzine Brush
 1 Hickory Mallet
 1 Large and 2 Small Type Planers
 1 Proof Planer
 1 Dozen Quoins and Quoin Key
 1 Dozen Spring Tongue Gauge Pins

Another good type series might be substituted, if desired. If another press is added, size 12x18 is most practical. Advanced instruction requires more typographic material.

GLOSSARY

Technical and Trade Terms

Ad—The abbreviation for advertisement; now in common use.

Alignment—Type is in alignment when the bottoms of the letters print in a direct line horizontally. These types are out of alignment

Agate—The name given to $5\frac{1}{2}$ point type used in classified advertising. Agate is fourteen lines to an inch.

Alley—The space between facing type cabinets, or case racks, in the composing room.

Ascender—The portion of a type which rises above the common height of the lower-case letters. These letters have ascenders—b, d, f, h, k, l, and t.

Author's corrections—Changes or corrections made in the proof by the author after the compositor's errors have been corrected.

Bastard—Composing material cut to odd or unusual lengths.

Bind—Any part of the type form is said to bind when its size or position prevents a square and even lock-up in the chase.

Bleed—A sheet or page is said to be bled when it has been trimmed into the printed portion.

Bourgeois—The name of 9 point type; a term now little used.

Boxes—The compartments in the type cases, for individual letters.

Brevier—The name of 8 point type. This section is set in brevier.

Caption—The heading of a chapter, of a division of text matter, or of a page.

Clean proof—Proof which contains very few or no errors.

Condensed type—Type narrower than that of standard proportion.

Column rules—Vertical rules used to separate the columns of type matter in newspapers, etc.

Dead matter—Type forms which are not to be used again are said to be dead. To kill a form is to designate it for distribution.

Descender—The portion of a letter which descends below the line of the printing face, in g, j, p, q, and y.

Devil — The apprentice or errand boy in the printing plant is often known as the printer's devil.

Dirty case — A type case in which the letters are badly mixed.

Dirty proof—Proofs are dirty when they contain numerous errors.

Display type — Type of comparatively heavy face, and of more pronounced design than regular body type, used for headlines, or for open display work.

Distribution—The work of replacing the type and other composing material into the cases after the printing has been completed.

Draw-sheet—The top sheet of the the tympan, or packing, on the platen of a job press, or cylinder of a cylinder press.

Dummy — A general lay-out for a folder or booklet, or a preliminary sketch of an advertisement.

Electros, or electrotypes, are metal printing plates, made in duplication of type forms or plates, by securing an impression of the pattern in wax, building a copper shell upon it by the electroplating process, then "backing" the shell with type metal.

Em—The square of any type body. When widths are designated in ems, ems pica (12 pt.) are meant.

Embossing—The process of raising letters or designs above the surrounding surface of the paper by the impression of matched dies.

Expanded—Type whose characters are slightly wider than standard.

Extended—Type whose characters are considerably wider than the standard proportion for lettering.

Font—An assortment of type, in a single style and size, as put up by type founders. The quantity of each letter varies in accordance with the frequency of its use.

Form—One or more pages of type which have been locked up in a chase, ready to be printed.

Furniture—Pieces of wood or metal, less than type-high, and very accurately dimensioned, that are placed about the type matter in a chase, or inserted within the job itself for blanking out large areas.

Galley—A flat, rectangular tray of brass or steel used as a receptacle for type as comes from the stick. Forms are assembled and made up in the galley, and are tied up, proofed, and then removed to the stone, to be locked for the press.

Gingerbread—A common printers' term for useless or meaningless ornament applied to a job.

Hair-spaces —Spaces thinner than 5-em, furnished with some of the larger sizes of type.

Halftone — A printing plate made by the photoengraving process, in which the copy is photographed through a screen, thus breaking the matter up into diminutive dots which reproduce all the different depths of tone, as in the copy.

Hanging indention—A manner of composition in which the first line of the paragraph is set full width and all the succeeding lines are uniformly indented. This style of composition is used on this page.

Hell-box—A container into which broken and battered types, leads, and rules are thrown.

Imposition—The operation of arranging forms in proper order on the stone, and of locking them in the chase, for the press.

Imprint—The name or trade mark of a printer or publisher, placed on a piece of printed matter.

Journeyman—A printer who has served his apprenticeship, and is received into the craft as a finished tradesman.

Justification—Accurate, uniform spacing out of lines of type.

Kerned letters—Types on which a part of the face projects beyond the body. Some Italic types are kerned, in order that the proper slope of the letters may be had without separating the individual letters too widely.

Leaders—Type characters cast in en, em, 2-em, and 3-em widths, the face of which prints a dotted or intermittent line. as follows:

Hyphen _____ Leaders
Dot .... Leaders

Letter-spaced—Words in which spaces have been inserted in the intervals between the letters, as: This line is letter-spaced.

Ligatures — Two or more letters conjoined and cast on one body, as: ff, fi, fl, ffi, ffl, ct, st, &.

Line gauge—The printers' measuring stick, or rule, graduated by nonpareils and picas.

Lower-case letters—The small letters, or minuscules—not capitals; so-called because they occupy the lower news case.

Make-ready—Work of securing an even impression of a form in the press, by building up lower parts and cutting down higher ones.

Make-up—Assembling and spacing out of jobs, or pages, on a galley.

Miters—Corner pieces of rules or borders, cut to an angle of ninety degrees, to form a corner.

Nonpareil — The name of 6 point type. In the printers' measure, it is half a pica, or approximately one-twelfth of an inch.

Off its feet—Type is said to be off its feet when the individual letters lean toward either side of the line, resulting in an imperfect print.

Offset — A sheet is said to offset when fresh ink from its surface is transferred to another sheet.

Point—Unit of the printers' measure, approximately one seventy-second of an inch.

Points—The punctuation marks of a font of type (. , ; : - ! ?) are frequently designated as points.

Pi—Type matter that has become mixed up, or jumbled into a mass.

Pica—The name of 12 point type. It is approximately one-sixth of an inch. Widths of type columns, and the dimensions of forms, are always measured in picas.

Quoins—Steel wedges, usually triangular, and less than than type-high, used to lock forms rigidly in the chases, for the press.

Quotes—Printers' term for quotation marks. (" " or " ").

Register—A form in the press is said to register when its impression comes exactly in the proper position on the sheet. When two forms are printed, one over the other on the sheet, as in tabular, or two-color, jobs the second must be made to register with the first. This is called close-register work.

Reglet—Narrow strips of wood, the thickness of a nonpareil or pica, less than type-high, used for the spacing out of forms in the chase.

Retouching—Art work on photographs used as copy for halftones, to insure clearer details in the finished plate.

Running-heads—Page headings of books, which carry the title or other suitable wording together with the folios, or page numbers.

Scored—Cardboard or heavy cover paper is scored when it has been given a heavy impression from a rule, without ink. It is frequently necessary to score stiff covers or cards in order to secure a neat fold without breaking the stock.

Script—A style of letter fashioned in the manner of handwriting. It is used largely in society printing.

Serifs—Short cross-lines put as a finish at the ends of the unconnected body strokes of the letters. Serifs:

Shoulder—The portion of the upper surface of a type or plate which surrounds the printing face, and which is less than type-high.

Slip-sheeting—In printing on hard finished papers which offset very easily, it is often necessary to insert sheets of soft paper between the printed sheets as they come from the press. This interleaving of sheets is called slip-sheeting.

Sorts—Type characters not secured in regular fonts, or in standard assortments, but which are obtained individually, as desired.

Stereotypes—Printing plates made by pouring molten lead into type-high molds, on one side of which matrices of the desired patterns are placed. Stereotyping is used largely in newspaper work.

Swash letters—Special characters included in some fonts, which are embellished by elongated strokes or additional curves or flourishes. Swash letters: *A D M N R*

Tympan—The packing placed on the platen of a job press, or the cylinder of a cylinder press, consisting of paper, pressboard, etc., and covered with a draw-sheet, against which the form is printed.

INDEX